Fire, Light and Light Equipment in the Graeco-Roman World

Edited by

Denis Zhuravlev

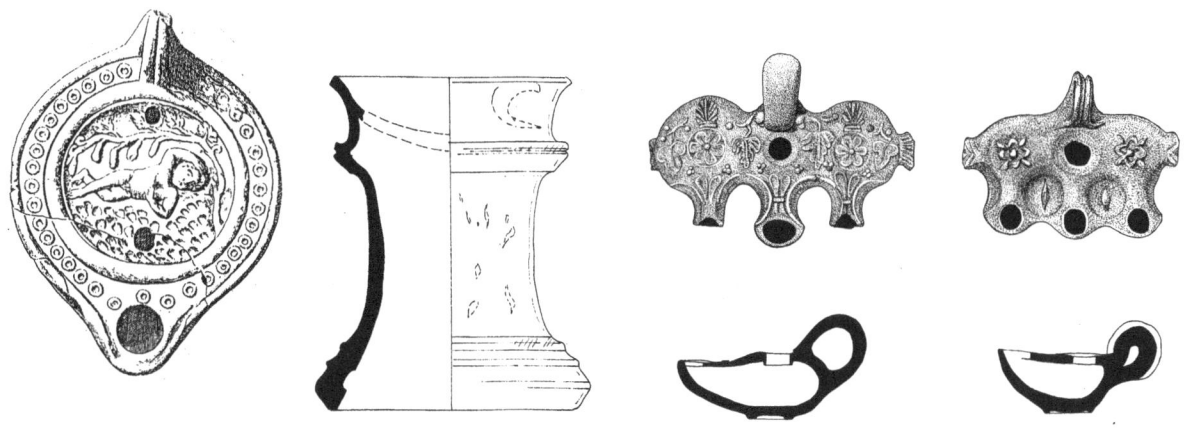

BAR International Series 1019
2002

Published in 2016 by
BAR Publishing, Oxford

BAR International Series 1019

Fire, Light and Light Equipment in the Graeco-Roman World

ISBN 978 1 84171 400 4

© The editor and contributors severally and the Publisher 2002

The authors' moral rights under the 1988 UK Copyright,
Designs and Patents Act are hereby expressly asserted.

All rights reserved. No part of this work may be copied, reproduced, stored,
sold, distributed, scanned, saved in any form of digital format or transmitted
in any form digitally, without the written permission of the Publisher.

BAR Publishing is the trading name of British Archaeological Reports (Oxford) Ltd.
British Archaeological Reports was first incorporated in 1974 to publish the BAR
Series, International and British. In 1992 Hadrian Books Ltd became part of the BAR
group. This volume was originally published by Archaeopress in conjunction with
British Archaeological Reports (Oxford) Ltd / Hadrian Books Ltd, the Series principal
publisher, in 2002. This present volume is published by BAR Publishing, 2016.

Printed in England

PUBLISHING

BAR titles are available from:

        BAR Publishing
        122 Banbury Rd, Oxford, OX2 7BP, UK
EMAIL   info@barpublishing.com
PHONE +44 (0)1865 310431
  FAX   +44 (0)1865 316916
        www.barpublishing.com

Contents

Introduction		iii
Abbreviations		iv
Denis Zhuravlev, Natalia Zhuravleva (*Moscow, Russia*)	Bosporan Late Hellenistic Multi-nozzled Lamps: a prelimenary report	1
Laurent Chrzanovski (*Geneva, Switzerland*)	Bullhead Lamps: An attempt at typological and chronological classification	13
Laurent Chrzanovski (*Geneva, Switzerland*)	Harpocrates on a new lamp handle-ornament recently found in Leptis Magna (Libya)	37
Yuriy Zaitsev (*Simpheropol, Ukraine*)	Imported lamps and candelabra from Ust'-Alma necropolis (Crimea, Ukraine).	41
Yuriy Zaitsev (*Simpheropol, Ukraine*)	Light and fire in the palace of Scythian King Skilur.	61
Denis Zhuravlev (*Moscow, Russia*)	Late scythian grave with a lamp from Belbek IV necropolis in the South-Western Crimea	75
Corinne Sandoz (*Geneva, Switzerland*)	Scènes vetero-testamentaires sur les lampes à huile tardo-antiques	81
Sergey Sorochan (*Kharkov, Ukraine*)	Light for life and death in early Byzantine Empire	111

Introduction

This volume is based on the papers read and discussed on 17 September 1999 at the session of the 5th Annual Meeting of the European Association of Archaeologists in Bournemouth, United Kingdom. The session title was "Trade and clay lamps in the Graeco-Roman World", but when all the articles had been gathered I thought it would be expedient to change the title of the volume, for it did not reflect exactly all the problems the authors addressed. In addition to these articles the text of the paper made in Lisbon (6th Annual Meeting of EAA, 2000) by Y. Zaitsev was added to this volume, as it is directly connected with his report about recent finds of lamps from the Late Skythian necropolis Ust'-Alma in Crimea.

Despite many investigations that have been devoted to this theme, interest for studying the ancient lamps still exists. The articles written by the archaeologists from Russia, Switzerland and Ukraine tackle problems from different aspects - there are papers considering contexts in which the lamps were found recently (Y.Zaitsev, D.Zhuravlev), papers suggesting new classifications of different lamp groups (L.Chrzanovski, D.Zhuravlev, N.Zhuravleva), papers on iconography (C.Sandoz) and papers discussing the problems connected with new types of lighting equipment, i.e. candles (S.Sorochan). The article of Y. Zaitsev is devoted to the role fire played in the life of Late Skythian royal palace. A large group of articles is devoted to the North Pontic area, which is still an area not well known outside the boundaries of the former USSR.

All the authors helped to prepare the volume for publishing by force of their possibilities. I would like to express all my thankfulness to Professor Timothy Darvill, the head of the organising Committee of the Congress for his proposal to hold this section and his friendly help during the Congress. My great thanks goes to Dr.David Davison, for his kind invitation to publish this volume in BAR International Series. I am also thankful to Mrs. Natalia Zhuravleva for her help during the preparation of this volume.

Moscow, October 15, 2001   Denis Zhuravlev

Abbreviations

ADSV	Antichnaya drevnost' i srednie veka. Sverdlovsk.
IAK	Izvestiya Imperatorskoy Arkheologicheskoy Komissii. Sankt-Peterburg.
MAIET	Materialy po arkheologii, istorii i etnographii Tavriki. Simpheropol.
MIA	Materialy i issledovaniya po arkheologii SSSR. Moscow.
OAK	Otchet Imperatorskoy Arkheologicheskoy Komissii. Sankt-Peterburg.
PG	Patrologiae cursus completus. Series graeca. P.
RA	Rossiyskaya arkheologiya. Moscow.
RAN	Russian Academy of Science
SA	Sovetskaya arkheologiya. Moscow
SAI	Svod arkheologicheskih Istochnikov. Moscow
VDI	Vestnik drevnei istorii. Moscow.

Bosporan Late Hellenistic Multi-Nozzled Lamps: A prelimenary report

Denis Zhuravlev, Natalia Zhuravleva
(Moscow, Russia)

Multi-nozzled lamps were used as lighting equipment in many cities of the Greek and Roman world. A great amount of Late Hellenistic multi-nozzled lamps was found in the capital of the Bosporan Kingdom - in Panticapaion (the modern city of Kertch in Crimea). No special investigation was devoted to this group of material up to date. There are only a few lines written by O.Waldhauer in the catalogue of lamps of the Hermitage Museum (Waldhauer 1914: 25-26). He proposed Egyptian origin for the lamps. A small chapter in an article by V. Zabelina was dedicated to the lamps from Panticapaion while discussing Late Hellenistic lamps. However this group of lamps is very numerous and deserves a special study. We consider this article to be just a preliminary investigation, the first one devoted only to this problem and we hope to continue the work with other materials.[1]

All the lamps of this type were made from grey (Munsell Soil Colour Charts 2.5Y 4/1-3/1) quite dense clay (sometimes there are can exist small wholes) with lime inclusions; there is no slip. Lamps were produced rather carefully. However, defects on some examples — a handle attached crookedly, a rough surface and so on can be noticed.

Two-nozzled lamps

Two-nozzled lamps (fig. 1, *1-2*; 4, *1-3*) were formed by mechanical connection of two nozzles to the body of a standard Bosporan mould-made lamp of Hellenistic time. These lamps have one receptacle for oil, whose shape does not differ from that on single-nozzled lamps, two nozzles with volutes and a little loop-shaped handle. Such lamp is published among others from the collection of the State Historical Museum (Zhuravlev & Chrzanovski: 2000, fig. 1, *9*). Its length is 8.1 cm., width - 5.5 cm., height - 2.9 cm. We should note that two-nozzled lamps are not all the same - some have almost no volutes (Zabelina 1982, Pl. VII, *10*). Width of nozzles differs - artefacts from excavations of V. P. Tolstikov (fig.1, *2*) have long and narrow ones. The hole for pouring oil of this lamp is decorated only sparingly.

Besides Panticapaion, two-nozzled lamps come (Waldhauer 1914: N 57, 62; Zabelina 1992, Pl. VII, *5, 10*) from some other Bosporan cities: Kepoi (Kuznetsov, 2001, fig. 14), Mirmekion (Gaidukevitch 1959, fig. 93, p. 82). Bosporan two-nozzled lamps are close to the ones from Italy from the collection of the British Museum (Bailey 1975, Q 728 - 732) dating to the 1st century B.C. There are also some parallels in decoration, for example, with the Egyptian lamp Q 577 from the collection of the same Museum (Bailey 1975) dating to the 1st century B.C. Many bronze lamps of the similar shape were also widespread (see Bailey 1996, Q 3771-3776 and others) and they date to the Roman time in general.

Multi-nozzled lamps

Local one-nozzled lamps found very often at the site of ancient Panticapaion might have been the prototypes for multi-nozzled ones (see for example: Zabelina 1992, Pl. 7, *1-4*). It should be noted, that the number of wick-holes of Bosporan multi-nozzled lamps was usually odd (three or five or nine), although there are some examples with even (four or six) amount of holes. We may suppose that these groups of lighting equipment existed simultaneously during some period of time, because we found different types of lamps in same layers.

TYPE I (fig.1, *3*; 4, *4*). Three-nozzled lamps were formed by mechanical connection of three one-nozzled lamps. The nozzles of these lamps were not joined with each other and the hole for pouring oil was drilled only in the central part. The two other filling-holes are absent and the places for them were decorated with rosettes. The bottom is a little bit concave. The nozzles were decorated with volutes. This type of decoration makes three-nozzled lamps close to two-nozzled, as well as to one-nozzled ones. There are grape leaves and palmettos around rosettes. Small stylised triangular handles decorated sometimes with grooves were attached to the sides of such lamps. The vertical handle, at the place where it connects with the body of the lamp, is decorated with applications by its sides. The length of such lamps is 11,2 cm., the width - 8 cm., the height - 2,7 cm. (the height with the handle - 4,3 cm.). Very similar to this type is the lamp M-1133 from Pushkin Museum (fig. 2, *2;* 5, *4*) with a less rich decoration (there are only rosettes in the places intended for pouring oil). Their sizes are: length - 10, 1 cm., width - 5,7 cm., height - 2,5 cm.

The lamp from the Athenian agora, dating to the end of the 4th - 5th century A.D. (Perlzweig 1961, N 2031, Pl. 33) or to the end of the 5th - beginning of the 6th century A.D. (Kariveri 1996: 241, pl. 23, N 263) is also very close to this type. Lamp Q 1121 from the collection of the British Museum is made according to the same scheme (joined side by side) and dates to the end of the 1st - beginning of the 2nd century A.D. (Bailey 1975, Pl. 43, p. 251).

TYPE II. All the multi-nozzled lamps were moulded and then they could have been finished by hand (a vertical handle could have been added or ornament could be made on the side handles). Despite the fact that all the lamp-parts were joined with each other it is possible to notice that the

---

[1] The preliminary Russian version of this article was published by one of the authors: Zhuravlev, 2001

body of each one is round. The bottom is slightly concave. The handles, similar to the ones of type I, are attached on the sides. The filling-hole is only one, the other intended holes are just marked.

II.1 *Three-nozzled lamps* (1, *4*; 2, *1,3,4*; 5). The filling hole is also only one; the intended holes are decorated with different rosettes. It is interesting to note that other lamps do not have rosette decoration. The round places between nozzles are pressed and are decorated with relief leaf-shaped applications in the centre. Some examples from the State Historical Museum, former I. Zabelin collection (fig. 2, *3-4*), are not decorated so well and pressed places between nozzles do not have any applications. Their sizes: length - 9-9,7 cm.; width (including the handle) - 5,7 - 6,9 cm. An interesting peculiarity should be noted - the handles could be moulded in the same form as the whole lamp was or could be added afterwards.

II.2. *Four-nozzled lamps.* The nozzles are decorated with palm-branches. The only known lamp of this type is from the collection of the State Hermitage Museum (Waldhauer 1914, Pl. VII, N 73, p. 25). Length - 8,5 cm.; height - 3 cm. Although we do not know exactly its origin, the lamp must have been found in Kertch. Unfortunately for the moment we do not have an illustration of this lamp.

II.3. *Five-nozzled lamps* (fig. 3, *2*; 6, *1-2*). Sometimes the indented holes for pouring oil are marked, but not perforated. Rosettes decorating the lamps of other types are absent (The Pushkin Fine Art Museum, N M-1111). Shallow decorative round depressions separating one part from another were made between nozzles. There are round applications similar to ones of type I decorating the handle at the place of its connection with the lamp's body. Dimensions: length - 10, 9 cm.; width - 5,7 cm.; height - 2,7 cm.

II.4. *Six-nozzled lamps* (fig. 3, *1*; 6, *3*) are represented by only one example (The Pushkin Fine Art Museum, N M-1112). Dimensions: length - 15, 4 cm.; width - 6,6 cm.; height - 3 cm. The handle is broken off. Volutes of this lamp are well made, places for supposed holes are marked with circles and the hole for pouring oil is not in the centre - the craftsman ignored the rules of symmetry.

II.5. *Nine-nozzled lamp* (fig.7, *1*). The nine-nozzled lamp from the collection of the Hermitage Museum (Waldhauer 1914, N 77). Dimensions: the length - 20 cm.; the height - 2,6 cm. Details of decoration are close to ones of three-nozzled and five-nozzled lamps.

TYPE III. Nine-nozzled mould-made lamp (fig. 3, *3*; 7, *2*) with a body of rectangular (close to trapezium) shape. The filling hole is only one and places for others are unmarked. The surface is flat with three shallow incisions by the sides. Side handles are absent and each nozzle is marked with a shallow channel. Dimensions: length - 20, 6 cm.; width - 5 cm.; height - 3 cm. (including the handle - 3,7 cm.).

This type is significantly different morphologically from the lamps of Types I - III described above, although it has the same scheme of nozzles joining.

The places of manufacture. At his time O. Waldhauer thought that multi-nozzled lamps were produced in Egypt, wheres the two-nozzled ones he considered to have been of local origin (Waldhauer 1914: 8, 24-25). However, Egyptian lamps have different shape and decoration and were made from different clay. Further, the amount of filling- holes in Egyptian lamps is always multiple of 5 (10, 20) (Bailey 1988: 220), while Bosporan multi-nozzled lamps usually have even number of holes. All the known Egyptian lamps date to the 1st century A.D. and during the Hellenistic period quadrangular multi-nozzled lamps might have been lacking in Egypt (Mlynarczyk 1997). The first one to have written about the local production of Bosporan multi-nozzled lamps was V. S. Zabelina (Zabelina 1992: 322-323).

We do not have any doubts that this type of lamps was a local product, most probably from Panticapaion. As many lamps have similar elements of decoration we can suppose that there was one workshop producing all the lamps which supplied both the capital and other poleis of the state. Although no moulds for such lamps were found within the territory of the Bosporan Kingdom, the fact that these lamps were made of clay similar to the one of Bosporan "Megarian" bowls and Bosporan sigillata[2] proves this supposition. The predomination of these lamps in the Kertch peninsula during the Late Hellenistic period also testifies to their local production.

Distribution. Multi-nozzled lamps of the types described above are known only from the territory of the Bosporan Kingdom (there is no information about the finds of such lamps from the other sites). The majority come from Panticapaion (see Zabelina 1992, Pl. VII; AGSP 1984, Pl. CXXXII, *17-18*). Some were found in the territory of European Bosporus - in Mirmekion (Gaidukevitch 1959, fig. 94), in Ilurat (Gaidukevitch 1981: 118-119, fig. 32, *3*), Nymphaion (Drevniy gorod Nimphey 1999: 66-67, N 156,) and in Zenon Chersonesos (Maslennikov 1992, fig. 16, *1*). Only one lamp of this type comes from Phanagoria in the territory of the Asian part of Bosporus[3] and none from Tanais. Unfortunately there are no general publications of the material from other Bosporan sites.

Looking at foreign collections, there are two three-nozzled and a nine-nozzled lamp from the exhibition of the Museum of Chartoryszhki in Krakow, where they might have come from south Russia. We did not find any publications of these lamps. Two lamps in fragments kept in the collection of the Istanbul Museum and determined as having been produced in Pontic area in the 1st century B.C.

---

[2] There were no special physic-chemical investigations of this pottery yet.
[3] It should be noted that the remains of production of round multi-nozzled lamps dating to the 4th century A.D. were found in Phanagoria (Kobylina 1966: 179, fig. 9). We do not know finds of lamps of this type from any other Bosporan site besides Phanagoria.

(Kassab Tezgör & Sezer 1995: 157-158, N 418-419) are, to our mind, of the Egyptian origin, as well as the lamp published by O. Waldhauer (Waldhauer 1914, Pl. VII, N 78). There is a difficult question concerning a lamp from Hermitage collection published by O. Waldhauer (Waldhauer 1914, VII, N78). On one hand it resembles Egyptian lamps, but the fact that it has 9 wick holes testifies to its non-Egyptian origin. We have not had an opportunity to see this lamp yet - it may be Dacian or Pannonian product of Roman period. And we are not allowed to retract the supposition that it is one more type of Bosporan lamps.

Multi-nozzled lamps from the Mediterranean area. As it was noted above, multi-nozzled lamps were spread quite widely. Their shapes are various - the earliest multi-nozzled lamps from Knidos are round and their nozzles are situated around the body (the amount of nozzles could be both odd and even, ranging from 3 to 21). These lamps have one round receptacle for oil with nozzles joined to it. Round lamps of similar shape come also from Troy (Barr 1996, Fig. 23, N 92), from some Roman sites (see Loeschke 1919: 150 - 151, Abb. 21) and from other places.

Some lamps were made by simple joining of several one-nozzled lamps in the multi-nozzled one. The lamp, whose shape is rather similar to the shapes of lamps of Type I, but having 5 nozzles, is kept in the Museum of the National Library in Paris (Hellmann 1987, N 233). The other lamps have bodies of rectangular shape with one or several filling-holes and with nozzles situated by the perimeter (for example, artefacts of Egyptian or Dacian production).

Among the earliest multi-nozzled lighting equipment we should name Athenian lamps of the second - third thirds of the 5th century B.C. (Bailey 1975, Q 37bis) and Corinthian multi-nozzled lamps (Bailey 1975, Q 108 - 109). There are also some lamps of this type from Knidos (Bailey 1975, Q 291 - Q 299) dating to the end of the 3rd - 2nd centuries B.C. It is interesting that the same lamp types existed both for multi-nozzled lamps and for one-nozzled ones, i.e. there were no serious differences in their construction. Only lamps from Rhodes and Ephesos (Bailey 1975, Q 152, Q 368) that must have been used in sanctuaries were not made in this way.

The largest region producing multi-nozzled rectangular lamps in Roman period was Egypt. Lamps of this origin come from Warsaw (Bernhard 1955, Tabl. LXXVI, N 277), London (Bailey 1988, Q 1971 - Q 1976) and Paris (Hellmann 1985, N 52bis - with a stamp **ΚΑΙΕΙCΩPA (C)**). Besides, multi-nozzled rectangular lamps consisting of several joined lamps are known from Samaria (Crowfoot, Crowfoot, Kenyon 1957, fig. 87, *8*; p. 371) and from Libya (Bailey 1985: 7, N 23, Pl. II).

Some traces of production of five-nozzled lamps were discovered in Moesia, in Butovo workshop - their body is decorated with ten rosettes and there is a filling-hole in one of them (approximately in the lamp centre). The supervisor of excavations dates these lamps to the 3rd- 4th centuries A.D. (Sultov 1976: 75). Multi-nozzled lamps were very wide spread in the territory of Roman Dacia. These lamps have from 2 to 9 nozzles (it should be noted that their number is also odd - 3, 5, 7 or 9 nozzles) and the body is divided into two symmetrical parts with different decoration. They belong to the type VI of D. Aliku (Aliku & Nemes 1977: P. 24 - 25; Aliku 1994, Type VI; there are analogues from the other Dacian sites) and were produced by *Ianuarius* in the local workshop in the 2nd century A.D. There are a lot of various multi-nozzled lamps in Pannonia (Iványi 1935, Taf. XVII - XXIV, XXIX - XXXIII). The rectangular lamps of type IX (Iványi 1935: 13, Taf. XXXII - XXXIII). These lamps were wide spread in Roman provinces (Šubic 1976, N 17, 18; Kuzmanov 1992: 38, N 282). Several multi-nozzled lamps of different types are kept in the Römisch-Germanischen Zentralmuseum in Mainz (Menzel 1954, Abb. 26, 1; 30; 56 - 58 and others) and in many other collections.

The special group is made by multi-nozzled lamps of Jewish origin (Goodenough 1953, Vol. 2, P. 101-108; Vol. III, N 259, 261, 273 - 275, 282, 285 - 287, 289 and others). These lamps have different amounts of filling-holes - from 3 to 8. There are some seven-nozzled lamps among them. (Goodenough 1956, Vol. V, N 6) and ones with images of menorah (Goodenough 1953, Vol. III, 340, 344 - 347, 352). It should be noted also that there were no finds of Bosporan seven-nozzled lamps up to date.

Dating. Unfortunately there are only a few contexts in the territory of Panticapaion acropolis that have already been excavated with layers of the 1st century B.C. in situ - most of them were disturbed as a result of acropolis reconstruction in the first two centuries A.D. Thus, it is not possible to date these lamps exactly and we can only state that they existed in the 1st century B.C. The nine-nozzled lamp from Mirmekion was found in a layer dated not later than to the beginning of the 1st century A.D. (Gaidukevitch 1959b: 82) and the three-nozzled one dates to the Late Hellenistic period (Gaidukevitch 1987, fig. 137, *4*, p. 109). Multi-nozzled lamps were not found in Panticapaion in the same contexts with light clay amphorae with double-barrelled handles that appeared in the 1st century B.C. The fact that multi-nozzled lamps are absent in the contexts of the end of the 1st century B.C. in the house of Chrysaliskos (Sokolskiy 1976), for example, also proves this dating.

Unfortunately there are no finds of such lamps in the other cities of the Bosporan kingdom in the contexts that are dated well. Therefore dating is not always valid. For example, M. Kobylina dates a multi-nozzled lamp from Phanagoria to the 1st –2nd centuries A.D. (Kobylina 1956: 75). However, we are not able to rule out the possibility of their existence until the 1st century A.D. A multi-nozzled lamp, although a very rough one (it must date to the later period as compared with artefacts described above) was found in Ilurat, where the layers of the Hellenistic period are absent (Gaidukevitch 1981: 118-119, fig. 32, *3*). A nine-nozzled lamp from Panticapaion comes from a layer of the 1st-2nd centuries A.D. (Blavatskiy 1957: 72).

A similar multi-nozzled lamp from Libya dates to the second half of the 2nd - the first quarter of the 1st century B.C. (Bailey 1985: 7) and a lamp from Samaria also does to the 2nd-1st centuries B.C. (Crowfoot, Crowfoot, Kenyon 1957: 371).

Production of multi-nozzled lamps seems to have started in Panticapaion in the beginning of the 1st century B.C. and continued for about a century. Some two-nozzled volute lamps could have existed in the first half of the 1st century B.C. All the types of multi-nozzled lamps must have existed simultaneously. We have not found out any chronological difference between various types yet.

Survivals. It is very difficult to explain the independent appearance of large series of multi-nozzled lamps in the 1st century B.C. In spite of the fact that two nozzled lamps were used in Panticapaion from the 6th century B.C., they were spread most widely in the Late Hellenistic period. Besides their use in everyday life, such lamps might have had some sacral functions. A rather small cubic capacity of oil receptacle and a great number of nozzles demanded frequent pouring of oil into the lamp; furher, premises would be lighted much better with the help of several one-nozzled lamps. The most of multi-nozzled lamps from Athens come not from sanctuaries and temples, but from private houses of the 3rd - 2nd centuries B.C. (Howland 1958: 107). Some of them might have been used at domestic sanctuaries. The finds of different types of multi-nozzled lamps are known from all the territory of the city.[4] It is interesting, that the majority of multi-nozzled lamps found in Ulpia Traiana Sarmitizegetuza come from the sanctuary of Asklepios and Gigeia (Alicu & Nemes 1977: 24; Alicu 1994: 121) and the lamp from Lybia was found in a small temple (Bailey 1985: 7). At excavations of the sanctuary near the settlement Beregovoy - 4, where life continued until the middle of the 1st century B.C., a great amount of fragments of round multi-nozzled lamps was found (excavations of A. A. Zavoykin).

Also we do not know about finds of such lamps in the graves of Panticapaion, Nymphaion (Gratch 1999) or Zolotoye (Korpusova 1983) necropoleys, although lamps of other types were often found in them.

In Panticapaion multi-nozzled lamps were spread everywhere and are among ordinary and frequent finds at the territory of the city. They are not found only in temples (it should be noted, that there are only a few excavated temples of the 1st century B.C. in Panticapaion). In the temple of the 1st century which was excavated some years ago there were no finds of multi-nozzlled lamps.[5] V. D. Blavatskiy supposed that such lamps could have been used for lighting of public buildings (Blavatskiy 1957: 72), but we do not have any arguments to prove this.

According to the above, it is very difficult to say what multi-nozzled lamps were used for in the capital of the Bosporan Kingdom. We are able only to suppose that some of multi-nozzled lamps might have been used in home sanctuaries or have played some other sacral role. And there is no ground to suppose that they were not used in everyday life.

As a conclusion we would like to note that new publications of multi-nozzled lamps (among them of ones from closed contexts) would make it possible not only to correct these scheme, but also to define dates more exactly and to return to the question concerning their using.

Acknowledgements

We would like to thank Dr. Vladimir Tolstikov for the possibility to publish materials from the excavation of Panticapaeum, preserved in the Pushkin Museum of Fine Arts (Moscow). We are very thankful to Laurent Chrzanovski (Geneva) for some bibliographical notes.

All the drawings were done by Anna Kotova and Maria Tkachenko, photos by Denis Zhuravlev and ©Hermitage Museum.

Bibliography

AGSP, 1984. *Antichnye gosudarstva Severnogo Prichernomorya. Arkheologiya SSSR*. Moscow. (in Russian)

D. Alicu 1994. *Opaitele Romane Ulpia Traiana Sarmizegetusa*. Bucuresti.

D. Alicu & E. Nemes. 1977. *Roman Lamps from Ulpia Traiana Sarmizegetusa*. BAR Suppl. Ser. 18.

T.M. Arsen'eva. 1988. *Svetil'niki Tanaisa*. Moscow. (in Russian)

D.M. Bailey. 1975. *A Catalogue of the Lamps in the British Museum. I. Greek, Hellenistic, and Early Roman Pottery Lamps*. L.

D.M. Bailey. 1980. *A Catalogue of the Lamps in the British Museum. II. Roman Lamps Made in Italy*. L.

D.M. Bailey. 1985. *Excavatios at Sidi Khrebish Benghazi (Berenice)*. Vol. III, Part 2. Tripoli.

D.M. Bailey. 1988. *A Catalogue of the Lamps in the British Museum. III. Roman Provincial Lamps*. L.

R.L. Barr. 1996. Greek and hellenistic lamps from Ilion. In: *Studia Troica*. Band 6. 159 — 200.

M.L. Bernhard.1955. *Lampki starozytne*. Warszawa.

V.D. Blavatskiy. 1957. Stroitelnoe delo Pantikapeya po dannum raskopok 1945-1949 i 1952-1953 gg. In: *MIA*, Vol. 56. Moscow. 5-95. (in Russian)

---

[4] Information of Dr. Miron Zolotarev, vice-director of Chersonesos Archaeological Museum.

[5] Information of Dr. Victor Zin'ko, Director of the excavations.

O. Broneer. 1930. *Corinth IV, 2. Terracotta Lamps.* Cambridge.

J.W. Crowfoot, G.M. Crowfoot., K.M. Kenyon. 1957. *The Objects from Samaria.* L.

Drevniy gorod Nimphay. 1999. *Ancient city Nimphaion. Catalogue of the exhibition in the State Hermitage.* Sankt-Peterburg (in Russian).

V.F. Gaidukevitch 1959. *Mirmekiy. Sovetskie raskopki v 1956 g. 1934 — 1956.* Warsaw. (in Russian)

V.F. Gaidukevitch. 1981. *Bosporkie goroda. Ustupchatye sklepy. Ellinisticheskaya usad'ba. Ilurat.* Leningrad. (in Russian)

V.F. Gaidukevitch. 1987. *Antichnye goroda Bospora. Myrmekiy.* Leningrad. (in Russian)

E.R. Goodenough. 1953-1956. *Jewish Symbols in the Greco-Roman Period.* N.Y.

N.L. Grach. 1999. *Nekropol Nimfeya.* Sankt-Peterburg. (in Russian)

M.-C. Hellmann. 1985. *Lampes antiques de la Bibliothèque Nationale. I. Collection Froehner.* Paris.

M.-C. Hellmann. 1987. *Lampes antiques de la Bibliothèque Nationale. II. Fonds général: lampes pré-Romaines et Romaines.* Paris.

R.H. Howland. 1958. *Greek Lamps and Their Survivals. The Athenian Agora. Vol. IV.* Princeton, New Jersey.

D. Iványi. 1935. *Die pannonischen Lampen.* Budapest.

A. Karivieri. 1996. *The Athenian Lamp Industry in Late Antiquity.* Helsinki.

D. Kassab Tezgör, T. Sezer 1995. *Catalogue des lampes en terre cuite du Musée Archéologique d'Istamboul. Tome 1. Epoques protohistorique, archaïque, classique et hellénistique. Varia Anatolica VI, 1.* Istamboul-Paris.

M.M. Kobylina. 1956. *Phanagoria. MIA, Vol. 57.* Moscow. (in Russian)

M.M. Kobylina. 1966. Keramicheskoe proizvodstvo Phanagorii v IV v. In: *Sovetskaya arkheologiya N 3.* 172–186. (in Russian)

V.N. Korpusova. 1983. *Nekropol Zolotoe (K etnokulturnoy istorii evropeyskogo Bospora).* Kiev. (in Russian)

G. Kuzmanov. 1992. *Antike Lampen. Sammlung des Nationalen Archäologischen Museums.* Sofia.

V.D. Kuznetsov 2001. Archaeological investigations in the Taman Peninsula. In: G. Tsetskhladze (Ed.). North Pontic Archaeology. Recent Discoveries and Studies. *Colloquia Pontica.* 6. Brill. Leiden, Boston, Köln. 319-344.

S. Loeschcke. 1919. *Lampen aus Vindonissa. Ein Beitrag zur Geschichte von Vindonissa und des antiken Beleuchtungswesens.* Zürich.

A.A. Maslennikov. 1992. Zenonov Khersones – gorodok na Meotide. In: Koshelenko (Ed.) *Otcherki archeologii i istorii Bospora.* Moscow. 120-173. (in Russian)

H. Menzel. 1969. *Antike Lampen in Römisch-Germanischen Zentralmuseum zu Mainz.* Mainz.

J. Mlynarczyk. 1997. *Alexandrian and Alexandria-Influenced Mould-Made Lamps of the Hellenistic Period.* BAR International Series 677.

J. Perlzweig. 1961. *Lamps of the Roman Period. The Athenian Agora, Vol. VII.* Princeton.

N.I. Sokolskiy. 1976. *Tamanskiy tolos i rezidentsiya Khrisaliska.* Moscow (in Russian).

Z. Šubic. 1976. Rimske oljenke v Sloveniji. In: *RCRF Acta XVI.* 82-99.

B. Sultov. 1976. *Ancient Pottery Centres in Moesia Inferior.* Sofia.

V.S. Zabelina. 1992. *Antichnye glinyanye svetil'niki iz Pantikapeya.* Soobscheniya GMII, Vol. 10, Moscow, 298 — 328 (in Russian).

D. Zhuravlev. 2001. Pozdneellinisticheskie mnogorozhkovye svetil'niki Bospora. In: A. Maslennikov, A. Zavoikin (Eds). *Drevnosti Bospora,* Vol. 4. Moscow. 131-149 (in Russian)

D. Zhuravlev, L. Chrzanovski. 2000. Kollektsiya antichnykh svetilnikov Gosugarstvennogo Istoricheskogo Muzeya. In: *Vestnik drevney istorii* N 3. 159-166 (in Russian).

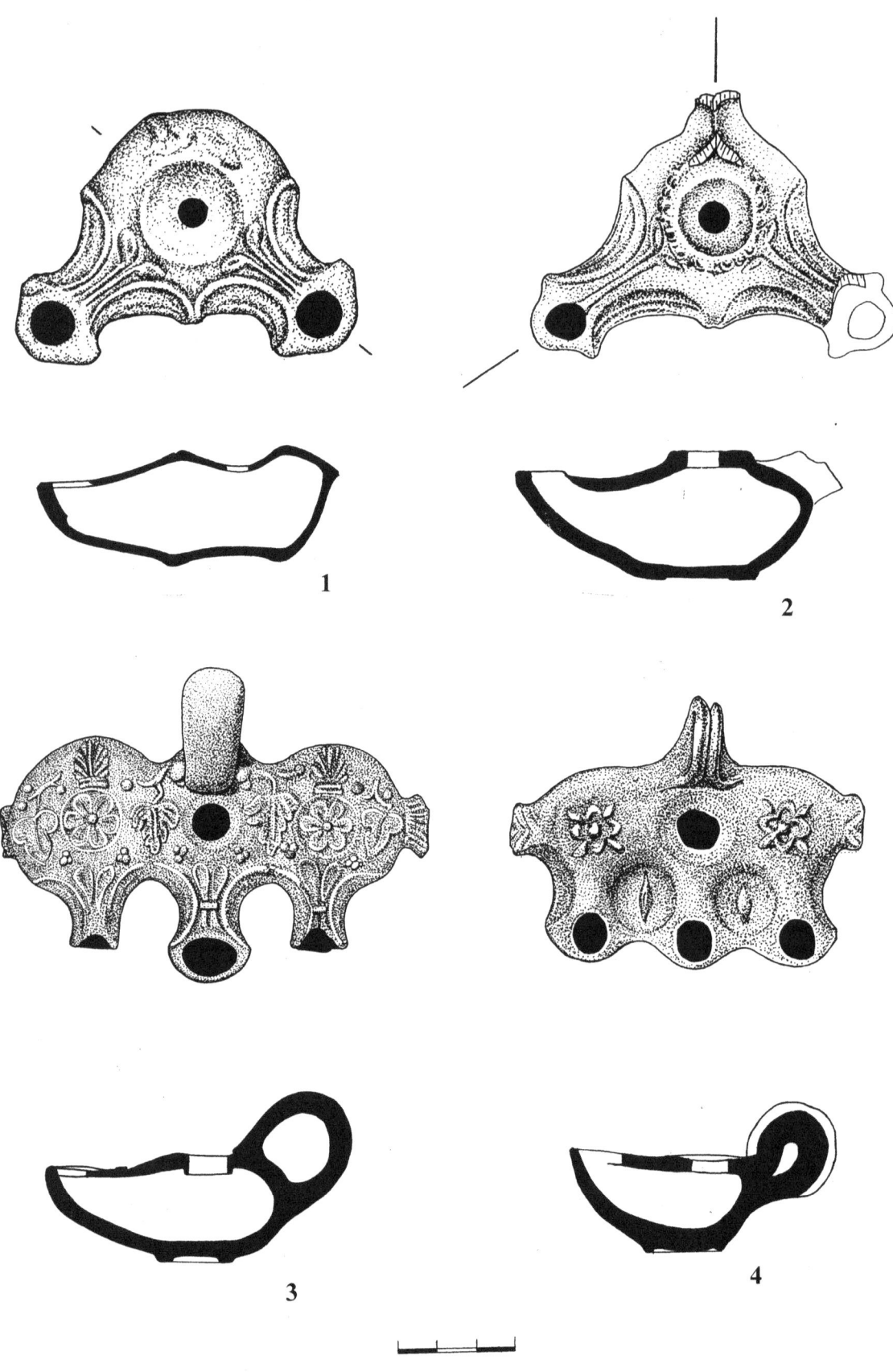

Fig. 1. Bosporan multi-nozzled lamps: 1- State Historical Museum, Moscow; 2- Kertch Archaeological Museum; 3 – Pushkin Fine Arts Museum, Moscow, M-1134; Pushkin Fine Arts Museum, M-1110. Clay.

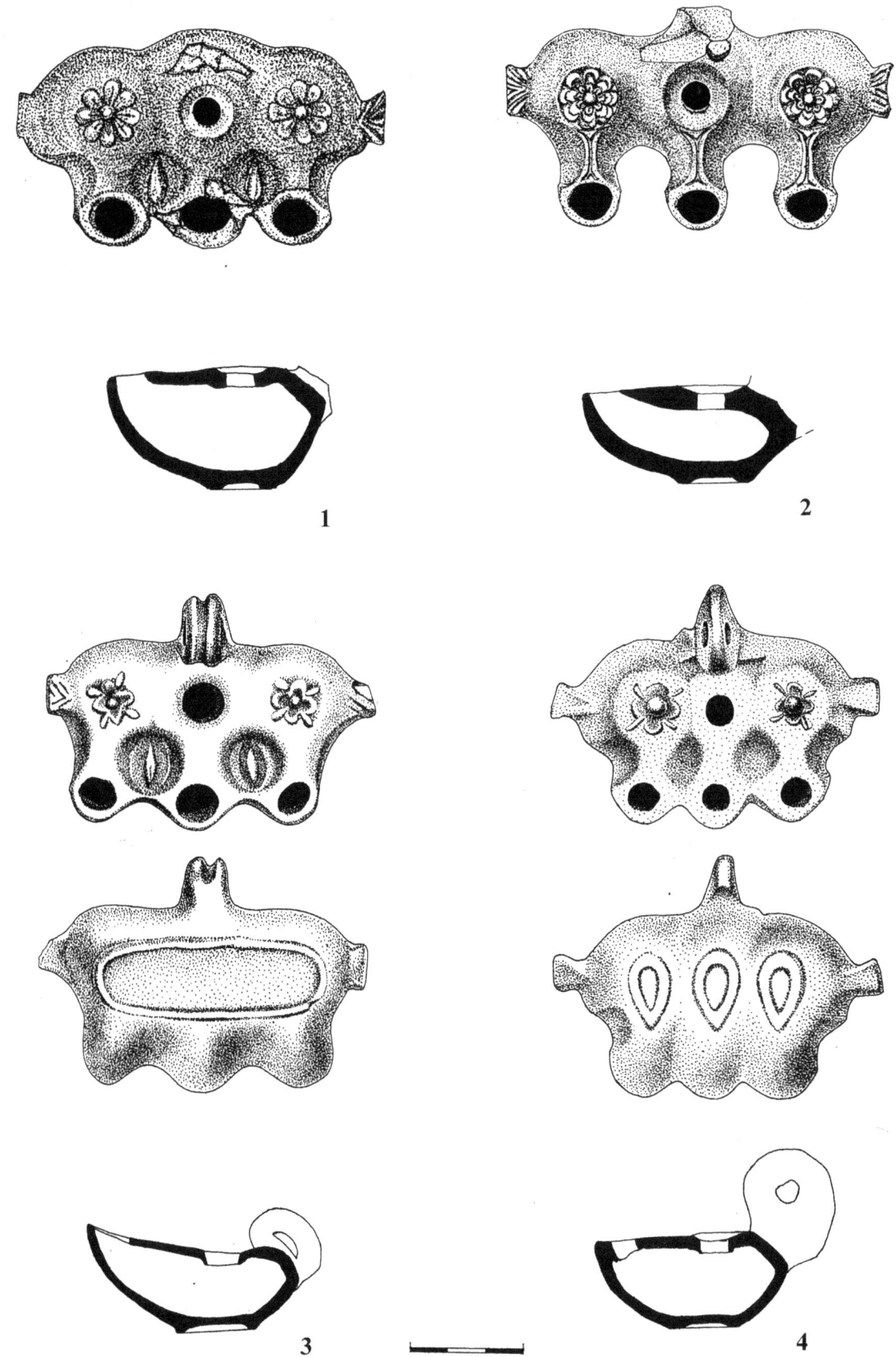

Fig. 2. Bosporan multi-nozzled lamps: 1-2 - Pushkin Fine Arts Museum, M-35; M-1133; 3-4- State Historical Museum. Clay.

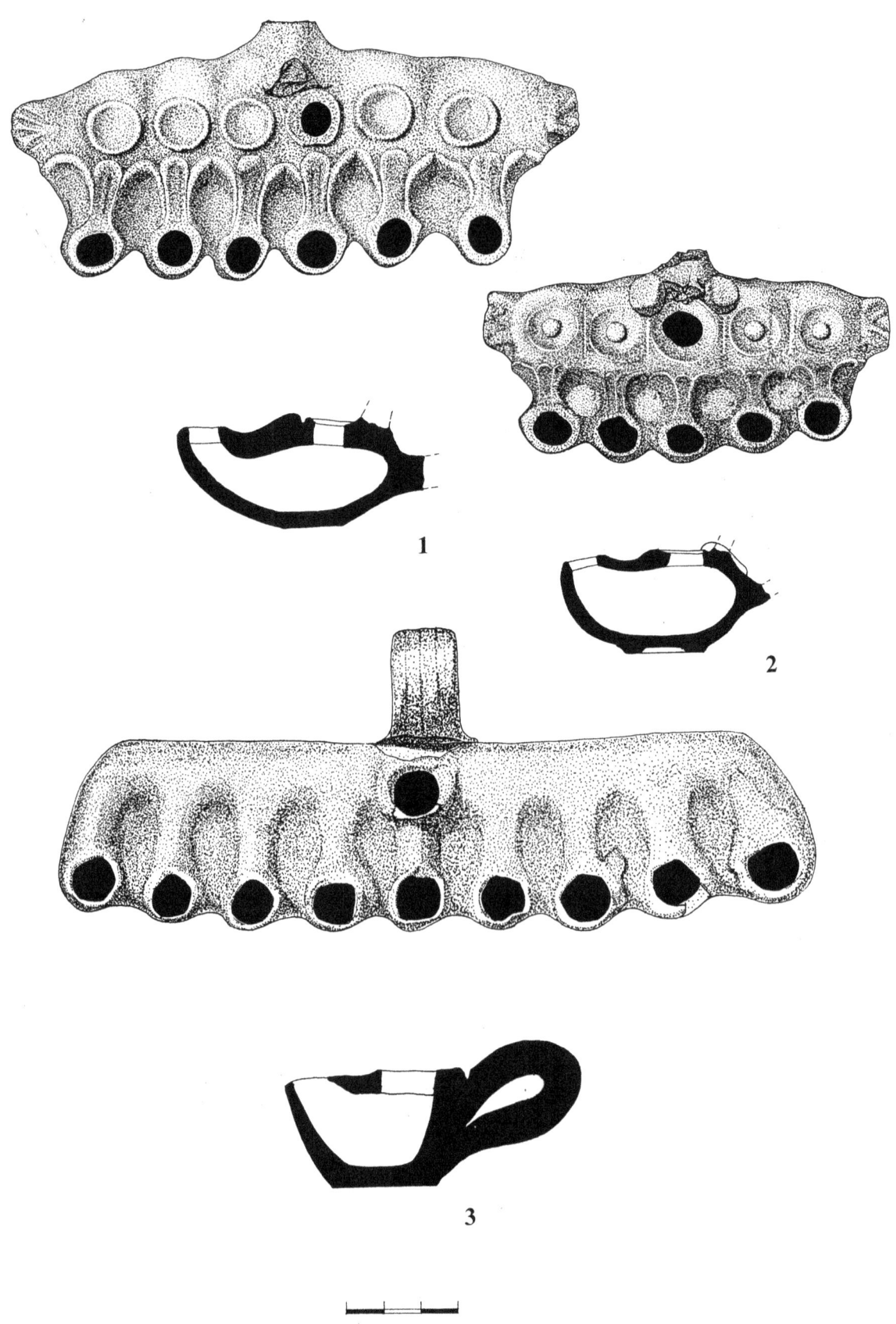

Fig. 3. Bosporan multi-nozzled lamps: 1-3- Pushkin Fine Arts Museum, M-1112; M- 1111; M-192. Clay.

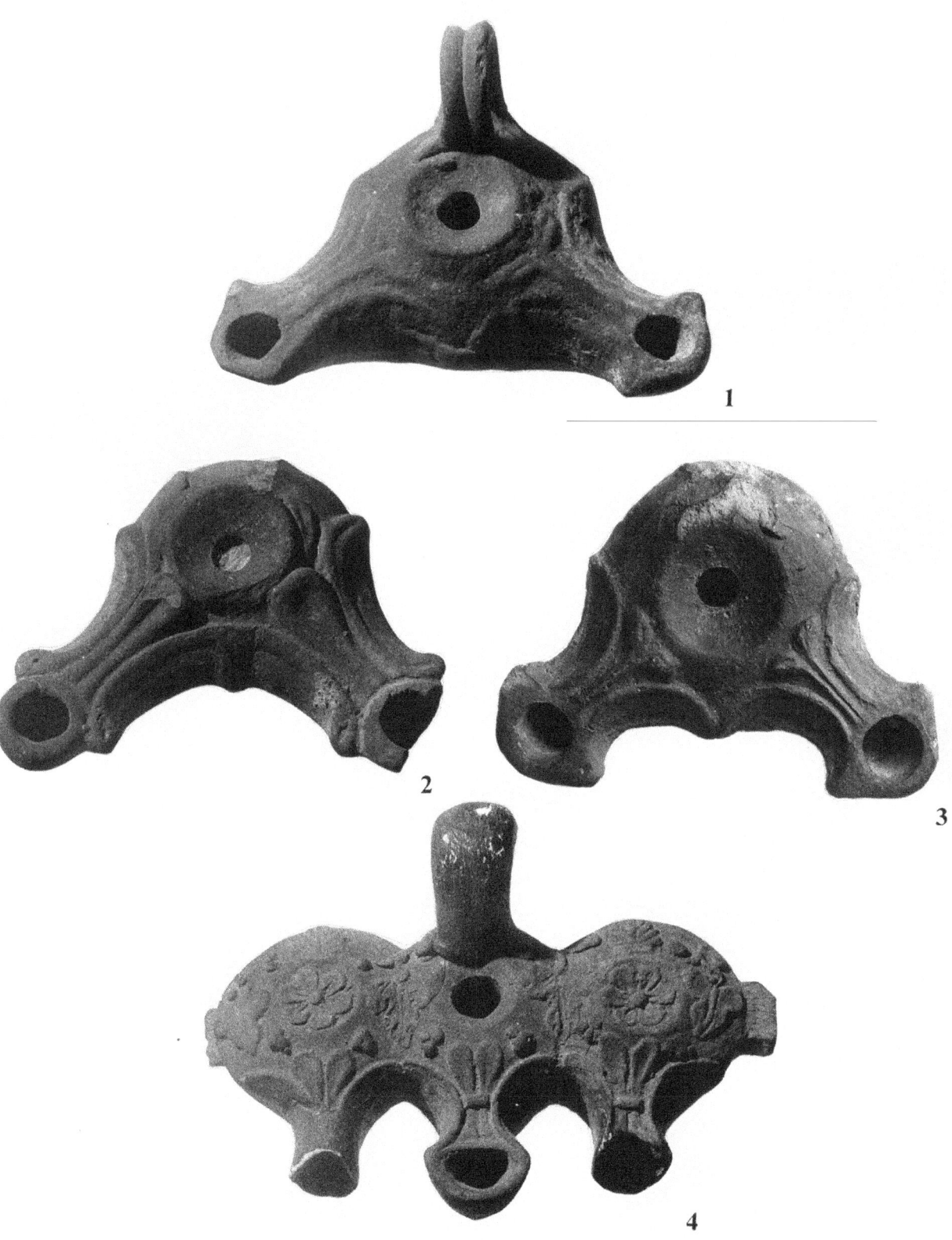

Fig. 4. Bosporan multi-nozzled lamps: 1,2,4 – Pushkin Fine Arts Museum; 3 – State Historical Museum. Clay.

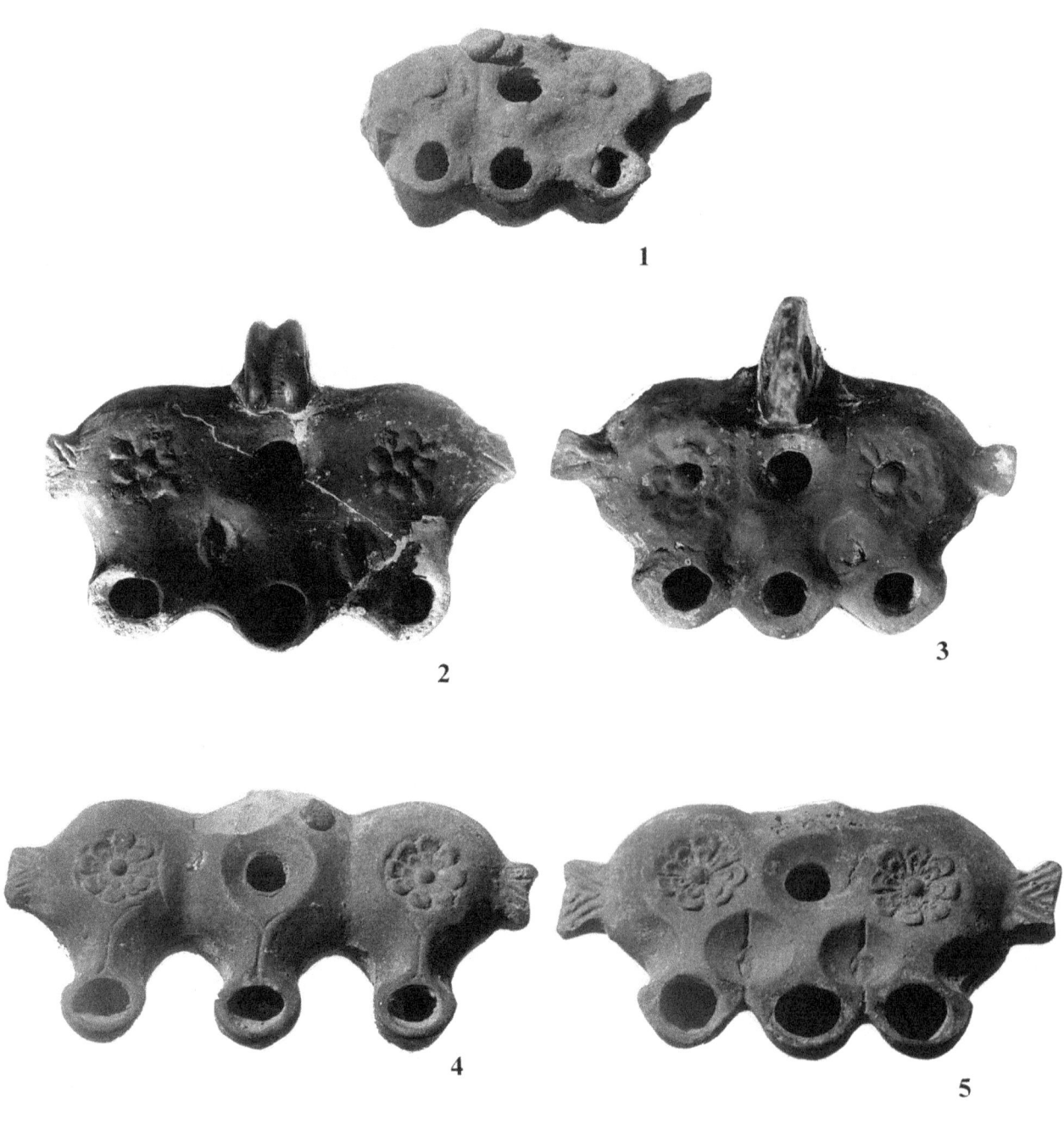

Fig. 5. Bosporan multi-nozzled lamps: 1- the Hermitage, Sankt-Peterburg; 2-5 – Pushkin Fine Arts Museum. Clay.

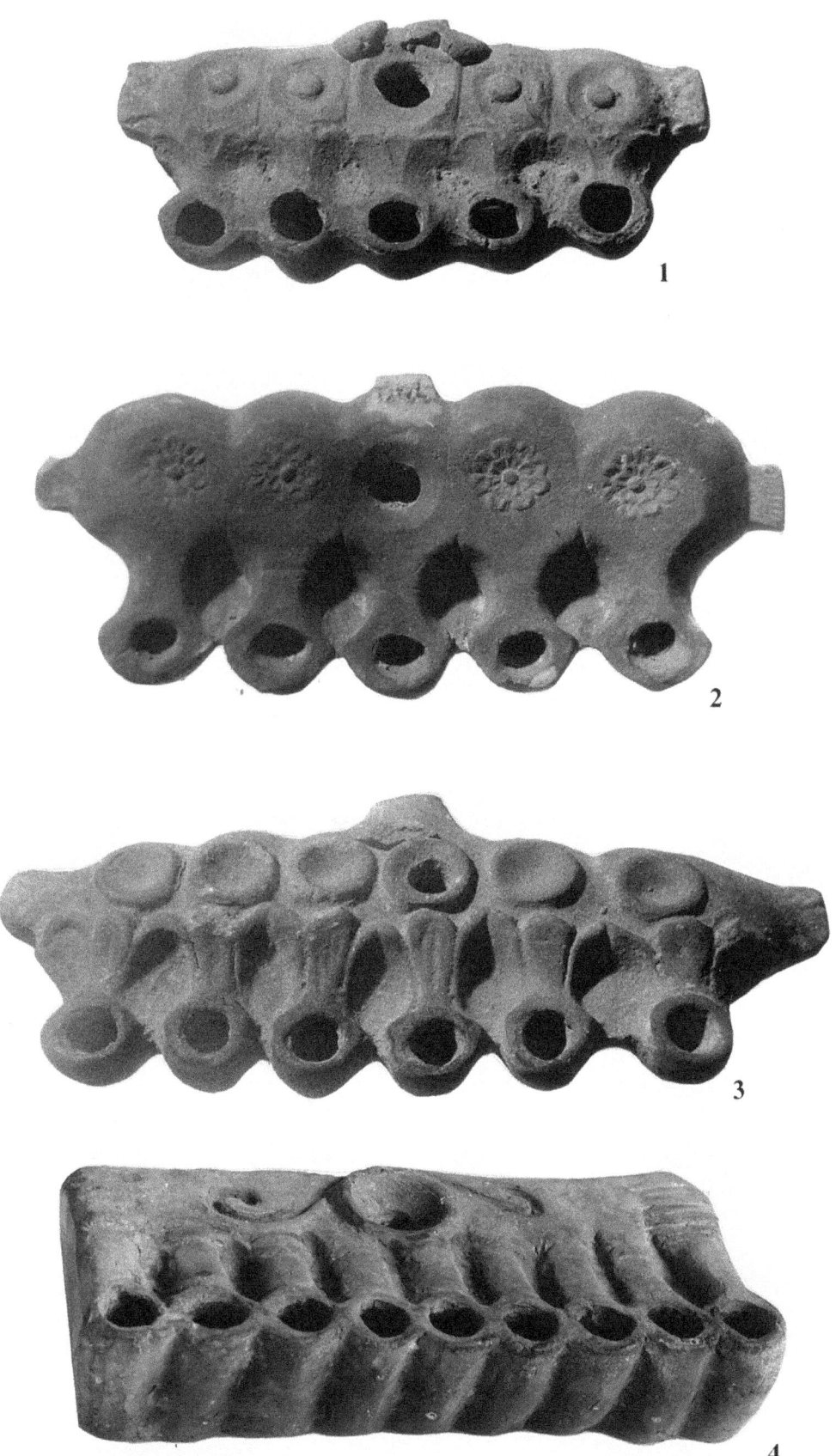

Fig. 6. Bosporan multi-nozzled lamps: 1-3- Pushkin Fine Arts Museum; 4- the Hermitage. P-1896. Op. N 1. Clay.

Fig. 7. Bosporan multi-nozzled lamps: 1- the Hermitage, P-1864 N 1004; 2- Pushkin Fine Arts Museum. Clay.

Bullhead Lamps: An attempt at typological and chronological classification

Laurent Chrzanovski
(Geneva, Switzerland)

1. The state of research:

Among all the Greek and Roman ceramics, clay lamps have been the object of many typological classifications, maybe more than any other category of artefacts.

As a matter of fact, since 1899 and Dressel's first attempt at a general typological classification of these items, over fifty different typologies have been published, some of them born from the catalogue of a museum; some of them following the analysis of the materials of an archaeological site; some of them created to fit the material of a precise antique or modern geographical region; finally, some of them completing or modifying some types of the preceding ones.

Among all these proposed classifications, some criteria are always followed to create and define a specific type, such as the chronological unity of the exemplars and the geographical location of the production centres, but, above all, a canon of shape common to all the lamps included in the same type (and canons of small differences to establish sub-types if necessary).

Following this methodology, none of the most commonly used general typologies (Dressel, Loeschcke, Dressel-Lamboglia, Deneauve, Bailey, etc.) proposed an apposite type for bullhead lamps. Most frequently, this kind of lamps is classified among the very general group of 'plastic lamps' (for example Bailey type L). The very small number of these lamps found and, moreover, published up to date probably explains this shortcoming.

Nevertheless, we can note that these exemplars represent a precise and well-defined category among the plastic lamps for three main reasons: the characteristics of their shape, the period of production, and the production centres.

The most interesting observation that can be made on bull-head lamps is that they always follow a very strict canon of shape specific to the type to which they belong (among the eight main ones that we propose), and this, despite the numerous different workshops.

Furthermore, we can see among other common types of plastic lamps (for example Negroid head-lamps, theatrical mask-lamps, fish-lamps), that there are very few canons, and each exemplar, even while keeping some common characteristics with its contemporaries, seems to be an original creation of the workshop that produced it.

If we consider all the exemplars we were able to find, we can see that the extent of their period of production is really impressive, lasting (without even including the bronze prototypes) from the IInd century BC to the IInd century AD.

The production centres (or rather: the production regions, as the exact centres have not as yet been located precisely) are also very interesting testimonies to their expansion throughout the ancient world. As a matter of fact, we can note the first productions in Greece, Asia Minor and Egypt (Alexandria), then a massive Italian production, and also an intensive production on the Northern shores of the Black Sea (essentially Crimea and South Russia).

All these peculiarities lead us to consider that the bullhead lamps fulfil all the criteria of a specific lamp type, and therefore should have their own place in the very general group of plastic lamps.

Moreover, it should be investigated whether other kinds of plastic lamps fit or not the same criteria, in order to leave, in future lamp catalogues, the 'type' designated as 'plastic lamps' only for original, chronologically or locally limited and well-defined productions.

To conclude this introduction, it is also interesting to mention the numerous discussions held about the social and religious interpretation of bullhead lamps (see for example Moehring 1988: 279), a certainly much more delicate point than for other types of lamps, and still the object of contradictory debates. As it is not the aim of this article, we will just provide here a short summary of the most significant theories.

Some scholars consider these lamps as witnesses of the cult of the Egyptian god Apis, confirming this hypothesis by the location of some of the early workshops in Egypt, and by the frequent presence, among the Italian lamps, of the plastic lunar crescent shaped handle. This theory is interesting, and probably applicable to some of these lamps, but we must not forget the bronze lamp (Cat. n. 60) from Thessalia, also with a lunar crescent, and dedicated to the goddess Artemis.

Then, numerous authors see the lamps from the imperial period as a testimony of the cult of the god Mithra.

Lastly, some consider also these lamps as Christian (Conticello De' Spagnolis, De Carolis 1986: 97), but we think that the arguments in favour of this hypothesis are very weak due to the dating of the last exemplars, too early for including them among the first groups of Christian lamps.

By looking at the decorative details of the first Greek types, and of the early Italian types, we would rather suggest that these lamps were a simple witness of religious cults, without linking them to a specific deity. As a matter of fact, the flamboyant floral patterns, palmettes, and the rich fillets of the Greek types, as well as the accurate rendering of festive (and hence non-functional) harnessing tend to show these bulls as realistic witnesses of sacrificial ceremonies, in which the animals (the bulls being the most prestigious ones) were sumptuously adorned before being led to the altar.

Thus as these lamps are bereft of any precise detail linking them to a specific cult (always with the exception of bronze lamp Cat. n. 60), they can be seen, and probably were seen at their time of production, through the eyes of each of their owners, who could give their own religious significance to the animal.

We can also notice that representations of bulls, even if quite rare, are also present on the discus of Italian lamps of Loeschcke types IV and VIII, from Tiberian times to the middle of the IIIrd century AD (Chrzanovski & Zhuravlev 1998: 86-87 and notes 224 to 237).

2. A classification attempt:

Following the principle" *Faute avouée est à moitié pardonnée*", as we commonly say in French, it is essential to indicate, as a foreword, that the present research does not claim to establish a precise typology. Rather it tries to divide the few bullhead lamps into some main groups, established by common criteria of shape and chronology, in order to observe, step by step, the evolution and the dissemination of this unique kind of artefact in the different areas of the Hellenistic and Roman worlds.

As a matter of fact, the very limited number of these lamps found and published to date (see the complete inventory in Moehring 1988:273-274), associated to the extremely rare specimens issued from precise and well-dated archaeological contexts, make it impossible to reach any reliable conclusions for the time being.

It is also important to remember that the actual shape of these lamps increases the difficulty of their study. The early exemplars were extremely fragile due to the quality and fineness of their prominent details and were thus found in very fragmentary condition, most of them being without handle or nozzle. Moreover, the richness of the details, some of them added by the ceramists on the single exemplars after withdrawing them from the mould, also contributes to give to each production a vast range of small variations (See for example Bailey 1980, Q 1142 and 1143, p. 258-259).

Finally, in the descriptions of the single exemplars, we tried to edit them in the most synthetic way, without giving any detail of the decoration when it did not represent particular innovations in respect to the general description of the type. The analysis concentrated on the functional parts such as filling-hole, nozzle, handle and base, when the authors of the publications provided this information or when it was possible to extrapolate from photographs.

Type I:
Attic productions: IInd to Ist century BC.

Description: Type I bullhead lamps are moulded lamps, very finely modelled and with very realistic details. They are large, usually about 13 cm. long. They are characterised by a triangular shape, ending with a small rounded nozzle projecting from the bull's mouth.

Their rich decoration starts with a large, raised, floral pattern between the two horns, below this is the large filling-hole, located on the top of the head and often provided with a strainer pierced with five holes in a cross pattern. Almost all the forehead, beneath the filling-hole, is covered with very accurate locks of hair. Then, the large muzzle is rendered with numerous wrinkles, and ends with the two nostrils.

The filling-hole and the hairs are flanked on either side by two fillets, extending from the large floral pattern, and ending on the sides of the lamp, near the animal's eyes. On each side of the lamp, the ear is rendered under the horn.

A separately made ring-handle is often applied at the rear.

The flat base is generally raised or defined by a ring foot.

Dating and production centres: The first bullhead shaped clay lamps are an original creation of Attic (and maybe also Pergamenian) ceramists. It started at the very beginning of the IInd century B.C, as confirmed by the dating (190 to second quarter of the IInd century BC.) provided by the archaeological context in which our Pergamenian lamp (cat. n. 1) was found (De Luca 1968: 139).

These wonderfully crafted productions are probably the result of the copying and adaptation, in clay, of bronze lamps of the late IIIrd century BC (Howland 1958: 156). The ceramists successfully achieved a very difficult work, as their prototypes succeeded in preserving the richness of the decoration patterns (and even the elegance of the small, rounded nozzle projecting from the mouth of the animal), specific to the metal lamps.

Furthermore, they also added some characteristic elements of the most common contemporaneous types of clay lamps. As a matter of fact, we can observe that their triangular shape is very close to the so-called" Ephesian"lamps (Cahn-Kleiber 1977: 178), and that some of them have a double-coiled and knotted handle at their back identical to those of" Cnidian"lamps of Howland type 50A (Howland 1958: 56).

Cat. 1:
Origin: Pergamon, Turkey; Excavations of theAsclepeion (from the temple, building phase 10) (Inv. n.: 458 L 59/63)

Dimensions: L. max: 6.90
Clay and slip: Red-brown clay; black slip.
Description: Mouldmade lamp, very fragmentary: only a part of the forehead and one horn are preserved. The filling-hole, with a stainer now almost completely lost, is on the top of the head.
Place of manufacture: Probably local production.
Proposed dating: 190 to second quarter of the IInd century BC
Bibliography: De Luca 1968, n. 266, pp. 136, 139 and pl. 49.

Cat. 2 (fig.1):
Origin: Athens, Greece; Excavations of the Agora (D 19:2, well: use filling) (Inv. n.: L. 3908)
Dimensions: L.: 7.20; B.: 13.40; H.: 9.40
Clay and slip: Pinkish buff clay, fine light brownish-red slip.
Description: Mouldmade lamp, intact except for the end of the nozzle and a small part of the floral ornament. The filling-hole, with a stainer with five holes, is on the top of the head. A double-rolled and knotted handle was added at the rear. A ring foot defines the flat base, decorated with moulded rings.
Place of manufacture: Attic production according to the clay.
Proposed dating: Second half of the second century BC
Bibliography: Howland 1958, n. 617, pp. 156-157; pl. 48.

Cat. 3 (fig.2):
Origin: Delos, Greece; Excavations (found in the southern part of the Agora of Theophrastos)
Dimensions: L.: 11.90; B.: 9.10
Clay and slip: Pinkish clay; brown slip.
Description: Mouldmade lamp, intact except for the end of the nozzle and a small part of the floral ornament. The filling-hole, with a stainer with five holes, is on the top of the head.
Place of manufacture: Attic production according to the clay.
Proposed dating: Second half of the second century BC
Bibliography: Deonna 1909: 168 and pl. II, 4; Bruneau 1965, n. 4771, p. 153; pl. 36.

Cat. 4:
Origin: Delos, Greece; Excavations
Dimensions: L. (max.): 4.80
Clay and slip: Pinkish-beige clay, orange-brown slip.
Description: Mouldmade lamp, very fragmentary: only a part of the forehead is preserved.
Place of manufacture: Attic production according to the clay.
Proposed dating: Second half of the second century BC
Bibliography: Bruneau 1965, n. 4772, p. 153; pl. 36

Cat. 5:
Origin: Delos, Greece; Excavations (found in the Aphrodision)
Dimensions: L. (max.): 4.60

Clay and slip: Grey clay, black slip.
Description: Mouldmade lamp, very fragmentary: only a part of the forehead is preserved.
Place of manufacture: Attic production according to the clay.
Proposed dating: Second half of the second century BC
Bibliography: Bruneau 1965, n. 4773, p. 153; pl. 36.

Cat. 6:
Origin: Delos, Greece; Excavations
Dimensions: L. (max): 8.20; H. (max.): 7.00
Clay and slip: Grey clay, black sometimes greenish slip, only partly preserved.
Description: Mouldmade lamp, very fragmentary: only a part of the forehead and one horn are preserved. The filling-hole, with a stainer, is on the top of the head.
Place of manufacture: Attic production according to the clay.
Proposed dating: Second half of the second century BC
Bibliography: Bruneau 1965, n. 4774, p. 153; pl. 36.

Type II:
Late Attic productions: Ist century BC to Ist century AD.

Description: Type II bullhead lamps are moulded lamps with very realistic details, but poorer decoration than the type I lamps. They are large, generally about 13 cm. long and are characterised by a triangular shape, ending with a small rounded nozzle projecting from the bull's mouth.
Their decoration starts with a raised palmette between the two horns (in some exemplars replaced by the moulded, pierced, ring-handle), below this, in the centre of the forehead, is the large filling-hole with a moulded edge. Stylised locks of hair occupy almost all the forehead all around the filling-hole. Then, the large muzzle is rendered without any decoration, and ends with the two nostrils.
On each side of the lamp, the ear is rendered under the horn.
The flat base is generally raised or defined by a ring foot.

Dating and production centres: the type II lamps are a later and simplified variant of type I lamps and should be considered as an Attic production. They are difficult to date precisely, as none of the exemplars belonging to this type come from a chronologically precise excavation context. Nevertheless, we can suggest, following what has already been noted about the presence of the raised palmette (Bruneau 1965: 153) or by observing the moulded ring-handle (as well as the nozzle of our cat. n. 9, very near to some late" Ephesian" lamps), that a dating extending from the late Ist century BC to the Ist century AD should fit this type, obviously waiting for the publication of exemplars recently found in excavations.

Cat. 7:
Origin: Delos, Greece; Excavations (found in the House of the Trident)
Dimensions: L.: 10.20; B.: 7.00

Clay and slip: Brick-red clay, Greyish slip with mica inclusions.
Description: Mouldmade lamp, intact except for the end of the nozzle. The large filling-hole, with a moulded edge, in the centre of the forehead, under a large, raised palmette acting as a handle.
Place of manufacture: Attic production?
Proposed dating: First century BC to first century AD
Bibliography: Bruneau 1965, n. 4775, p. 153; pl. 36.

Cat. 8:
Origin: Delos, Greece; Excavations
Dimensions: L.: 10.70; B.: 7.70
Clay and slip: Grey-yellowish clay, black slip only partly preserved.
Description: Mouldmade lamp, intact except for the end of the nozzle. The large filling-hole, with a moulded edge, in the centre of the forehead. A moulded, pierced handle is situated at the rear.
Place of manufacture: Attic production?
Proposed dating: First century BC to first century AD
Bibliography: Bruneau 1965, n. 4776, p. 153; pl. 36.

Cat. 9:
Origin: Magnesia (Museum collection: Rijksmuseum, Leiden, The Netherlands) (Inv. not indicated)
Dimensions: L.: 11.00
Clay and slip: not indicated.
Description: Mouldmade lamp, intact except for the handle, broken and the handle-ornament, now lost. The filling-hole is pierced through the forehead, in a concave moulded edge; the large, triangular nozzle projects from the mouth of the animal.
Place of manufacture: Attica (?)
Proposed dating: Second half of the Ist to IInd century AD
Bibliography: Brants 1913, n. 450, p. 30, pl. 4

Type III:
Egyptian productions: Ist century BC to Ist century AD.

Description: Type III bullhead lamps are moulded lamps, with poorer decoration than type I lamps, where the absence of realism gives place to a much more stylised rendering, in which any rich ornament has disappeared, except, sometimes, the harnessing or a simple frontal fillet. They are generally about 8 cm. long.

They are characterised by a broad triangular shape, ending with a large oval nozzle projecting from the bull's mouth. The main details of these lamps are the two large curved horns, raised above the head.

The filling-hole, with a moulded edge, is in the centre of the forehead. Horns and ears are rendered without details and, on the forehead, numerous small-incised points represent the hair. A very important place is given to the eyes, they are very accurately treated and are no longer situated on each side of the lamp but in an almost frontal position, dominating the large muzzle, rendered with two or three wrinkles, and ending with the two nostrils.

In some exemplars the filling-hole between the horns is preceded by a larger hole, also with a moulded edge, interpreted as a thumb-grip (Bailey 1975: 278); in others, by the beginning of a large, moulded, pierced handle decorated with three grooves.

The flat base is generally raised, pointed-oval in shape.

Dating and production centres: Sometimes wrongly considered as the first bullhead shaped clay lamps (Szentleleky 1969: 73), the earliest Egyptian productions seem to appear only in the Ist century BC.

As we have seen in the analysis of their shape and decoration, these lamps are far from the original bronze prototypes, and, moreover, seem to have no relation with the Type I and II Pergamene and Attic productions. Thus we should consider them as original Egyptian productions, specifically made for the local market.

They are also difficult to date precisely, as none of the exemplars belonging to this type comes from a chronologically precise excavation context. Nevertheless, by observing their characteristics, we can suggest that a dating extending from the late Ist century BC to the Ist century AD should fit this type, obviously waiting for the publication of exemplars recently found in excavations.

Cat. 10 (fig.3):
Origin: Egypt (?) (Museum collection: British Museum, London, United Kingdom)
(Inv. n.: 1963.7-15.2)
Dimensions: L.: 8.0; B.: 4.70
Clay and slip: Brown, micaceous clay, with a few white grits; red slip except under the base.
Description: Mouldmade lamp, intact. The filling-hole, with a moulded edge, is in the centre of the forehead. Behind the filling-hole, between the horns, is a larger hole, probably a thumb-grip. Projecting from the bull's muzzle is an oval nozzle, with a flat rim round the wick-hole. The lamp stands on a raised base, pointed-oval in shape and flat below.
Place of manufacture: Egypt.
Proposed dating: 1st century BC
Bibliography: Bailey 1975, n. Q 607; p. 278; pl. 114.

Cat. 11:
Origin: Alexandria (Museum collection: Archäologisches Institut der Universität Tübingen, Tübingen, Germany)
(Inv. n.: Sch. 5150/25)
Dimensions: L.: 6.20; B.: 4.80; H.: 3.10
Clay and slip: Black-brown clay with white inclusions, no slip.
Description: Mouldmade lamp, intact except for the end of the nozzle. The filling-hole, with a moulded edge, is in the centre of the forehead. Behind the filling-hole, between the horns, is a larger hole, probably a thumb-grip. Projecting from the bull's muzzle is an oval nozzle, with a flat rim round the wick-hole. The lamp stands on a raised base, pointed-oval in shape and flat below.

Place of manufacture: Egypt.
Proposed dating: First century BC
Bibliography: Cahn-Klaiber 1977, n. 153, pp. 177-178, 332; pl. 13.

Cat. 12:
Origin: Unknown (Museum collection: Akademisches Kunstmuseum der Universität Bonn, Bonn, Germany) (Inv. n.: 2183)
Dimensions: L.: 4.20; B.: 4.90; H.: 2.00
Clay and slip: Red-brown clay, brick-red slip.
Description: Mouldmade lamp, intact except for the handle, now lost. The filling-hole, with a moulded edge, is in the centre of the forehead. A Lotus flower is represented on the forehead.
Place of manufacture: Egypt .
Proposed dating: First to second century AD
Bibliography: Hübinger 1993, n. 326, p. 158; pl. 38.

Cat. 13:
Origin: Unknown (Museum collection: Institute of Archaeology, Hebrew University, Jerusalem, Israel; from Shloessinger collection) (Inv. n.: 6188)
Dimensions: L.: 8.00; H.: 5.00
Clay and slip: Brown clay, white slip.
Description: Mouldmade lamp, intact except for the handle, partly broken. The filling-hole, with a moulded edge, is in the centre of the forehead. Raised triangular base. A double-grooved, pierced, moulded ring-handle is situated at the rear.
Place of manufacture: probably Egypt.
Proposed dating: First to second century AD
Bibliography: Rosenthal, Sivan 1978, n. 606, p. 147.

Cat. 14:
Origin: Alexandria (Museum collection: Musée Gréco-Romain, Alexandria, Egypt) (Inv. n.: not indicated)
Dimensions: not indicated.
Clay and slip: not indicated.
Description: Mouldmade lamp, intact except for the end of the nozzle. The filling-hole, with a moulded edge, is in the centre of the forehead.
Place of manufacture: Egypt.
Proposed dating: First century AD
Bibliography: Joly 1995: 331-332 and pl. LIII, 5.

Type IV:
First Italian prototypes: Ist century BC.

Description: Type IV bullhead lamps are moulded lamps, with very similar shape and characteristics as the type II Attic productions. Their size is variable, from about 8 cm. to over 16 cm. long.

They are characterised by a triangular shape, ending with a large rounded trumpet shaped nozzle projecting from the bull's mouth.

The decoration is very carefully and realistically treated, with the hairs occupying all the top of the head and surrounding the filling-hole. The rest of the decoration consists of numerous wrinkles on the forehead and on the muzzle which ends with two very large nostrils, and giving the lamp a very lively aspect, accentuated by the indication of the lower jaw teeth.

On each side of the lamp, the ear is rendered under the horn.

A moulded, vertical handle is situated at the back.

The flat base is generally raised or defined by a ring foot.

Dating and production centres: This very rare type of lamp seems to have been produced in Italy at the beginning of the first century BC.

Cat. 15 (fig.4):
Origin: Italy (?) (Museum collection: British Museum, London, United Kingdom)
(Inv. n.: 1926.2-16.39)
Dimensions: L.: 16.70; B.: 10.90
Clay and slip: Brown clay, containing mica, with a grey core. An orange-coloured slip is applied over all, varying in the intensity of its colour.
Description: Mouldmade lamp, intact except for a small part of the forehead and the vertical handle, now lost. The filling-hole is pierced through the forehead and the trumpet mouth of the nozzle projects from the mouth of the animal; the teeth of the lower jaw are indicated. The lamp stands on a flat base of pointed oval shape.
Place of manufacture: Italy.
Proposed dating: Second half of the second century or first half of the first century BC
Bibliography: Bailey 1975, n. Q 705, pp. 334; pl. 130.

Type V:
"Big horns" Italian productions: Ist century AD.

Description: Type V bullhead lamps are moulded lamps with rich details. Their size is variable, from about 8 cm. to over 16 cm. long.

They are characterised by a triangular shape ending with a large rounded trumpet shaped nozzle, and with the wick-hole surrounded by a flat rim projecting from the bull's mouth. The main details of these lamps are the two curved horns, raised high above the head.

The filling-hole, with a moulded edge, is in the centre of the forehead. The horns are decorated with numerous incisions. In many of these lamps, the ceramists have paid special attention to the rich harnessing, starting from the horns, occupying the main part of the forehead, (the hair is treated in a very discrete way), and ending on the muzzle. A very important place is given to the eyes and the shaggy eyebrows, very accurately treated, dominating the large prominent muzzle, rendered with two or three wrinkles, and ending with the two nostrils.

A large moulded, pierced, ring-handle decorated with three grooves is almost always situated at the back.

The flat, almost circular base is raised or defined by a base-ring.

Dating and production centres: The lamps of this type have been produced in Italy during the first century AD. Their characteristics may suggest an amalgam of the general shape of the late type II Attic lamps (through the type IV Italian prototypes, from which they adopt the nozzle) and the decoration of the type III Egyptian lamps, where the large curved raised horns and the harnessing represented the essential points of interest.

The last productions (cat. n. 16 and 17) indicate the transition towards type VI: the horns begin to be smaller and the details are simplified: the harnessing disappears and is replaced by a rich representation of the hair.

Cat. 16:
Origin: Rome, Viminale (Museum collection: Antiquarium Comunale, Rome, Italy)
(Inv. n.: 5136)
Dimensions: L.: 18.00; B.: 11.00; H.: 6.60
Clay and slip: not described.
Description: Mouldmade lamp, intact except for the horns and the vertical handle, now lost. The filling-hole is pierced through the forehead and the trumpet mouth of the nozzle projects from the mouth of the animal.
Place of manufacture: Italy.
Proposed dating: First century AD
Bibliography: Mercando 1962, n. 12, p. 40; pl. 15:2 (The author mentions five other exemplars preserved in the same museum (nn. 7 - 11), but without providing any indication or illustration).

Cat. 17:
Origin: Saliceta S. Giuliano, Modena, Italy; Excavations
Dimensions: L.: 8.80; B.: 8.00; H.: 4.50
Clay and slip: not described.
Description: Mouldmade lamp, intact except for the end of the nozzle, a part of the right horn and the vertical handle, now lost. The filling-hole is pierced through the forehead and the trumpet mouth of the nozzle projects from the mouth of the animal.
Place of manufacture: Italy.
Proposed dating: First century AD
Bibliography: Forte 1988: 108 and fig. 72:8, p. 106 and fig. 78, p. 111.

Cat. 18 (fig.5):
Origin: Unknown (Italy?) (Museum collection: Civico Museo Archeologico, Milano, Italy) (Inv. n.: A 2097)
Dimensions: L.: 5.50; B.: 3.70
Clay and slip: Light brown clay, red-brown slip.
Description: Mouldmade lamp, very damaged: horns, handle and nozzle are now lost. The filling-hole is pierced through the forehead.
Place of manufacture: Italy.
Proposed dating: First century AD
Bibliography: Sapelli 1979, n. 340, p. 145; pl. 39.

Cat. 19 (fig. 6):
Origin: Italy (Rome?) (Museum collection: British Museum, London, United Kingdom)
(Inv. n.: 1991.6-24.1)
Dimensions: L.: 18.00; B.: 10.40
Clay and slip: Grey clay, black slip.
Description: Mouldmade lamp, intact. The filling-hole is pierced through the forehead and the trumpet mouth of the nozzle projects from the mouth of the animal. The lamp stands on an almost circular base-ring, within which is an incuse letter N decorated with small impressed circles.
Place of manufacture: Italy.
Proposed dating: Ist century AD
Bibliography: Bailey 1996, n. Q 732bis, p. 128; pl. 168, 178 (the author proposes a dating around the second half of the first century BC).

Cat. 20 (fig. 7,8):
Origin: Italy (?) (Museum collection: Museum für Vor- und Frühgeschichte - Archäologisches Museum, Frankfurt, Germany) (Inv. n.: x 18479)
Dimensions: L.: 9.20; B.: 5.20; H.: 2.20
Clay and slip: Light red clay, no slip.
Description: Mouldmade lamp, intact. The filling-hole is pierced through the forehead and the trumpet mouth of the nozzle projects from the mouth of the animal. A moulded, pierced, ring handle is situated at the rear, under a plastic handle-ornament in shape of lunar crescent.
Place of manufacture: probably Italy.
Proposed dating: Second half of the Ist to IInd century AD
Bibliography: Schäfer, Marczoch 1990, n. 70, p. 64.

Type VI:
"Standard" Italian productions: Ist to IInd century AD.

Description: Type VI bullhead lamps are moulded lamps, with few details, attention being drawn to the hairs of the animal. Their size is very variable, from about 10 cm. to over 20 cm. long.

They are characterised by a less triangular and more compact shape than the preceding types, and by the almost imperative presence of a moulded, pierced ring-handle at their back above which is large moulded handle-ornament, often in lunar crescent shape.

The filling-hole is always situated in the centre of the forehead, surrounded by the hairs of the animal, rendered in relief. The horns and the ears are almost united, and the horns are often very small, not much larger than the ears themselves. The eyes and the shaggy eyebrows are very accurately treated with small incisions. The large prominent muzzle, rendered with two or three wrinkles, ends with the two nostrils and dominates the nozzle.

There are two main nozzle shapes in this type of lamps: single, round nozzles and double, round nozzles, generally very short in respect to the size of the lamp and with smaller wick-holes than in all the preceding types.

The bases are generally flat, in a broad oval or triangular shape, often defined by a groove.

We can notice, throughout the examples proposed here, the accurateness of details in the lamps we should consider as 'first generations' and some later, much less accurate exemplars.

Dating and production centres: The lamps of this type (the main part of the bullhead lamps found and published till now) have been produced in Italy from the middle of the first century to the end of the second century AD. Their simpler shape and details have certainly permitted a less expensive and consequently more intensive production, and have also ensured more solidity than the other types.

The different locations of findings, as well as the differences of clay and slip between the exemplars found, also suggest a wide dissemination of these lamps not only on the Italian market, but also abroad, where they were sometimes also produced, as we can observe by the presence of some African, Gaulish and German copies.

A. Single-nozzled lamp with plain semi-circular nozzle:

This variation is very rare, and is witnessed only by the magnificent exemplar preserved in the British Museum, and maybe by the two fragments found in Cosa, if we accept the reconstructive drawing proposed by the authors.

Cat. 21 (fig.9):
Origin: Italy (?) (Museum collection: British Museum, London, United Kingdom) (Inv. n.: 1840.12-15.42)
Dimensions: L.: 20.30; B.: 12.30; H.: 9.1
Clay and slip: Orange clay, orange-brown slip.
Description: Mouldmade lamp, intact. The filling-hole is pierced through the forehead, situated in the centre of a rosette; the plain semi-circular nozzle projects from the mouth of the animal.
At the rear is situated a pierced handle, above which is a decorative ornament, elliptical in plan, decorated with a palmette in flat relief. Flat base, broadly oval.
Place of manufacture: Italy.
Proposed dating: Late Tiberian to Antonine.
Bibliography: Bailey 1980, n. Q 1140, p. 258 - 259; pl. 47.

Cat. 22:
Origin: Cosa, Italy; Excavations (found in the basilica) (Inv. n.: not indicated)
Dimensions: L. (max.): 6.50 and 6.00
Clay and slip: Light buff clay, brown slip.
Description: Mouldmade lamp, very fragmentary. Only two fragments of the forehead are preserved, showing the eyes and a part of the large filling-hole, with a moulded edge.
Place of manufacture: Italy.
Proposed dating: The context is dated 50-100 AD
Bibliography: Fitch & Goldman 1994, n. 985, fig. 103.

B. Single-nozzled lamp with plain heart-shaped nozzle:

This variation is very rare, and is witnessed only by the magnificent exemplar preserved in the Musée d'Histoire de Marseille. Such nozzles are very common on round lamps of Loeschcke type VIII (Loeschcke nozzle-form H)

Cat. 23 (fig.10):
Origin: Marseille, found in the Roman harbour (Museum collection: Musée d'Histoire de Marseille, Marseille, France) (Inv. n.: 83.7.38)
Dimensions: L.: 15.00; B.: 6.00
Clay and slip: not indicated.
Description: Mouldmade lamp, intact. The filling-hole is pierced through the forehead, with a moulded edge; the plain heart-shaped nozzle projects from the mouth of the animal. An air-hole is situated between the muzzle and the nozzle.
At the rear is situated a pierced handle, above which is a handle ornament in lunar crescent shape.
Place of manufacture: Italy (?)
Proposed dating: Middle of the Ist to IInd century AD
Bibliography: Marseille 1988, n. 631, p. 125.

C. Single-nozzled lamp with large nozzle surrounded by a flat rim:

This variation is the most common among the single-nozzled lamps.

Cat. 24 (fig.11):
Origin: Unknown (Museum collection: Bibliothèque Nationale, Paris, France) (Inv. n.: 4183)
Dimensions: L.: 13.20; B.: 12.20; H.: 6.20
Clay and slip: beige clay, red slip.
Description: Mouldmade lamp, intact except for the handle and handle-ornament, now lost. The filling-hole is pierced through the forehead, with a moulded edge; the large nozzle projects from the mouth of the animal.
Place of manufacture: Italy (?)
Proposed dating: Second half of the IInd century AD
Bibliography: Hellmann 1987, n. 224, p. 59; pl. 26.

Cat. 25 (fig.12):
Origin: Unknown (Museum collection: Museo Civico, Biassono, Italy) (Inv. n.: A.99.66.14)
Dimensions: L: 12.98; B.: 10.54; H.: 4.81
Clay and slip: Beige clay; orange-brown slip.
Description: Mouldmade lamp, intact except for the left horn, broken, and the handle and handle-ornament, now lost. The filling-hole is pierced through the forehead, with a moulded edge; the large nozzle (almost heart-shaped) projects from the mouth of the animal. Flat triangular base.
Place of manufacture: Italy (?)

Proposed dating: IInd century AD
Bibliography: Unpublished. Our best thanks to the director Museum, Professor E.A. Arslan, for the kind permission of taking a picture and of publishing this lamp for the first time.

Cat. 26 (figs.13,14):
Origin: Italy (Museum collection: Hermitage, St. Petersburg, Russia) (Inv. n.: 1120)
Dimensions: L.: 8.00; H.: 5.70
Clay and slip: Yellow clay; black slip.
Description: Mouldmade lamp, intact. The filling-hole is pierced through the forehead, with a moulded edge; the large nozzle projects from the mouth of the animal. Flat, almost triangular base. At the rear is situated a pierced handle, above which is a handle ornament in lunar crescent shape.
Place of manufacture: Italy.
Proposed dating: Ist century AD
Bibliography: Waldhauer 1914, n. 502, p. 64, pl. XLVII.

Cat. 27:
Origin: Unknown (Museum collection: Museum of Fine Arts, Budapest, Hungary) (Inv. n.: 50.1148)
Dimensions: L.: 13.20; H.: 6.90
Clay and slip: Creamy-yellow clay; streaky red slip.
Description: Mouldmade lamp, intact except for the lower part of the nozzle. The filling-hole is pierced through the forehead, with a moulded edge; the large nozzle projects from the mouth of the animal. Flat, almost triangular base, in the middle of which are inscribed the letters PAR. At the rear is situated a pierced handle, above which is a handle ornament in lunar crescent shape.
Place of manufacture: Italy (?)
Proposed dating: Ist century AD
Bibliography: Szentleleky 1969, n. 86, p. 73.

Cat. 28 (fig.15):
Origin: Unknown (Museum collection: Museum für Vor- und Frühgeschichte - Archäologisches Museum, Frankfurt, Germany) (Inv. n.: 90, 1.2)
Dimensions: L.: 5.70; B.: 3.30; H.: 2.70
Clay and slip: Light brown clay, brown slip.
Description: Mouldmade lamp, intact except for the handle, broken and the handle-ornament, now lost. The filling-hole is pierced through the forehead, with a moulded edge; the large nozzle projects from the mouth of the animal.
Place of manufacture: Italy (?)
Proposed dating: Second half of the Ist to IInd century AD
Bibliography: Schäfer, Marczoch 1990, n. 69, p. 63.

Cat. 29 (fig.16):
Origin: Unknown (Museum collection: Museo Archeologico al Teatro romano, Verona, Italy) (Inv. n.: 24368)
Dimensions: L.: 9.10; B.: 7.90; H.: 4.30 (B. Crescent : 6.00)
Clay and slip: Light orange clay, orange-brown slip.
Description: Mouldmade lamp, intact except for the nozzle, completely lost, and for the handle and handle-ornament, partly broken. The filling-hole is pierced through the forehead, with a moulded edge. At the rear is situated a pierced handle, above which is a handle ornament in lunar crescent shape. Flat, triangular base.
Place of manufacture: Italy (?)
Proposed dating: Second half of Ist century AD
Bibliography: Larese, Sgreva 1996, n. 266, pp. 173-174.

Cat. 30 (fig.17):
Origin: Unknown (Museum collection: Museo Civico Archeologico, Bologna, Italy) (Inv. n.: 6123)
Dimensions: L.: 9.5; B.: 8.00; H.: 5.50
Clay and slip: Ocra clay, red slip.
Description: Mouldmade lamp, intact except for the handle-ornament, now lost. The filling-hole is pierced through the forehead, with a moulded edge; the large nozzle projects from the mouth of the animal. Oval, flat base, with inscribed mark : IVN (= IVNI?) in irregular letters.
Place of manufacture: Italy (?)
Proposed dating: Ist century AD
Bibliography: Gualandi Genito 1977, n. 509, p. 185; pl. 67.

Cat. 31:
Origin: Unknown (Museum collection: Museo Biscari, Catania, Italy)
Dimensions: L.: 17.80; B.: 11.50
Clay and slip: Dark clay, slip not described.
Description: Mouldmade lamp, intact except for the nozzle, now lost. The filling-hole is pierced through the forehead, with a moulded edge. At the rear is situated a pierced handle, above which is a handle ornament in lunar crescent shape.
Place of manufacture: Italy (?)
Proposed dating: Ist century AD
Bibliography: Libertini 1930, n. 1483, p. 296 and pl. 130.

Cat. 32 (fig.18, 19):
Origin: Unknown (Museum collection: Museum für Vor- und Frühgeschichte - Archäologisches Museum, Frankfurt, Germany; from the collection of F. Beyer) (Inv. n.: x 21109)
Dimensions: L.: 12.00
Clay and slip: Red-brown clay, no slip.
Description: Mouldmade lamp, intact except for the nozzle, completely lost, and for the handle and handle-ornament, partly broken. The filling-hole is pierced through the forehead, with a moulded edge. At the rear is situated a rough, unpierced handle, above which was probably a handle ornament. Flat, raised, almost triangular base.
Place of manufacture: Italy (?)
Proposed dating: Ist to IInd century AD
Bibliography: Unpublished. Our best thanks to the Museum, and especially to D. Stutzinger, for the kind permission of publishing this lamp for the first time.

Cat. 33 (fig.20):
Origin: Italy (?) (Museum collection: Kestner-Museum,

Hannover, Germany) (Inv. n.: 1893.17)
Dimensions: L.: 10.20; B.: 8.10; H.: 4.80
Clay and slip: Light red clay; slip has disappeared.
Description: Mouldmade lamp, intact except for the handle, partly broken and the handle-ornament, totally lost. The very large filling-hole is pierced through the forehead, with a moulded edge. At the rear is situated a rough, pierced ring-handle, above which was probably a handle ornament. Flat, raised, almost triangular base.
Place of manufacture: Italy (?)
Proposed dating: Second half of the IInd century AD
Bibliography: Mlasowski 1993, n. 409, pp. 418-419.

D. Double-nozzled lamp with large nozzle surrounded by a flat rim:

This category contains the greatest number bull-head lamps.

Cat. 34 (fig.21):
Origin: Italy (?) (Museum collection: British Museum, London, United Kingdom) (Inv. n.: 1756.1-1.20)
Dimensions: L.: 13.90; B.: 8.80
Clay and slip: Orange-buff clay, worn orange-red slip
Description: Mouldmade lamp, intact except for the right nozzle, partly broken. The filling-hole is pierced through the forehead, with a moulded edge. The nozzle projects from the bull's muzzle and terminates in two wick-holes, each pierced through adjacent oval flat areas. At the rear is situated a pierced handle, above which is a handle ornament in lunar crescent shape. Broadly triangular flat base.
Place of manufacture: Italy (?)
Proposed dating: Second half of the first century AD
Bibliography: Bailey 1980, n. Q 1141, p. 258; pl. 47.

Cat. 35 (fig.22):
Origin: Italy (?) (Museum collection: British Museum, London, United Kingdom) (Inv. n.: 1945.11-29.1)
Dimensions: L.: 14.50; B.: 8.00
Clay and slip: Buff clay, traces of an orange slip.
Description: Mouldmade lamp, intact except for a small part of the handle-ornament. The filling-hole is pierced through the forehead, with a moulded edge. The nozzle projects from the bull's muzzle and terminates in two wick-holes, each pierced through adjacent oval flat areas. At the rear is situated a pierced handle, above which is a handle ornament in lunar crescent shape. Broadly triangular flat base.
Place of manufacture: Italy (?)
Proposed dating: Second half of the first century AD
Bibliography: Bailey 1980, n. Q 1142, pp. 258 - 259; pl. 47.

Cat. 36 (fig.23):
Origin: Italy (?) (Museum collection: British Museum, London, United Kingdom) (Inv. n.: 1814.7-4.99)
Dimensions: L.: 11.00; B.: 8.00
Clay and slip: Orange-buff clay, traces of an orange-brown slip.
Description: Mouldmade lamp, intact except for the handle and handle-ornament, now lost. The filling-hole is pierced through the forehead, with a moulded edge. The nozzle projects from the bull's muzzle and terminates in two wick-holes, each pierced through adjacent oval flat areas. At the rear was situated a pierced handle, above which was the handle ornament. Broadly triangular flat base.
Place of manufacture: Italy (?)
Proposed dating: Second half of the first century AD
Bibliography: Bailey 1980, n. Q 1143, p. 259; pl. 47.

Cat. 37:
Origin: Italy (?) (Museum collection: Musées Royaux d'Art et d'Histoire, Belgium) (Inv. n.: not indicated)
Dimensions: not indicated.
Clay and slip: not indicated.
Description: Mouldmade lamp, intact except for the handle and handle-ornament, now lost. The filling-hole is pierced through the forehead, with a moulded edge. The nozzle projects from the bull's muzzle and terminates in two wick-holes, each pierced through adjacent oval flat areas. At the rear was situated a pierced handle, above which was the handle ornament. Broadly triangular flat base.
Place of manufacture: Italy (?)
Proposed dating: First century AD
Bibliography: Skinkel-Taupin 1980, n. 7a, p. 8.

Cat. 38 (fig. 24):
Origin: Italy (?) (Museum collection: Kestner-Museum, Hannover, Germany) (Inv. n.: 1935.200.892)
Dimensions: L.: 9.40; B.: 6.70; H.: 3.70
Clay and slip: Light beige clay; rests of dark slip.
Description: Mouldmade lamp, intact except for the handle and handle-ornament, now lost, and for the right nozzle, partly broken. The filling-hole is pierced through the forehead, with a moulded edge. The nozzle projects from the bull's muzzle and terminates in two wick-holes, each pierced through adjacent oval flat areas. At the rear was situated a pierced handle, above which was the handle ornament. Broadly triangular flat base.
Place of manufacture: Italy (?)
Proposed dating: Second half of the first century AD
Bibliography: Mlasowski 1993, n. 410, pp. 420-421.

Cat. 39:
Origin: Unknown (Museum collection: Museum of Fine Arts, Budapest, Hungary) (Inv. n.: 50.1149)
Dimensions: L.: 7.40; H.: 6.10
Clay and slip: Greyish-yellow clay, brown slip.
Description: Mouldmade lamp, intact except for the nozzles, completely lost, and for the handle and handle-ornament, partly broken. The filling-hole is pierced through the forehead, with a moulded edge. At the rear is situated a pierced handle, above which is a handle ornament in lunar crescent shape. Flat, triangular base, defined by a groove.
Place of manufacture: Italy (?)
Proposed dating: Second half of Ist century AD

Bibliography: Szentleleky 1969, n. 87, p. 73.

Cat. 40:
Origin: Limoges, France; Excavations of a urban domus in the Rue du Chaudron
Dimensions: not indicated.
Clay and slip: not indicated.
Description: Mouldmade lamp, intact except for the nozzles, almost completely lost. The filling-hole is pierced through the forehead, with a moulded edge. The nozzle projects from the bull's muzzle and terminated in two wick-holes, now lost. At the rear is situated a pierced handle, above which is a handle ornament in lunar crescent shape.
Place of manufacture: Italy (?)
Proposed dating: First century AD
Bibliography: A.A.V.V., *Informations archéologiques, Circonscription de Poitiers*, in Gallia XXIII (1965), p. 383 and fig. 54, p. 385

Cat. 41 (fig.25):
Origin: Unknown (Museum collection: Museo Archeologico, Genova-Pegli, Italy) (Inv. n.: 1192)
Dimensions: L.: 21.00; B.: 11.5; H.: 7.50
Clay and slip: Light beige clay, red-brown slip.
Description: Mouldmade lamp, intact. The filling-hole is pierced through the forehead, with a moulded edge. The nozzle projects from the bull's muzzle and terminates in two wick-holes, each pierced through adjacent oval flat areas. At the rear is situated a pierced handle, above which is a handle ornament in lunar crescent shape.
Place of manufacture: Italy (?)
Proposed dating: Second half of the Ist century AD
Bibliography: Pastorino 1989, n. 14, p. 136 and fig. 4, p. 135.

Cat. 42 (fig.26):
Origin: Unknown (?) (Museum collection: Museo Civico, Biassono, Italy) (Inv. n.: A.99.65.4)
Dimensions: L: 22.50 (with handle 26.00); B.: 18.50; H.: 11.2 (with handle 15.4)
Clay and slip: Light beige clay; dark orange-brown slip.
Description: Mouldmade lamp, intact except for the left horn and the handle, broken and reconstructed. The filling-hole is pierced through the forehead, with a moulded edge. The nozzle projects from the bull's muzzle and terminates in two wick-holes, each pierced through adjacent oval flat areas. At the rear was situated a pierced handle, and probably a handle-ornament (visible handle is a modern reconstruction). Broadly triangular flat base.
Place of manufacture: Italy (?)
Proposed dating: First century AD
Bibliography: Unpublished. Our best thanks to the director Museum, Professor E.A. Arslan, for the kind permission of taking a picture and of publishing this lamp for the first time.

Cat. 43:
Origin: Unknown (Museum collection: National Museum, Prague, Czech Republic) (Inv. n.: P. 1812)
Dimensions: L.: 4.60; B.: 4.90; H.: 2.40 (H. with handle: 3.90)
Clay and slip: Light brown clay, red slip.
Description: Mouldmade lamp, intact except for the nozzles, completely lost. The filling-hole is pierced through the forehead, with a moulded edge. At the rear is situated a pierced handle, above which is a handle ornament in lunar crescent shape. Flat, triangular base.
Place of manufacture: Italy (?)
Proposed dating: First century AD
Bibliography: Haken 1958, n. 86, p. 80-81 and pl. 12.

Cat. 44 (fig. 27):
Origin: Unknown (Museum collection: Kestner-Museum, Hannover, Germany) (Inv. n.: 1250)
Dimensions: L. (max.): 8.70; B. (max.): 7.50
Clay and slip: Yellow-grey clay; red-brown slip.
Description: Mouldmade lamp, very damaged: only a part of the head subsists. The filling-hole is pierced through the forehead, with a moulded edge.
Place of manufacture: Italy (?)
Proposed dating: Second half of Ist century AD
Bibliography: Mlasowski 1993, n. 412, pp. 420-421.

Cat. 45 (fig. 28):
Origin: Augst, Insula 31 (Museum collection: Römermuseum, Augst, Switzerland) (Inv. n.: 63.7790)
Dimensions: L. (max.): 6.4
Clay and slip: Yellowish clay, no description of slip.
Description: Mouldmade lamp, very damaged: only a part of the head and the beginning of the handle-ornament subsists. The filling-hole is pierced through the forehead, with a moulded edge. A lunar crescent handle-ornament was situated at the rear.
Place of manufacture: Italy (?)
Proposed dating: Ist to IInd century AD
Bibliography: Leibundgut 1977, n. 936, p. 51 and 292; pl. 14.

E. Provincial productions:
A Few lamps, all single-nozzled, can be classified in this category, one from Africa, one from Gaul and some from Germany (for these last, see Moehring 1988: 274, note 4).

Cat. 46 (fig. 29):
Origin: Carthage, Tunisia (Museum collection: British Museum, London, United Kingdom) (Inv. n.:1857.12-18.168.)
Dimensions: L.: 13.30; B.: 7.30; H.: 5.60
Clay and slip: Grey clay, with traces of mica in small particles; a very worn dark grey slip is applied over all.
Description: Mouldmade lamp, intact except for the nozzle and part of the handle, now lost. The filling-hole is pierced through the forehead, surrounded by a plain rim. Oval base ring. A grooved, vertical ring handle was applied to the rear.
Place of manufacture: Africa (?)
Proposed dating: Second half of the Ist to IInd century AD
Bibliography: Bailey 1975, n. Q 626, p.289; pl. 118 (the author suggested a probable dating on the Ist century BC).

Cat. 47 (fig. 30):
Origin: Gaul (?) (Museum collection: British Museum, London, United Kingdom) (Inv. n.: 1885.4-18.4.)
Dimensions: L.: 9.20; B.: 4.80; H.: 4.60
Clay and slip: Orange, micaceous clay; red slip.
Description: Mouldmade lamp, intact except for the handle, now lost. The filling-hole is pierced through the forehead. The lamp stands on three stubby feet, and is signed []TIBERI.
Place of manufacture: Africa (?)
Proposed dating: IInd century AD
Bibliography: Bailey 1988, n. Q 1580, p. 165; pl. 5, fig. 129; for the signature: p. 101 and fig. 130, p. 126.

Cat. 48:
Origin: Germany (Museum collection: Germanischen Nationalmuseum, Nürnberg, Germany) (Inv. n.: R 317)
Dimensions: L.: 11.50; B.: 6.50; H.: 7.40
Clay and slip: Red clay; red-brown slip.
Description: Mouldmade lamp, intact except for the handle, now lost, and the horns, damaged. The filling-hole is pierced through the forehead.
Place of manufacture: Germany
Proposed dating: middle of the IInd century AD
Bibliography: Moehring 1988

Type VII:
Early Northern Pontic productions: Ist century AD.

Description: Type VII bullhead lamps are moulded lamps with very realistic details. They are about 8 cm. long.

They are characterised by an oval and elongated shape. The filling-hole is in the middle of a concave undecorated zone, defined by a raised rim, and situated in the middle of the top of the head, itself surrounded by the hair of the animal, rendered in relief and falling to the forehead. Horns and ears are carefully treated in relief, as well as the eyes, situated on the sides of the lamp.

The large prominent muzzle rendered without wrinkles, ends with the two nostrils that dominate the large rounded nozzle. The careful rendering of the mouth all around the nozzle and, beneath it, of the lower jaw, give the lamp a very lively aspect

A raised, moulded handle or a grooved, moulded ring-handle is situated at the back.

The raised bases are generally flat and almond-shaped.

We can notice, throughout the few examples proposed here, the accurateness of details in the lamps we should consider as 'first generations' and a later, much less accurate exemplar.

Dating and production centres: This type of lamps has been produced in the Northern Pontic area during the first century AD.

The nozzle, the details of the lower jaw, and the important place played by the hair remind us of the first type IV Italian prototypes.

This fact is of the utmost interest, because we can thus actually ask whether there has been a direct link between these two groups through commercial exchanges or, a possibly more reasonable suggestion, that both the first Pontic and the first Italian productions followed a similar evolution starting from the same Attic production prototypes.

Cat. 49 (fig. 31):
Origin: Kertch (Museum collection: Hermitage, St. Petersburg, Russia) (Inv. n.: 1859.7)
Dimensions: L.: 6.50; H.: 3.30
Clay and slip: Grey-black clay; no slip.
Description: Mouldmade lamp, intact except for the handle and part of the nozzle, now lost. The filling-hole is pierced through the forehead, with a moulded edge. The base is raised and almond-shaped.
Place of manufacture: Northern Pontic area.
Proposed dating: Ist century AD
Bibliography: Waldhauer 1914, n. 512, p. 65, pl. XLVIII.

Cat. 50 (fig. 32):
Origin: (Museum collection: State Historical Museum, Moscow, Russia) (Inv. n.:)
Dimensions: L.:; H.:
Clay and slip:
Description: Mouldmade lamp, intact except for the handle and part of the nozzle, now lost. The filling-hole is pierced through the forehead, with a moulded edge. The base is raised and almond-shaped.
Place of manufacture: Northern Pontic area.
Proposed dating: Ist century AD
Bibliography: Unpublished.

Cat. 51:
Origin: Kertch (Museum collection: Hermitage, St. Petersburg, Russia) (Inv. n.: 28)
Dimensions: L.: 8.70; H.: 4.50
Clay and slip: Grey clay; no slip.
Description: Mouldmade lamp, intact except for the left horn, broken. The filling-hole is pierced through the forehead, in a moulded concave edge. The base is raised and almond-shaped. A pentagonal, raised, moulded handle is situated at the rear.
Place of manufacture: Northern Pontic area.
Proposed dating: Ist century AD
Bibliography: Waldhauer 1914, n. 508, p. 64, pl. XLVIII

Type VIII:
Late Northern Pontic productions: Ist to IInd century AD.

Description: Type VIII bullhead lamps are moulded lamps with few details. They are rather small, about 5 cm. long.

They are characterised by an ovoid compact shape, where the filling-hole is situated in the middle of a concave undecorated zone that occupies the main part of the bull's head, rendered in a very globular way, from which only the two small raised horns are prominent. The ears are very badly indicated. The rest of the head is decorated with numerous incisions rendering the hair.

The eyes also occupy an important place, often in low relief, and looking frontally towards the nozzle.

The large prominent muzzle, rendered with two or three wrinkles, ends with the two nostrils, from which starts the small round nozzle. They constitute the upper edge of the wick-hole.

A small semi-oval, raised, moulded handle or, in some exemplars, a grooved ring-handle is often added at the back, after the withdrawal from the mould.

The bases are generally flat and almond-shaped.

Dating and production centres: The lamps of this type were produced in the Northern Pontic area from the first to the second century AD. They can be seen as a degeneration of the early type, both in respect to the much more simplified shape as well as for the much poorer quality of the exemplars.

Cat. 52 (fig. 33):
Origin: Kertch (Museum collection: Hermitage, St. Petersburg, Russia) (Inv. n.: 1864.41)
Dimensions: L.: 5.50; H.: 3.30
Clay and slip: Grey-black clay; no slip.
Description: Mouldmade lamp, intact. The filling-hole is pierced through the forehead, in a large concave zone. The base is raised and almond-shaped. A grooved ring-handle is applied at the rear.
Place of manufacture: Northern Pontic area.
Proposed dating: Ist to IInd century AD
Bibliography: Waldhauer 1914, n. 510, p. 65, pl. XLVIII.

Cat. 53:
Origin: Kertch (Museum collection: Hermitage, St. Petersburg, Russia) (Inv. n.: 1896, N° 3)
Dimensions: L.: 5.10; H.: 3.40
Clay and slip: Grey-black clay; no slip.
Description: Mouldmade lamp, damaged: handle and nozzle are lost. The filling-hole is pierced through the forehead, in a large concave zone. The base is raised and almond-shaped.
Place of manufacture: Northern Pontic area.
Proposed dating: Ist to IInd century AD
Bibliography: Waldhauer 1914, n. 511, p. 65, pl. XLVIII.

Cat. 54:
Origin: Kertch (?) (Museum collection: National Museum, Warsaw, Poland) (Inv. n.: 138226)
Dimensions: L.: 6.00; B.: 4.20; H.: 3.00
Clay and slip: Grey-black clay; no slip.
Description: Mouldmade lamp, intact except for the handle, now lost. The filling-hole is pierced through the forehead, in a large concave zone. The base is raised and almond-shaped.
Place of manufacture: Northern Pontic area.
Proposed dating: Ist to IInd century AD
Bibliography: Bernhard 1955, n. 556, p. 378; pl. 156.

Cat. 55:
Origin: Unknown (Museum collection: Institute of Archaeology, Hebrew University, Jerusalem, Israel; from Shloessinger collection) (Inv. n.: 6212)
Dimensions: L.: 7.40; H.: 3.30
Clay and slip: Brown clay; no slip.
Description: Mouldmade lamp, intact except for the left horn, broken. The filling-hole is pierced through the forehead, in a moulded concave edge. The base is raised and almond-shaped. A moulded, grooved, pierced ring-handle is situated at the rear.
Place of manufacture: probably Northern Pontic area.
Proposed dating: Ist to IInd century AD
Bibliography: Rosenthal, Sivan 1978, n. 607, p. 147.

Unclassifiable lamps

Four exemplars had to be set in this section, three of them being probable fakes, and the last being because of its shape.

Cat. 56 (fig. 34):
Origin: Unknown (Museum collection: British Museum, London, United Kingdom) (Inv. n.: 1963.7-15.59)
Dimensions: L.: 7.50; B.: 4.50
Clay and slip: Brown clay, dark brown paint.
Description: Mouldmade lamp, intact. The filling-hole is pierced through the forehead, surrounded by a rim. Sub-triangular base-ring. Pierced handle with lunar crescent handle-ornament.
Place of manufacture: Naples.
Proposed dating: modern forgery.
Bibliography: Bailey 1988, n. Q 3418, p. 435; pl. 134.

Cat. 57 (figs. 35, 36):
Origin: Novocherkask, South Russia (?) (Museum collection: Hermitage, St. Petersburg, Russia; from Popoff collection) (Inv. n.: 9098)
Dimensions: L.: 8.70; H.: 3.80
Clay and slip: Grey clay; black slip.
Description: Mouldmade lamp, intact except for the right ear, now lost. The filling-hole is pierced through the forehead, and surrounded by a high rim in shape of a crown. Highly raised, curved horns. Ears and eyes in high relief. Large, round, widely open nozzle. Almond-shaped raised base. Triple-grooved, pierced, moulded ring-handle.
Place of manufacture: unknown.
Proposed dating: modern forgery.
Bibliography: Waldhauer 1914, n. 509, p. 65, pl. XLVIII (the author considers it as authentic).

Cat. 58:
Origin: Hungary (?) (Museum collection: Römisch-Germanisches Zentralmuseum, Mainz, Germany) (Inv. n.: O. 17593)
Dimensions: L.: 4.70; B.: 3.00; H.: 1.50
Clay and slip: No description of clay, red slip.
Description: Mouldmade miniature lamp, intact. The filling-hole is pierced through the forehead. Eyes in relief. Small, round nozzle. Circular raised base, defined by a groove. Grooved, pierced, moulded ring-handle. The head looks more like a bull's skull than like a bull's head.
Place of manufacture: unknown.
Proposed dating: modern forgery.
Bibliography: Menzel 1954, n. 510, p. 77; pl. 62:2.

Cat. 59:
Origin: Unknown (Museum collection: Institute of Archaeology, Hebrew University, Jerusalem, Israel; from Schloessinger collection) (Inv. n.: O. 6219)
Dimensions: L.: 9.50; H.: 11.50
Clay and slip: Brown clay, white slip.
Description: Mouldmade plastic lamp, in shape of a bull's head and chest, that stands on a half-round flat base, from which project two nozzles. The top of the head is broken. The large, triangular filling-hole is pierced in the plain bach of the animal.
Place of manufacture: unknown, maybe Egypt.
Proposed dating: Ist or IInd century AD
Bibliography: Rosenthal & Sivan 1978, n. 606, p. 147.

Bronze lamps

Even if these lamps are not the subject of this article, we propose here the two exemplars mentioned before in the text.

Cat. 60 (fig. 37):
Origin: Istanbul (?) (Museum collection: Bibliothèque Nationale, Paris, France; from the Froehner collection) (Inv. n.: 733)
Dimensions: L.: 14.00; H.: 5.30
Bronze lamp.
Description: The large filling-hole is pierced through the forehead. Raised, oval base-ring. Lunar crescent-shaped handle-ornament, linked at the rear, over a ring-handle. On the crescent is inscribed ΛΥΚΑΙΝΙΣ ΠΑΣΙΚΡΑΤΑΔΩΠΟΝ ("Lykainis, (as) gift to Pasikrata")
Place of manufacture: Thessalia (?)
Proposed dating: Ist century AD
Bibliography: Hellmann 1985, n. 80, pp. 81-82 (the author explains that Pasikrata was an adjective of Artemis in Ambrakia, and was also attested in all Thessalia, especially in Demetrias).

Cat. 61:
Origin: Unknown (Museum collection: Déri Museum, Debrecen, Hungary) (Inv. n.: R.V.8)
Dimensions: L.: 12.50; H.: 6.60
Bronze lamp.
Description: The large filling-hole is pierced through the forehead, surrounded by a rim. Narrow, flat ovoid base. Double nozzle. At the rear is the handle, curving forward and ending with a lion's head. The shape of the lamp is identical (with the exception of the handle) of clay lamps of type VI.
Place of manufacture: Unknown.
Proposed dating: Ist century AD
Bibliography: Szentleleky 1969, n. 277, p. 141 and 145.

Other well-preserved bronze lamps of the Ist century AD can be found in: Ivanyi 1935, n. 4337: 303; pl. 63:6 (National Museum, Budapest, Hungary); De' Spagnolis & De Carolis 1983, n. 6, type XXIV, pp. 81-2, 84, 93 (Museo Nazionale Romano, Rome, Italy; Inv. n.: 67482); Conticello De' Spagnolis & De Carolis 1986, n. 47, pp. 97-98 (Musei della Biblioteca Apostolica, Vatican; Inv. n.: 12120).

3. Conclusion:

A lot of questions and issues about the bullhead lamps remain open, above all regarding a more precise chronology of the appearance and period of production of all the different types. But, nevertheless, this research led us to a few (even if provisional) results. As a matter of fact, through the analysis of all the exemplars examined here, we can find some indications to understand the evolution and the spreading of this kind of lamp in the Hellenistic and Roman world.

As we have seen, through the different types, the first clay lamps (type I) were certainly created by Attic (and maybe also Pergamene) ceramists on the basis of some bronze prototypes.

Then, the richness of cultural and commercial exchanges starting from the Greek area and spreading throughout all the Mediterranean and the Black Sea brought the knowledge and subsequent appreciation of these lamps to Italy and to the Northern Pontic area. There, local workshops started to make their own productions as early as the first century BC for Italy, and from the beginning of the first century AD for Crimea.

Then the workshops of these three main regions began to develop their own variations (type II for Attica; types V and VI for Italy; type VIII for Northern Pontic area).

Meanwhile, Egyptian ceramists created their own version of bullhead lamps (type III), without any apparent link to the Attic prototypes, but achieving an innovative shape that probably later inspired some details to the Italian type V producers.

Finally, the extensive commercial and cultural exchange system between the provinces of the Roman Empire helped the less fragile Italian type VI to travel outside the peninsula, where it was copied by some local workshops in

Gaul and in Africa.

Another factor that emerges from this research is that, as for almost all other types of lamps, there are some internal evolutions within each type. Unfortunately, the exemplars described here are too few and their dating is too broad to enable us to propose definite sub-types (above all for the Italian type VI and the different nozzle-types).

In conclusion, we shall again underline, in our era in which 'communication' seems to be one of the buzzwords, that the simple invention of a lamp shaped like a bull's head, first met the interest and the taste of some Greek customers, then spread to almost all the Greco-Roman world.

Joking apart, and returning to a more scientific debate, we sincerely hope to see in a very near future more publications on bullhead lamps (and above all found in precise contexts), in order to gradually discover some new pieces to the too limited range of these admirable type of *lucernae*.

Acknowledgements and copyrights of illustrations:

The compilation of this article has been aided by a large number of people. I would particularly like to thank Dr. Anthony Cru (Geneva), who kindly corrected English manuscript. Professor Ermanno A. Arslan (director of the Civiche Raccolte Archeologiche e Numismatiche, Milan, and of the Museo Civico, Biassono), Dr. Silvia Fünfschilling (Römermuseum, Augst); Dr. Myriame Morel (Musée d'Histoire de Marseille), Dr. Cristiana Morigi Govi (director of the Museo Civico Archeologico, Bologna); Dr. Anne Viola Siebert (Kestner-Museum, Hannover); Dr. D. Stutzinger (Museum für Vor- und Frühgeschichte, Frankfurt am Main) kindly allowed me to publish free of charge the lamps of their collections. Finally, I would like to thank Professor Jean-Marc Moret and Mrs. Corinne Sandoz (Geneva), Dr. Denis Zhuravlev (Moscow) and Mrs. Olga Sokolova (St. Petersburg) for their help and constant encouragement.

Photographs of Cat. nn. 33; 38; 44 are © Landeshauptstadt Hannover Kestner-Museum

Photographs of Cat. nn. 26; 49; 52; 57 are © State Hermitage, St. Petersburg

Photographs of Cat. nn. 10; 15; 19; 21; 34; 35; 36; 46; 47; 56 are © Copyright The British Museum, London

Photographs of Cat. nn. 20; 28 are © Stadt Frankfurt am Main. Museum für Vor- und Frühgeschichte

Photographs of Cat. nn. 24; 60 are © Cliché Bibliothèque nationale de France, Paris

Photograph of Cat. n. 45 is © Römermuseum Augst and Mrs. Ursi Schild

Photograph of Cat. n. 41 is © Museo di Archeologia Ligure and Mr. P. Odone, Genova

Photograph of Cat. n. 29 is © Museo Archeologico al Teatro romano and Mr. Umberto Tomba, Verona

Photograph of Cat. n. 18 is © Civiche Raccolte Archeologiche e Numismatiche, Milano

Photograph of Cat. n. 23 is © Musée d'Histoire de Marseille, Marseille (from Marseille 1988, p. 125).

Photograph of Cat. n. 30 is © Museo Civico Archeologico, Bologna (from Gualandi Genito 1977, pl. 67).

Drawings of Cat nn. 2, 3 and 50 are © Anna Trifonova, Moscow.

Bibliography

D.M. Bailey 1975. *A catalogue of the lamps in the British Museum, 1. Greek, hellenistic, and early Roman pottery lamps*, London

D.M. Bailey 1980. *A catalogue of the lamps in the British Museum, 2. Roman lamps made in Italy*, London

D.M. Bailey 1988. *A catalogue of the lamps in the British Museum, 3. Roman provincial lamps*, London

BAILEY 1996 = D.M. Bailey, W.E.H. Cockle, D.R. Hook, *A catalogue of the lamps in the British Museum, 4. Lamps of metal and stone, and lampstands*, London

M.L. Bernhard 1955. *Lampki starozytne*, Warszawa

J. Brants, 1913. *Antieke Terra-cotta Lampen uit het Rijksmuseum van oudheden te Leiden*, Leiden

P. Bruneau 1965. *Exploration archéologique de Délos, 26. Les lampes*, Paris

E.M. Cahn-Klaiber 1977. *Die antiken Tonlampen des Archäologischen Instituts der Universität Tübingen*, (Tübinger Studien zur Archäologie und Kunstgeschichte, 2). Tübingen

L. Chrzanovski & D. Zhuravlev 1998 *Lamps from Chersonesos in the State Historical Museum - Moscow*. (Studia Archaeologica 94). Roma

M. Conticello De' Spagnolis & E. De Carolis 1986. *Le lucerne di bronzo*, Città del Vaticano, 1986 (Musei della Biblioteca apostolica vaticana. Inventari e studi, 1)

G. De Luca 1968. *Das Asklepeion XI, 1*, Berlin 1968

M. De' Spagnolis & E. De Carolis 1983. *Museo nazionale romano. I bronzi, 4, 1. Le lucerne*, Roma.

C.R. Fitch & N.W. Goldman 1994. *The Lamps. Cosa 5*, (Memoirs of the American Academy in Rome, 39). Rome.

M. Forte 1989. Lucerne, in *A.A.V.V., Modena dalle origini all'anno mille. Studi di archeologia e storia, II, Modena*, pp. 105-123

M.C. Gualandi Genito 1977. *Lucerne fittili delle collezioni del Museo civico archeologico di Bologna*, (Fonti per la storia di Bologna. Cataloghi, 3). Bologna.

R. Haken 1958. *Roman lamps in the Prague National Museum and in other Czechoslovak collections*, Sbornik Narodniho musea v Praze, Rada A, XII, 1-2, Praha.

M.C. Hellmann 1980. *Lampes antiques de la Bibliothèque nationale, 1. Collection Froehner*, Paris.

M.C. Hellmann 1987. *Lampes antiques de la Bibliothèque nationale, 2. Fonds général. Lampes pré-romaines et romaines*, Paris

R.H. Howland 1958. *Greek lamps and their survivals. The Athenian Agora 4*, Princeton

U. Hübinger 1993. *Die antiken Lampen des Akademischen Kunstmuseums der Universität Bonn*, Berlin.

D. Ivanyi 1935. *Die pannonischen Lampen*, Budapest.

A. Larese & D. Sgreva, 1996. *Le lucerne fittili e bronzee del Museo Archeologico di Verona, I.* (Collezioni e musei archeologici del Veneto), Roma.

A. Leibundgut 1977. *Die römischen Lampen in der Schweiz. Eine kultur- und handelsgeschichtliche Studie*, Bern.

G. Libertini 1930. *Il Museo Biscari*, Milano - Roma.

MARSEILLE 1988 = A.A.V.V., Musée d'Histoire de Marseille. L'antiquité, Marseille

H. Menzel 1969. *Antike Lampen im Römisch-Germanischen Zentralmuseum zu Mainz* (Römisch-Germanisches Zentralmuseum zu Mainz, Katalog 15), Mainz.

L. Mercando 1962. *Lucerne greche e romane dell'Antiquarium Comunale*, Roma.

A. Mlasowsky 1993. *Die antiken Tonlampen im Kestner-Museum Hannover*, (Kestner-Museum Hannover. Sammlungskataloge, 8). Hannover.

A. Möhring 1988. Eine römische Stierkopflampe im Germanischen Nationalmuseum Nürnberg, in *Bayerische Vorgeschichtsblätter 53*, pp. 273-279

A.M. Pastorino 1989. Le lucerne fittili della Collezione principe Oddone del Museo archeologico di Genova-Pegli, in *Rivista di studi liguri 55*, pp. 123-148.

R. Rosenthal & R. Sivan 1978. *Ancient lamps in the Schloessinger Collection*, Jerusalem (Qedem, 8)

M. Sapelli 1978. *Lucerne fittili delle civiche raccolte archeologiche*, (Notizie dal chiostro del monastero maggiore. Supplementi, 2). Milano

S. Schäfer & L. Marczoch, 1990. *Lampen der Antikensammlung. Auswahlkatalog*, (Museum für Vor- und Frühgeschichte Frankfurt a.M. Archäologische Reihe, 13). Frankfurt a.M.

C. Skinkel-Taupin 1980. *Lampes en terre cuite de la Méditerranée grecque et romaine*, Bruxelles

Szentléleky 1969. *Ancient lamps*, (Monumenta antiquitatis, 1). Budapest

O. Waldhauer 1914. *Kaiserliche Ermitage, die antike Tonlampen*, St. Petersburg

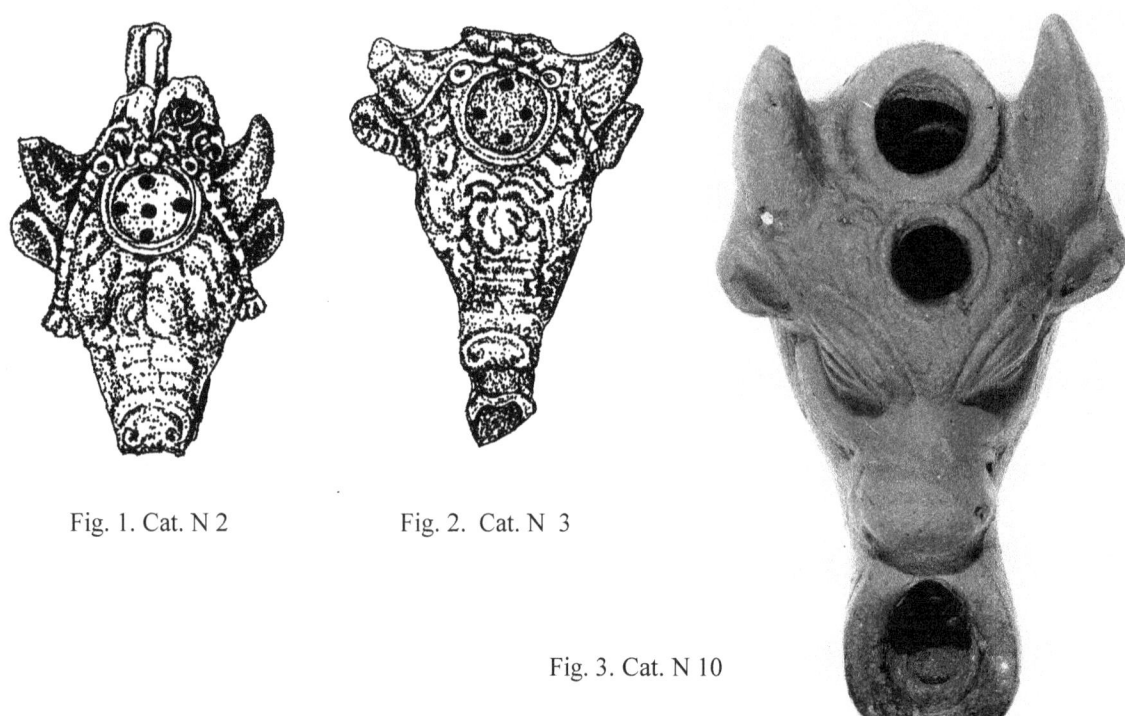

Fig. 1. Cat. N 2   Fig. 2. Cat. N 3

Fig. 3. Cat. N 10

Fig. 4. Cat. N 15

Fig. 5. Cat. N 18.

Fig. 6. Cat. N 19.

Figs. 7 & 8. Cat. N 20.

Fig. 9. Cat. N 21

Fig. 10. Cat. N 23

Fig. 11. Cat. N 24.

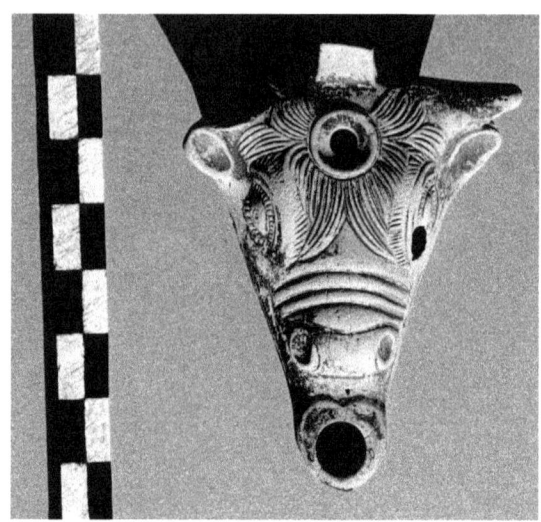

Fig. 12. Cat. N 25

Figs. 13 & 14. Cat. N 26

Fig. 15. Cat. N 28

Fig. 16. Cat. N 29

Fig. 17. Cat. N 30.

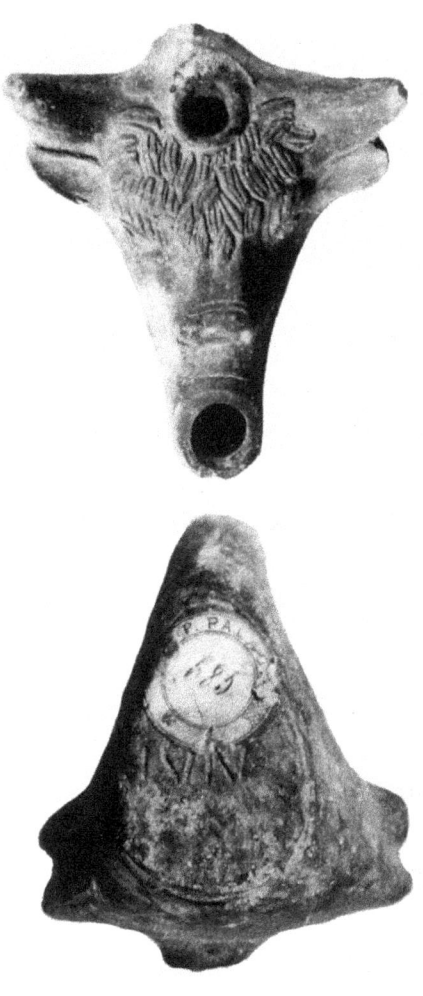

Figs. 18 & 19. Cat. N 32.

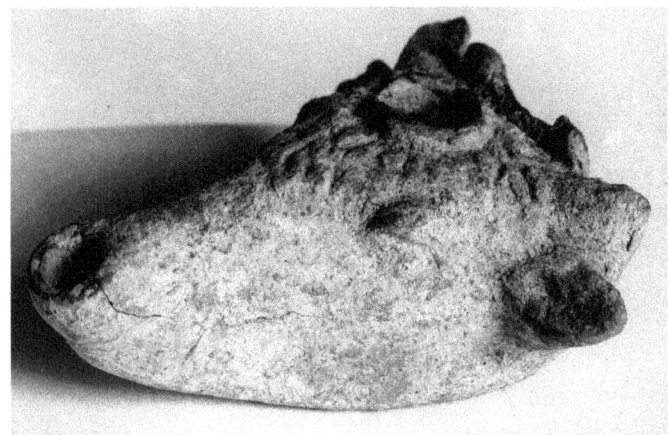

Fig. 20. Cat. N 33

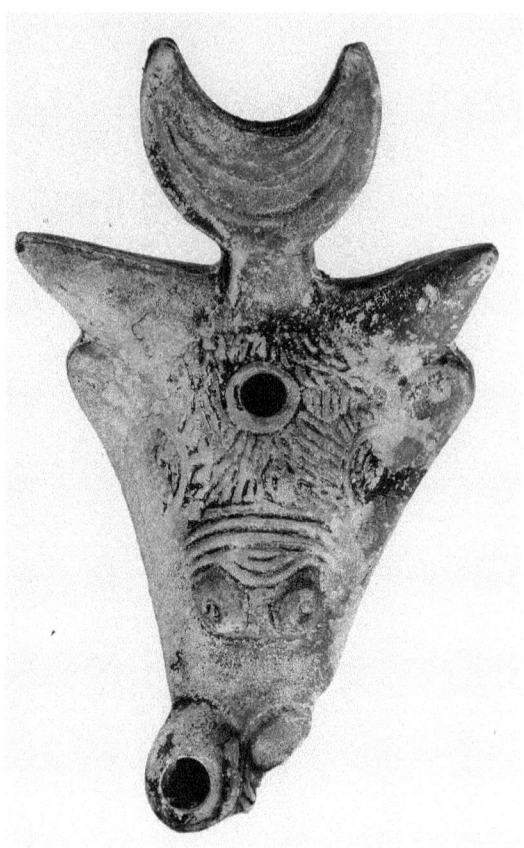

Fig. 21. Cat. N 34

Fig. 22. Cat. N 35

Fig. 23. Cat. N 36

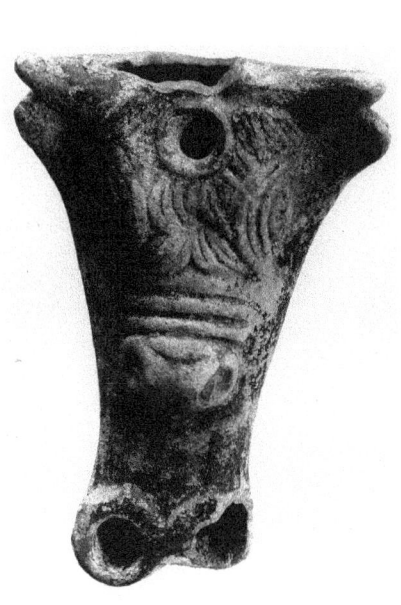

Fig. 24. Cat. N 38

Fig. 25. Cat. N 41

Fig. 26. Cat. N 42.

Fig. 27. Cat. N 44

Fig. 28. Cat. N 45

Fig. 29. Cat. N 46

Fig. 30. Cat. N 47

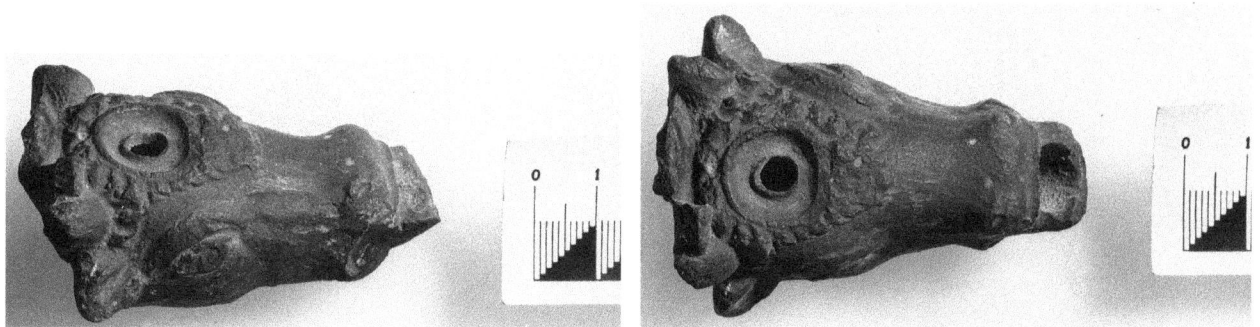

Fig. 31. Cat. N 49

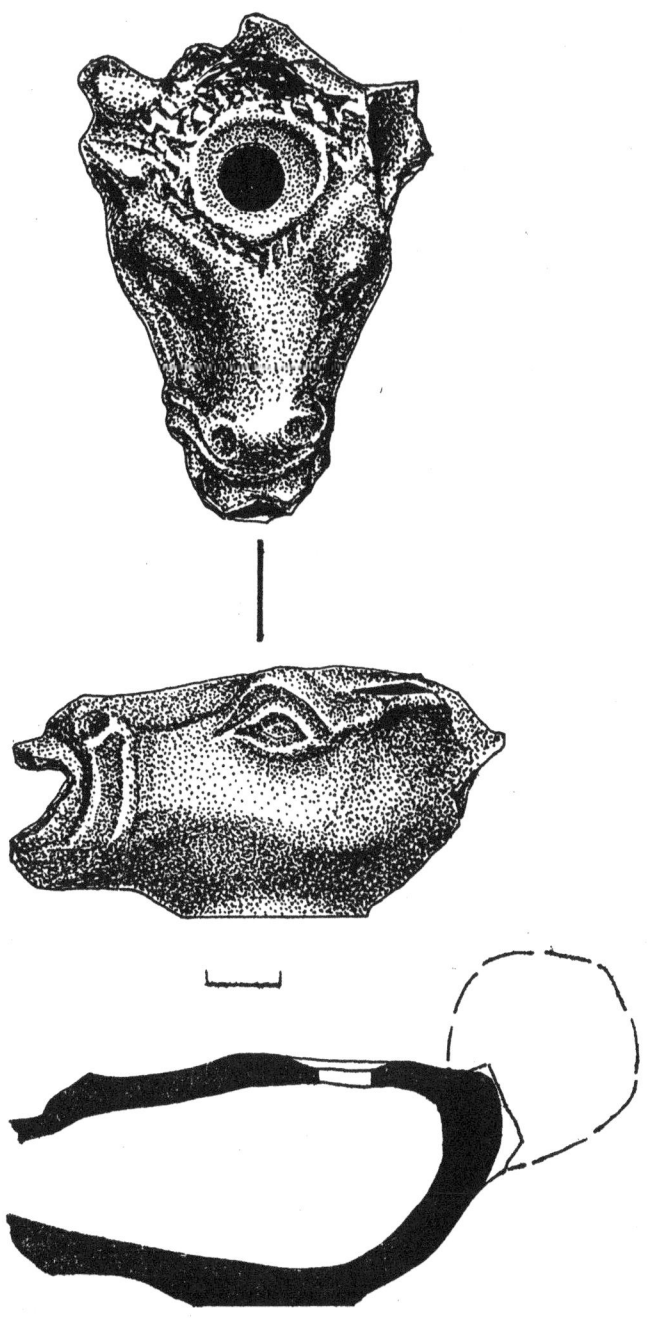

Fig. 32. Cat. N 50

Fig. 33. Cat. N 52

Fig. 34. Cat. N 56.

Fig. 37. Cat N 60

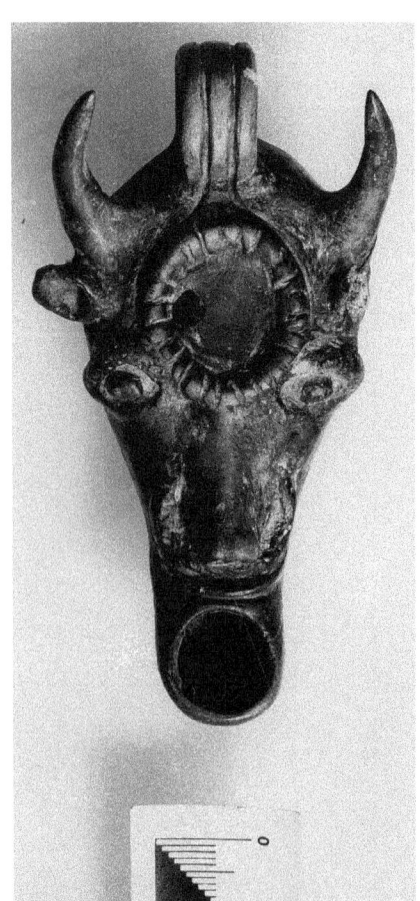

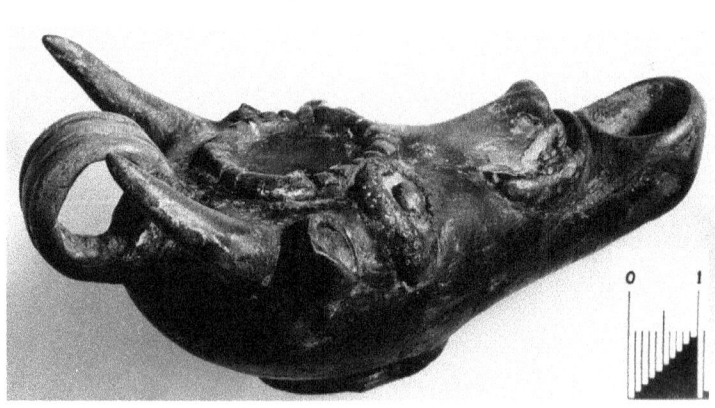

Figs. 35 & 36. Cat. N 57

Harpocrates on a new lamp handle-ornament recently found in Leptis Magna (Libya)

Laurent Chrzanovski
(Geneva, Switzerland)

Archaeological context:

This handle-ornament was unearthed in 1997 by the Italian Mission of the IIIrd University of Rome, directed by Professor Luisa Musso, on the excavations of the great suburban villa of Wadi Rsaf (Leptis Magna, Khoms, Libya). It was found in a waste-pit, filled with a remarkable quantity of fragments of different pottery: amphoras, common wares, fine wares, sigillata and lamps. First studies of the context (cf. Leptis 2000), suggest that all the items found belong to a period of no more than fifty years, which can be situated in the second half of the IInd century A.D.

There were 112 fragments of lamps, belonging to more than sixty exemplars, which can be divided into four different types: single- and double-nozzled volute-lamps (Deneauve types V A, B and D) and single-nozzled round lamps (Loeschcke type VIII). With the exception of the small number of double-nozzled volute-lamps, none of the other types seem to predominate over the others.

Types, potters' marks and iconography of the lamps confirm the date of the context provided by the study of other ceramics.

As a matter of fact, a few fragments of disks discovered show a bather Venus, a *scyphus* and a double *cornucopia*, three motifs very common on African and Italian lamps of the IInd century A.D.

Moreover, the seven potter's stamps found attest three workshops, all situated in Southern Tunisia: CIVNDRAC (Caius Iunius Draco) (2 fragments), a factory active from 120 to 200 A.D. (cf. Joly 1974: 88-89; Bailey 1985: 180; Bailey 1988: 98; Bailey 1994: 195); MNOVIVST (Marcus Novius Iustus) (1 fragment), a factory active from 120 to 180 A.D. (cf. Joly 1974: 93; Bailey 1985: 180; Bailey 1988: 98); and CIVNALEX (Caius Iunius Alexis), who was active from 120 to 200 A.D. (cf. Joly 1974: 91; Bailey 1985: 180; Bailey 1994: 195).

The handle-ornament:

The artefact, of remarkable size and quality, belongs to a fragmentary lamp, from which three pieces were unearthed: the handle-ornament itself (fig.1), a voluted nozzle (fig. 2) decorated with a mask and a pine-cone, and part of the round, flat base, defined by a raised circular band and marked, in its centre, with a double sunken circle.

By the first analysis of clay and slip, the lamp seems to be an Italian import, a fact confirmed by the iconographical interpretation of the motif.

As a matter of fact, the rendering of Harpocrates is executed in a Graeco-Roman way, very far from the original Egyptian representations. Harpocrates stands nude, in frontal position, with a drapery covering his left knee and part of his right leg. His head-dress seems to be very elaborate. He is sucking a finger of his right hand, and, with his left hand, he holds what seems to be a cornucopia (according to numerous other parlallels). The rest of the handle-ornament is richly decorated with floral patterns, among which we can observe a grape (near to the left shoulder of Harpocrates) and a lotus flower.

This handle-ornament is not only unusual for its shape and rendering, but is also an exceptional witness of the religious and cultural relations between Leptis and the rest of the Roman world.

In fact, we should imagine Leptis to have had intensive connections with the Alexandrine world, but the handle-ornament we are studying tends to prove the contrary. It is not the original Egyptian Harpocrates that we are observing, but his adaptation to the Graeco-Roman divinities. His representation, very near to some iconographical depictions of Dyonisos, attests that the rich Leptitan owners of the villa used to venerate oriental divinities (numerous other artefacts bearing the images of Sarapis and Isis were found) according to the Roman interpretation.

This phenomenon, well studied by Professor Tran tam Tinh in his numerous studies on the representations of Oriental divinities in the Roman world (Tram tam Ting 1970; 1984; 1990; 1992; 1993), is hence (in a surprising way) applicable to Leptis Magna, where the Alexandrine influence appears within numerous artistic forms (starting by architecture), but not within imported artefacts, where the preference was given (besides Tunisian productions) to Italian and, sometimes, Greek products.

To conclude this short article, we can again underline the words of Tran tam Tinh about Roman lamps with Isiac iconographies:

" *contrairement à d'autres produits, les lampes isiaques alexandrines et égyptiennes ne sont pas exportées à l'extérieur de l'Egypte. (...) En un mot, l'iconographie des lampes d'Egypte est un témoin de l'orthodoxie originelle de la religion d'Isis alors que celle des lampes non-égyptiennes exprime l'acculturation de cette conception religieuse dans les autres pays de la Méditerranée.*" (Tran tam Ting 1992: 435-437).

Acknowledgements

I would particularly like to thank Professor Luisa Musso (Rome), for her help and disponibility, and Mrs. Anna Trifonova (Moscow), author of the drawings.

Bibliography

D.M. Bailey, 1985. *Excavations at Sidi Khrebish, Benghazi (Berenice), 3, 2. The lamps*, Tripoli 1985 (Libya antiqua, Suppl.5, 3, 2)

D.M. Bailey, 1988. *A catalogue of the lamps in the British Museum, 3. Roman provincial lamps*, London.

D.M. Bailey, 1994. Part IV: Lamps, in M. Fulford, R. Tomber, *Excavations at Sabratha 1948 - 1951*, Tripoli, pp. 145 - 197

E. Joly, 1974. *Lucerne del Museo di Sabratha*, Roma (Monografie di archeologia libica, 11)

Leptis 2000. L. Chrzanovski, E. Cirelli, F. Felici et al., *Il contesto ceramico di età antonina dalla villa di Uadi Er-Rsaf (Leptis Magna)*, in Libya Antiqua 1988. Roma.

V. Tran tam Tinh, 1970. Isis et Sérapis se regardant, in *RA 1970*, pp. 55-80

V. Tran tam Tinh, 1984. Le baiser d'Hélios, in *Alessandria e il mondo ellenistico-romano. In onore di A. Adriani, 1*, Roma, pp. 318-328

V. Tran tam Tinh, 1990. Ex Oriente lux. Les dieux orientaux sur les lampes en terre cuite de la Campanie, in *RStPomp 4*, pp. 125-134

V. Tran tam Tinh, 1992. Les lampes isiaques du Musée Gréco-Romain d'Alexandrie, in *A.A.V.V., Alessandria e il mondo ellenistico-romano. I centenario del Museo Greco-Romano. Alessandria, 23-27 novembre 1992. Atti del II Congresso Internazionale Italo-Egiziano*, Roma 1995, pp. 432-437

V. Tran tam Tinh, M.O. Jentel. 1993, *Corpus des lampes à sujets isiaques du Musée gréco-romain d'Alexandrie*, Québec 1993 (Collection " Hier pour aujourd'hui", 6)

Laurent Chrzanovski: Harpocrates on a new lamp handle-ornament recently found in Leptis Magna (Libya)

Fig. 1

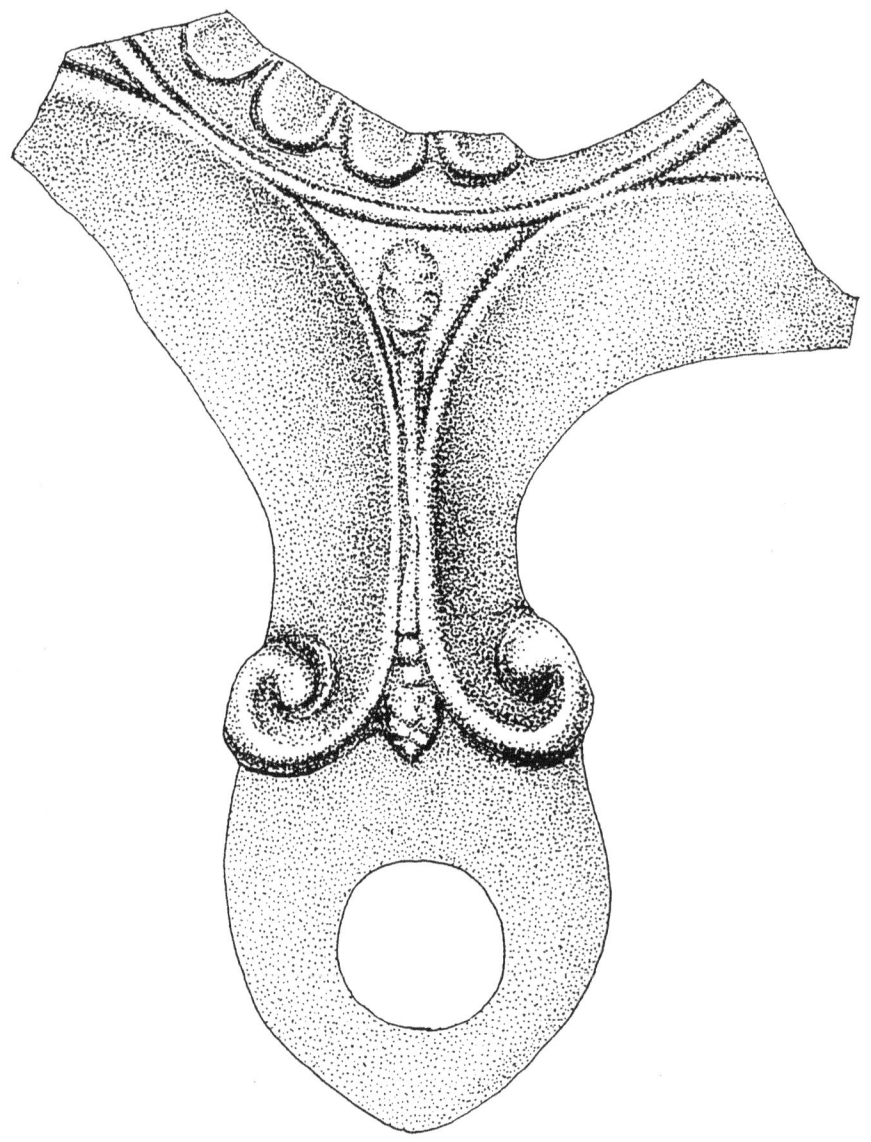

Fig. 2

Imported Lamps and Candelabra from Ust'-Alma Necropolis (Crimea, Ukraine)

Yuriy Zaitsev
(Simpheropol, Ukraine)

Ust' - Alma necropolis is situated at the site of the Late Scythian settlement, which carries the same name and was located on the steep cape of the left bank of the Alma river at the point where it flows into the Kalamitskiy gulf of the Black sea, to the west of the village of Peschanoe of Bakhchisaray district of the Autonomous Republic of Crimea (Ukraine). At the end of the 2nd century B.C. the Late Scythian settlement sprang up here and it existed until the middle of the 3rd century A.D. It was the largest centre of Crimean Scythia in the south-western part of the Crimean peninsula (Vysotskaya 1994).

Burial ground was located to the east of the settlement, its presumptive area was not less than 4 hectares. In 1964, and from 1968 to 1984, 220 burial constructions were discovered in the area of about 2000 sq. m. Alomst half of the burial ground area has been plundered. In 1998, and within 1992 to 1999 Alma expedition of the Crimean branch of the Archaeological Institute of the Ukraine National Academy of Sciences and Bakhchisaray Historical and Cultural Preserve, rescue excavations unearthed more than 500 burial constructions of the 2nd century B.C. - 3rd century A.D. (Zaitsev 2000).

Within burials a great number of red slip, hand made pottery, glass and bronze vessels, weaponry, metal ornaments and details of dress, beads, amulets and many other grave goods were discovered. However, a very few lighting appliances (lamps and candelabra) were found, although these items played a rather important role in the burial ceremonies of the ancient people. The article represents the publication of the burials, in which imported lamps were discovered, as well as the groups of metal candelabra that were found in the graves of nobility.

It is not the task of this paper to provide the detailed discussion on the chronology of these graves. The dating of burials in which the lamps and candelabra were found, was made on the basis of modern research on *terra sigillata*, fibulae and some other categories of finds. The most complex research on the chronology of Late Scythian culture of Crimea as a whole was also used (Eggers 1951; Ettlinger 1962; Hayes 1973; Chrzanovski & Zhuravlev, 1998; Tassinari 1993; Aibabin 1990; Alekseeva 1975, 1978, 1982; Ambroz 1966; Vnukov 1999; Guschina & Zhuravlev 1999; Zhuravlev 1997; Kosyanenko 1987; Kropotkin 1970; Novichenkova 2000; Skripkin 1977).

Crypt 424a was one of two chambers arranged in the opposite sides of same entrance hole. Not less than twenty burials, located in three tiers, were found. The numerous finds were dated to the second half of the 1st - 2nd centuries A.D. In such a context the group of grave goods lying on the floor at the entrance and not connected with the basic burials attracts attention. They are small crumpled sheets of gold foil, a large jug, an iron spear-head and a dark red slip lamp with the relief image of a dolphin and meander (cat. 1) (Fig. 1, *8-10*; 9). All these finds may have been the remains of earliest, unpreserved burials, dated to the 1st century B.C. - beginning of the 1st century A.D.

Tomb 430. It is of rectangular shape. The stone slabs leaned on the ledges along the long walls. Underneath further two ledges were constructed, on which a wooden overlap was probably laid in antiquity. The burial was of a c. 40-year-old woman, in a wooden coffin, with the head positioned towards southeast (Fig. 2). The vestiges of a pink paint - powder and rouge were traced on facial bones of the skull. Finds (Fig. 3); in the southern part of the tomb there was a red slip dish with the stamp in *planta pedis*, in which a bone of an animal and a red slip lamp with the image of the eagle on the plate lied (cat. 2). A red slip pitcher, a two-handled cup, a red slip flask with a handle, iron details of a box, a handmade spindle whorl, a lump of rouge and an iron awl were situated nearby. In jugular vertebrae and thorax area diverse beads were cleaned out and among them there was a bronze fibula. Two further fibulae were found on the left side of the breast. Near them bronze pincers, a touchstone and a bronze mirror were discovered. Three bronze finger-rings with glass inserts and fragments of a twisted glass ring and beads were found on the phalanxes of the right hand fingers and around the wrist of the left hand there were also beads of different materials. At the right hip a bronze brooch, a bronze engraved finger-ring, an iron and silver needles were lying. At the left hip a bronze ring, a ring with protrusions, beads, bronze pincers, a bronze core with a ring were found. At the ankles various beads were situated. Above the remains of the burial (on the top of the coffin cover?) a two-handled red slip kantharos broken in the antiquity with the riveting holes and a relief decoration on the handles was found in the north-western part of the tomb. This kantharos dates to the end of the 1st - first half of the 2nd centuries A.D.

Crypt 439. A large catacomb with multiple burials of the 1st –2nd centuries A.D. is typical for the necropolis. The chamber vault fell in the antiquity, and the gap, which had been formed, was filled with earth together with a great amount of breakage amphorae, handmade and red slip pottery. Here a red slip lamp with the relief image of a dog on the discus was found (cat. 3) (Fig. 9).

Crypt 449 (catacomb). The entrance hole is in the form of trapeze, it is orientated southeast-northwest and was completely filled with stones. In the south-eastern part three steps were constructed, the bottom lowered towards the chamber. The entrance was closed with a large limestone slab. The chamber was square in plan; one of the chamber walls was completely destroyed while the next chamber of the later crypt 439 was being erected.

15 burials were made in the crypt in three basic tiers. Within the framework of the publication it is appropriate to give the description of the 2nd tier burials. The second burial is a female one (30-55 years old). The burial was made in a wooden coffin, with the head towards southwest, arms clasped to the hips, the legs bent in the knees. Finds: around the neck the beads of cornelian and jet, the bronze fibula - brooch in the shape of bucranian were found, on the wrists there were beads of cornelian and jet, at the right hip there was a ring with protrusions, at the ankles there were Egyptian faience minute beads, at the right shoulder there was a red slip jug, under the pelvis there was a red slip plate, at the feet there were bronze and iron details of a box and an iron key. The burial N 3 was made at the southeastern wall of the chamber near burial 2. The dead woman was lying on her back, in the stretched position, with the arms along the body, the legs slightly ben in knees. Finds: around the neck beads of cornelian and jet, on the breast a fibula - brooch (bucrarian) and a fibula with sophisticated profile, on the left wrist a bronze bracelet with the flattened endings and beads of glazed earthware and glass, on the right hand a bronze ring, iron pincers and bronze clips were found. At the ankles the pile of faience beads was registered. In the northern corner a red slip lamp was found (cat. 4).

Tomb 510 was of rectangular plan, with ledges and a stone overlap, orientated northeast-southwest. The bones of a child were completely decayed, the position of the body could be determined only by the location of finds (Fig. 1, *3-7*): the head must have been directed north-east. At the left arm a red slip goblet and a red slip cup with two handles stood. On the breast a bronze fibula and beads of glass, jet, chalcedony, on the right arm a bronze bracelet with a glass bead were found. In the legs there was a red slip lamp with the relief image of the eagle on its discus (cat. 5) (Fig. 9). The date is 2nd century A.D.

Tomb 553. The tomb was of oval shape, with ledges and a stone overlap. A child's burial was made in it with the head of the child facing north-west. Finds (Fig. 1, *1-4*): at the decayed skull there was a red slip plate with a bone of an animal, nearby a red slip lamp with an image of a bull on the plate (cat. 6) (Fig.9), various beads and two bronze pendants in the shape of hatchets. In the centre of the tomb a bronze handbell was situated. Date: the 2nd century A.D.

Crypt 595. The complete publication of this interesting complex makes it unnecessary to give a detailed description. A deep catacomb, similar in its construction to the crypt 634, contained a twin female burial, which has been partially plundered nowadays. The remaining finds (a set of ritual wooden vessels and other objects, a set of ceremonial horse harness, gold ornaments etc.) made it possible to assume that the dead were of the high social status and that they were priestess. Among the objects that were found in the main burial, there was a red slip lamp (cat. 7) (Fig. 10). The date of the burials in the crypt is late 1st - early 2nd centuries A.D.

Crypt 634 (Fig. 4). The entrance hole in the catacomb was of trapezoid shape, and was orientated northwest-southeast. The bottom had a sloping path towards the entrance. The large blocking slab was lying inclined on the bottom, and the spherical entrance was covered with the friable stone blocking. The chamber was of the irregular quadrangular form. Among the stones that filled the chamber, two fragments of a limestone tomb with the primitive pediment were found. The pediment was decorated with rosettae. In the crypt there were four burials located in two tiers.

Tier 1. The burial 1 (a grown-up man) was made in a decayed oak log. The man was lying on his back, in stretched position, with his head towards the west, legs were straight and arms were stretched along the body. Finds: along the southern wall of the log some iron nails were situated, under the log an amphora of light clay similar to type C according to D. Shelov classification with a narrow neck was found. Burial 2 (an adult) was made in a half-sitting position, the head pointing to the east, the legs slightly bent; the spinal column was curled and the skull was displaced. Finds: (Fig. 4, *1-17*) under the pelvis a javelin tip and fragments of bronze plates were discovered.

Tier 2. Burial 3 (a grown-up man) was made in a large oak log. He was laying with his head towards the southeast, on his back, in stretched position; arms and legs were straight. Finds: At the top of the log there was a red slip lamp with an image of the Gorgon Medusa's head on the discus (cat. 8) (Fig. 10) and remains of the wooden staff with silver clips. In the neck area there were two small tubes of gold foil and an iron overlay of a box was situated under the left hand. Burial 4 (an adult woman) was made in a large oak log; the body laid on its back in stretched position, head towards southeast, legs were apart in the knees and were joined in the ankles. The bones of arms, pelvis and thorax were turned over. The log was put on a thick layer of large pieces of charcoal and decayed reed stalks.

Finds: at the top of the log the remains of four glass cups, a bone of an animal and a handmade conical vessel were situated. Near the wall of the log, on a layer of coal, a glass cup, a flask, and also a bronze mirror with a central handle - loop and hieroglyphs, two bronze small bells were lying. At the skull two scraps of gold foil were found, among the bones of arms and thorax beads of glass, amber, cornelian and chalcedony, two scraps of a gold chain, gold plaques, beads and pendants, a gold hook with a small loop, inserts of violet glass were found. In the region of feet there were many varied small beads.

Crypt 690 was a catacomb. The entrance hole was rectangular, orientated west-east. A gently sloping path led to the entrance. It was filled with thick homogeneous clay with a great number of small and middle stones. The spherical entrance was closed with a large slab. The chamber was of irregular oval form, orientated north-south.

In the crypt there were nine burials.

Burial 1 (an adult man) was made in a coffin at the entrance, with his head to the north, the legs were under the knees, arms clasped to the pelvis. Finds (Fig. 6, *16-28*): behind the skull, at the wall, there was a clay pitcher and a dark red slip dish with an iron knife and a bone of a cow. On the breast lay a bronze fibula and a scrap of gold foil, on the pelvis was an iron buckle, at the right hand a large bead of glass and a slate touchstone, at the right hip an iron dagger, and an iron awl was placed at the left knee. At the left shin there were two arrow-heads and an iron knife, between the shinbone and the fibula there were the remains of a red case with organic material, and an ivory button. At the feet an iron bit with curb bits, a large iron buckle and bronze rings – clips were found. Burial 2 (an adult) was in the centre of the chamber, in a coffin. The deceased was on his back in stretched position, the head facing to the north, the legs were slightly bent, and the bones of arms were displaced. The bones from the burials N 3-9 were shifted to the northern and western walls, the skulls were crushed. Among bones the remains of oak boards were noticed.

The finds (Fig. 6, *1-14*) discovered among isolated bones consisted of the fragments of a moulded pot, of a red slip dish and of a clay jug, a red slip flask and a dark red slip lamp with the relief images of dolphins (cat. 9) (Fig. 10), various beads, three iron buckles, three bronze fibulas, an iron finger-ring with a cornelian insert, a bronze bracelet, an iron arrowhead, a golden band with panel ornament and gold pendants in the shape of stylized amphora. The burial places in the crypt may be dated to the 1st century B.C. to the beginning of the 1st century A.D.

Crypt 703. The entrance hole was rectangular, orientated northwest-southeast; the chamber was of the extended quadrangular form (Fig. 7). In the east corner a niche (Fig. 12) was cut out, in which a ceramic incense-burner with charcoal, a red slip plate and a red slip lamp (cat. 10) (Fig. 10) were placed. The burial place was plundered in antiquity, its site fixed by a well - defined contour of the large decayed oak log.

Finds (Fig. 7, *1,3,4,7-10*): at the far wall a red slip krater, a bone of an animal, a flask of dark blue glass, alabaster vessel with a figure of an animal, a bone pixis and a glazed faience saucer were kept. Above the surface of the floor of the chamber a broken amphora, bronze buckles and a spring of a fibula, a large cornelian bead were found. The burial in the crypt could be dated to the late 1st - early 2nd century A.D.

Crypt 716. (Fig. 8) The entrance hole was of the trapezoid form orientated northwest-southeast, its lowest part was filled with large and small stones. A processed square slab partially broken by ancient robbers closed the entrance. Originally it was the face of some monumental construction. The chamber was of trapezoid form, the vault was semicylindrical. In the crypt one burial in a wooden log, standing along the southern wall, was found.

Finds (Fig.8, *1-4*): in the centre of the chamber a bone of an animal and an iron knife were lying, at the far wall there was a red slip cup with the a rosette stamp, in the south-eastern corner a red slip lamp with the image of Pegasus lay *in situ* (cat. 11) (Fig. 10) on a plate; a moulded lamp on a leg with remains of ashes at the bottom was also found. The burial place in a log was completely plundered in the antiquity. The date is late 1st - early 2nd centuries A.D.

Crypt 735 was a small catacomb, containing a child's burial in a large oak log. The numerous and rich finds - a bronze ladle, a silver cantor, an amphora, a red slip jug, beads, gild embellishments etc - allow us to date the burial to the mid 1st century A.D. In a special niche a red slip lamp with the vague image on the discus and large bucranian on the handle (cat. 12) (Fig.10).

Candelabra:

Crypt 603 was a large and deep catacomb containing the burial of a noble woman of the mid 1st century A.D., plundered in the antiquity. Among the remained intact finds were gold and silver ornaments, stone vessels, etc. Near one of the walls lay an open moulded lamp, under which two concave bronze plates with the holes in the centre were found. They were parts of a simple candelabrum (cat. 2/1) (Fig. 11, *2/1, 1a*).

Crypt 620. In the chamber there was one male and one female burial, found undisturbed in an oak log. Rich and diverse grave goods (the numerous gold and silver ornaments, weapons, amulets, Roman bronze utensils, Chinese varnished casket etc.) made it possible to date this complex to the mid 1st century A.D. In one of the corners of the chamber an iron candelabrum was standing (cat. 2/2) (Fig. 11, *2/2, 2a*), on the top of which there was a moulded (?) open lamp.

Tomb 700 was the largest tomb with a side niche on the burial ground. A middle-aged man, placed in the large pine coffin of a sophisticated design was here. A multitude of features suggest that the grave belonged to a high ranking priest. This grave is similar to the burial of priestesses in the crypt 595. Among diverse finds (a bronze cup, an amphora, wooden staffs, details of clothing, amulets etc.) a large iron candelabrum with a rectangular platform is worth mentioning (cat. 2/3) (Fig. 11, *2/3*).

Crypt 735 was a large catacomb, containing rich male and female burials in oak logs. The burials were plundered in modern times, but the some of the artefacts (an amphora, incense - burners, red slip painted jug, arrowheads) have survived. To the woman's interment belonged an iron candelabrum with a round platform (cat. 2/4) (Fig. 11, *2/4, 4a*), on which a moulded lamp on the leg stood. The date of burials in the crypt is c. id 1st century A.D.

Short analysis of the artefacts

Two major factors explain the use of lamps in funeral tradition of the ancient time. The first factor is lighting of underground chambers while funeral ceremonies were being performed. According to their conditions, the lamps from crypts 449, 634, 703, 716 and 735 fall into this category. The situation is not clear with crypts 424-a and 690 because the lamps in them were displaced in antiquity. The other factor is also possible in their cases. The necessity of the presence of "living" fire was stipulated by sacral purposes (Zubar & Sorochan 1984). The lamp decorated with an image of a dog was supposed to be part of the objects used and broken at the funeral feast. Their fragments were scattered with the earth into the gap of the crypt 439 chamber, and they are unlikely to have any bearing on it. Only in tombs 430, 510 and 553 the lamps with the images were undoubtedly placed as funeral stock and the latter two burials were children's. In these cases one can definitely speak about their cult purpose. Obviously, the lamps were to protect the dead's soul and to light up its way in the gloom of the other world. The diverse types of the images on their discuses (an eagle, the Gorgon Medusa, a bull, Pegasus, a dog) undisputably had some meaning. However, it is unknown whether this was kept at the funeral ceremonies. The lamp from the crypt 595 is significant in this sense. It was among the properties of a priestess of the high social rank. In the detailed publication of the tomb, the assumption was made that the "plain" (without an image) copy, which had no primary meaning, was specially chosen for ceremonial purpose (Zaitsev 2000).

Conclusion

The use of oil lamps was not widely spread among the Late Scythians, not even among those who lived in the close vicinity of Greek settlements and cities. The use of such objects was an isolated phenomenon which was caused by various reasons in each specific case. Even in the burials of nobility where there were plenty of expensive embellishments, bronze imported utensils and Chinese caskets, the large part of lamps were open moulded ones, fuelled by animal fat.

The other lighting object is metal candelabra, four examples of which were found in the necropolis. All of them were from the burials of nobility of the mid 1st - early 2nd centuries A.D and were, obviously, the objects of social prestige. The series of similar synchronous Sarmatian complexes, where the same objects were repeatedly found, also confirm this (Guschina & Zasetskaya 1989; Guschina & Zasetskaya 1994). The example from the grave 700 is probably not a candelabrum and served as a portable sacrificial altar (according to the design of the platform) or as an original fatty lamp.

Catalogue N 1 (lamps)

1. Mouldmade lamp. (Fig.13, *1*) The body is low, biconical, the nozzle is stretched, and a wick-hole is surrounded with a horizontal round rim. The discus is surrounded with a high crown and has four holes. On shoulders a relief ornament in the shape of meander is impressed carelessly, on the nozzle there is a stylised dolphin. Clay is grey, solid with infrequent calcareous inclusions, overburnt greatly. Slip is overburnt to dark grey with metal shine. L (length) - 12,1; B (breadth) - 6; H (height) - 2,9 (with a handle -4,5) cm.

2. (Fig.13, *2*) Mouldmade lamp. The body is low, the round discus is concave and is surrounded with a raised relief ring. The nozzle is short; the handle is in the shape of a loop, of a complex profile. On the discus there is a relief image of an eagle with wings folded. A print is careless and indistinct. Clay is solid, light, of brown-yellow tone, with minute golden sparkles. Slip is orange, dim with stains. It is overburnt in some places. L - 8,1; B - 5,7; H - 2,5 (3,4) cm.

3. Mouldmade lamp (Fig.13, *3*). The body is biconical, low. The nozzle is short, the handle is in the shape of a loop, of a complex profile. On the concave discus a relief image of a running dog is impressed surrounded with ornament of stylised small horseshoes. Clay is solid, light, of brown-yellow tone, without visible inclusions. Slip is dim, light orange with stains. L - 9,4; B - 7,2; H - 2,8 (3,8) cm.

4. Mouldmade lamp. The body is biconical, low. The lamp is made very carelessly; the joint of the top and bottom parts is well seen. The nozzle is protruded; its end is broad and lozenge-shaped. The shoulders are decorated with relief rosettae, which are impressed very badly. The handle was broken in the antiquity. Clay is light orange, solid. Slip is orange, thin, dim, covers the item unevenly. L - 8,7; B - 4,5; H - 2,8 (3) cm.

5. Mouldmade lamp. The body is low; the round discus is concave and is surrounded with a raised relief ring. The nozzle is short. The handle is vertical to the body. On the concave discus there is a relief image of an eagle with the folded wings sitting on an altar. The print is indistinct without details. Slip is orange, dim with stains. It is overburnt in some places. L - 7,4; B - 6; H - 2,9 (5) cm.

6. Mouldmade lamp (Fig.13, *4*). The body is biconical, low, the nozzle is short. On the concave discus there is a relief image of a bull, the details are not worked out. The lamp is stuck together. The handle is attached to the body at the angle of 45 degrees. L - 10,2; B - 7,4; H - 2,9 (5) cm.

7. Mouldmade lamp. The lamp is with the low round body, small nozzle, concave discus and loop handle. The discus is surrounded with the double ridge, without any images. Clay is solid, light, of brown - yellow tone. Slip is orange, with metal shine. L - 9,5; B - 7; H - 2,9 (4) cm.

8. Mouldmade lamp. The body is low; the round discus is concave and is surrounded with a raised relief ring. The nozzle is short; the handle is in the shape of a loop, of a complex profile. On the concave discus there is a relief image of the Gorgon Medusa's head (?). The details are not worked up properly. Clay is solid, light, of brown-yellow tone, with minute golden sparkles. Slip is orange, dim with stains. It is overburnt in some places. L - 7,7; B - 5,9; H - 2,5 (2,9) cm.

9. Mouldmade lamp identical to № 1. On the shoulders and nozzle the relief ornament fashioned as stylised dolphins is impressed carelessly. L - 8,2; B - 7; H - 3,2 cm.

10. Mouldmade lamp. The body is low; the round discus is concave and is surrounded with a raised relief ring. The nozzle is short, without the handle. The central part of the round discus, surrounded with the relief ridge, is broken. The shoulders in the spot of nozzle's attachment are decorated with the thin relief twisted spirals. Slip is orange, dim with stains. It is overburnt in some places. L - 12,4; B - 6,3; H - 3,2 (4,7) cm.

11. Mouldmade lamp (Fig.13, 5). The body is low; the round discus is concave and is surrounded with a raised relief ring. The nozzle is short; the handle is in the shape of a loop, of a complex profile. 0n the concave discus there is the relief image of Pegasus, the details are not worked up properly. Clay is solid, light, of brown - yellow tone. Slip is orange, glittering. L - 9,4; B - 6,5; H - 2,9 (4,2) cm.

12. Mouldmade lamp (Fig.13, 6). On the concave circular discus, surrounded with the double rindge there is a badly impressed relief composition of two figures (?). In the centre there is a round hole for filling oil. The sharp round nozzle is decorated with two volutes. The handle is moulded, in the shape of a massive stuck piece, decorated with a relief bucranian (head of a bull). Slip is dark orange, evenly spread. The object is greatly damaged with soil salts. L - 13,5; B - 7,6; H - 3 (4,8) cm.

Catalogue № 2 (Candelabra)

1. (Fig. 11, *2.1*). Two concave bronze plates with a hole in the centre. One of them is of the flat semispherical form, the other has a profiled edge. According to their location, one of them (the smaller one) served as a detail of the candelabrum basis, and the other was a platform for a lamp placing. Diameter (D) 1 - 7,5; H1 - 0,9; D2 - 5,4; H2 - 0,8 cm.

2. (Fig. 11, *2.2*). Forged iron candelabrum, consisting of a round in section vertical rod, a round stand with the raised edges and three legs ("paws"), that recede the main vertical basis almost horizontally. The edges of the "paws" are broadened, flattened and have superficial grooves in the end. The object's preservation is poor; all the metal is corroded. H - 34,5; D (top platform) - 8,3; B (base) - 11,3 cm.

3. (Fig. 11, *2.3*). The top platform is massive, of rectangular form, with the edges bent upwards. The details of the basis remained in fragments. It is determined, that there also were three square in section legs ("paws"), but the way they were attached to the central rod is not defined. H - 52; Top platform: 11,4 x 14,4 cm; B (base) - ?

4. (Fig. 11, *2.4*). Forged iron candelabrum, consisting of a round in section vertical rod, a round stand with the raised edges. Three legs of the basis recede the central rod horizontally. For stability their edges are bent at right angles and unriveted as pentagonal platforms. The object's preservation is poor, all the metal is corroded. H - 32; D (top platform) - 9; B (base) - 18,1 cm.

Bibliography

Aibabin A.I. 1990. Chronologiya mogilnikov Kryma pozdnerimskogo i rannesrednrvekovogo vremeni. In: *MAIET, N 1*, Simpheropol. (in Russian).

Alekseeva E.M. 1975. *Antichnye busy Severnogo Prichernomorya. SAI G1-12*. Moskow. (in Russian).

Alekseeva E.M. 1978. *Antichnye busy Severnogo Prichernomorya. SAI G1-12*. Moskow. (in Russian).

Alekseeva E.M. 1982. *Antichnye busy Severnogo Prichernomorya. SAI G1-12*. Moskow. (in Russian).

Ambroz A.K. 1966. *Fibuly yuga evropeiskoi chasti SSSR. SAI D1-30*. Moscow. (in Russian).

Chrzanovski L., Zhuravlev D. 1998. *Lamps from Chersonesos in the State Historical Museum - Moscow. Studia archaeologica, 94*. Roma.

Eggers H.J.1951. *Der römische Import im frein Germanien*, Bd.I-II. Hamburg.

Ettlinger E. 1962. *Die römischen Fibeln in der Shweiz*. Bern.

Gushchina I.I., Zhuravlev D.V. 1999. Pogrebeniya s bronzovoi posudoi iz mogilnika Belbek IV v Yugo-Zapadnom Kpymu. In: *Rossiyskaya arkheologia, N 2*. 157-171. (in Russian).

Gushchina I.I., Zasetskaya I.P.. 1989. Pogrebehiya zubovsko-vozdvizhenskogo tipa iz raskopok N.I. Veselovskogo v Prikubahye (1 v. do n. e. - nachalo 2 v. n. e.). In: *Arkheologicheskie issledovaniya na yuge Vostochnoy Evropu. Papers of the State Historical Museum, Vol. 70*. Moscow. 71-141. (in Russian).

Gushchina I.I., Zasetskaya I.P. 1994. *"Zolotoe kladbishche" Rimskoi epochi v Prikubanye*. Sankt Peterburg. (in Russian).

Hayes J.W. 1973. Roman pottery from the South Stoa at Corinth.In: *Hesperia, H.42*.

Kosyanenko V.M. 1987. Bronzovye fibuly iz nekropolya Kobyakova gorodishcha. In: *Sovetskaya arkheologiya, N 2*. 45-62. (in Russian).

Kropotkin V.V. 1970. *Rimskie importnye izdeliya v Vostocnoi Evrope (II v. do n. e. - V v. n. e.). SAI*

D1-27. Moscow

Loescke S. 1919. *Lampen aus Vindonissa*. Zurich.

Novichenkova N.G..2000. Fibuly iz svyatilishcha u perevala Gurzufskoe Sedlo. In: *Rossiyskaya arkhelogiya* N1. 154-166. (in Russian).

Raddatz K. 1957. Der Thorsberger Moorfund. Gürtelteile und Körperschmuck. In: *Offa-Bücher*, Bd. 13.

Skripkin A.S. 1977. Fibuly Nizhego Povolzhya (po materialam sarmatskich pogrebenyi). In: *Sovetskaya arkheologiya* N2. 100-120. (in Russian).

Tassinari S. 1993. *Il vasellame Bronzeo di Pompei. Cataloghi 5*. Roma.

Vnukov S.Yu. 1999. Chronologicheskie raznovidnosti svetloglinyannych amfor s dvustvolnymi ruchkami. In: *Donskaya archeologiya, N1*. Rostov. (in Russian).

Vysotskaya T.N. 1994. *Ust-Alminskoe gorodishche i nekropol*. Kiev. (in Russian).

Zaitsev Yu. P. 2000. "Sklep zhrits" Ust-Alminskogo nekropolya. In: *Zhertvoprinoshenie*. Moscow. (in Russian).

Zaitseva K.I. 1997. Kultovye chashi V-I vv. do n. e. iz Severnogo Prichernomorya. In: *Trudy Gosudarstvennogo Ermitazha. Vol. XXVIII*. 38-53. (in Russian).

Zhuravlev D.V., 1997. Krasnolakovaya keramika gruppy Eastern sigillata B iz mogilnika Belbek 1V v Yugo-Zapadnom Кpымu. In: S.Demidenko, D.Zhuravlev (Eds) *Drevnosti Evrazii*. Moscow. 227-250. (in Russian).

Zubar V.M., Sorochan S.B. 1984. Svetilniki v pogrebalnom obryade antichnych gorodov Severnogo Prichernomorya. In: *Antichnaya kultura Severnogo Prichernomorya*. Kiev.

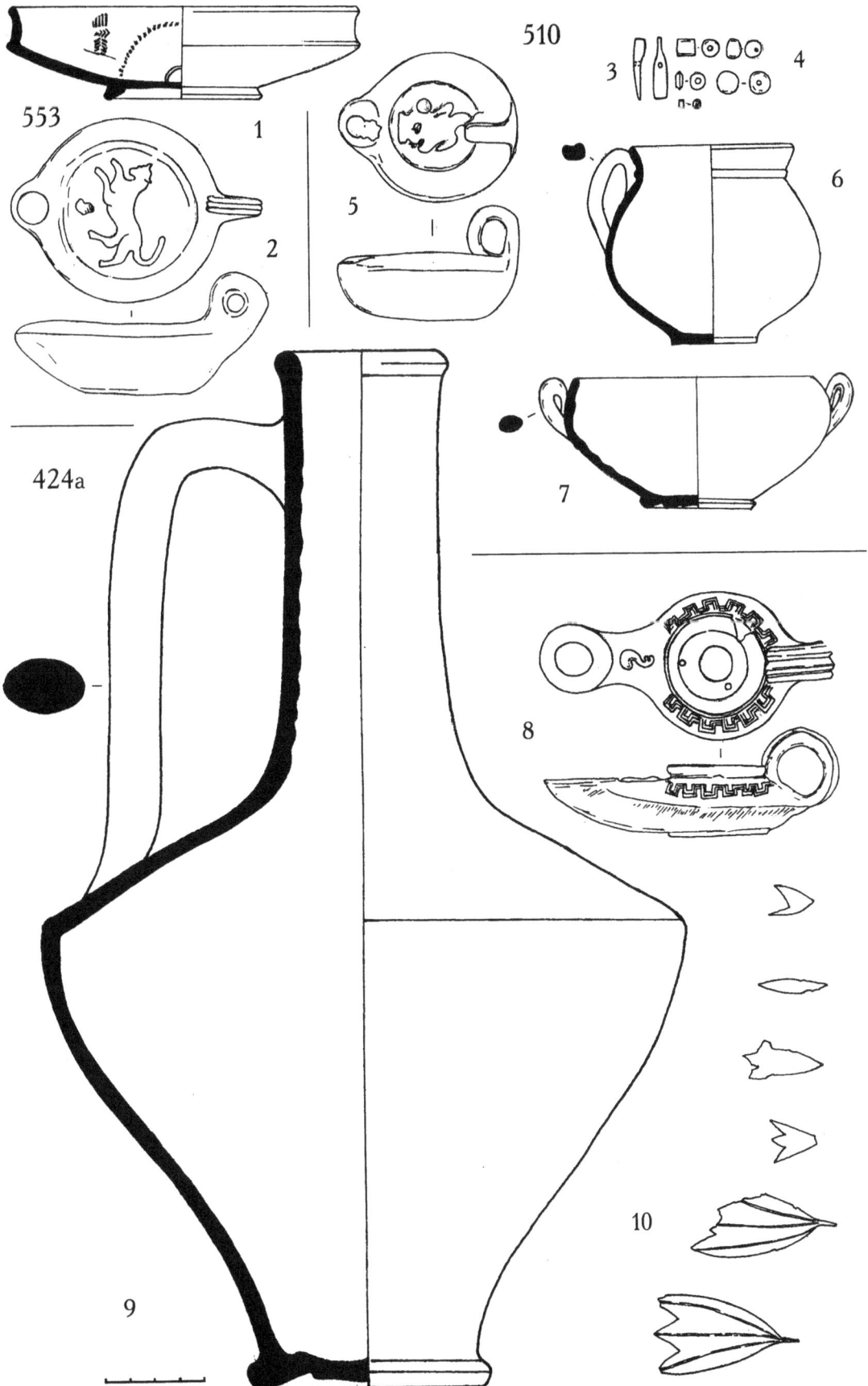

Fig. 1. Crypts 424a, 510, 533. Inventory.

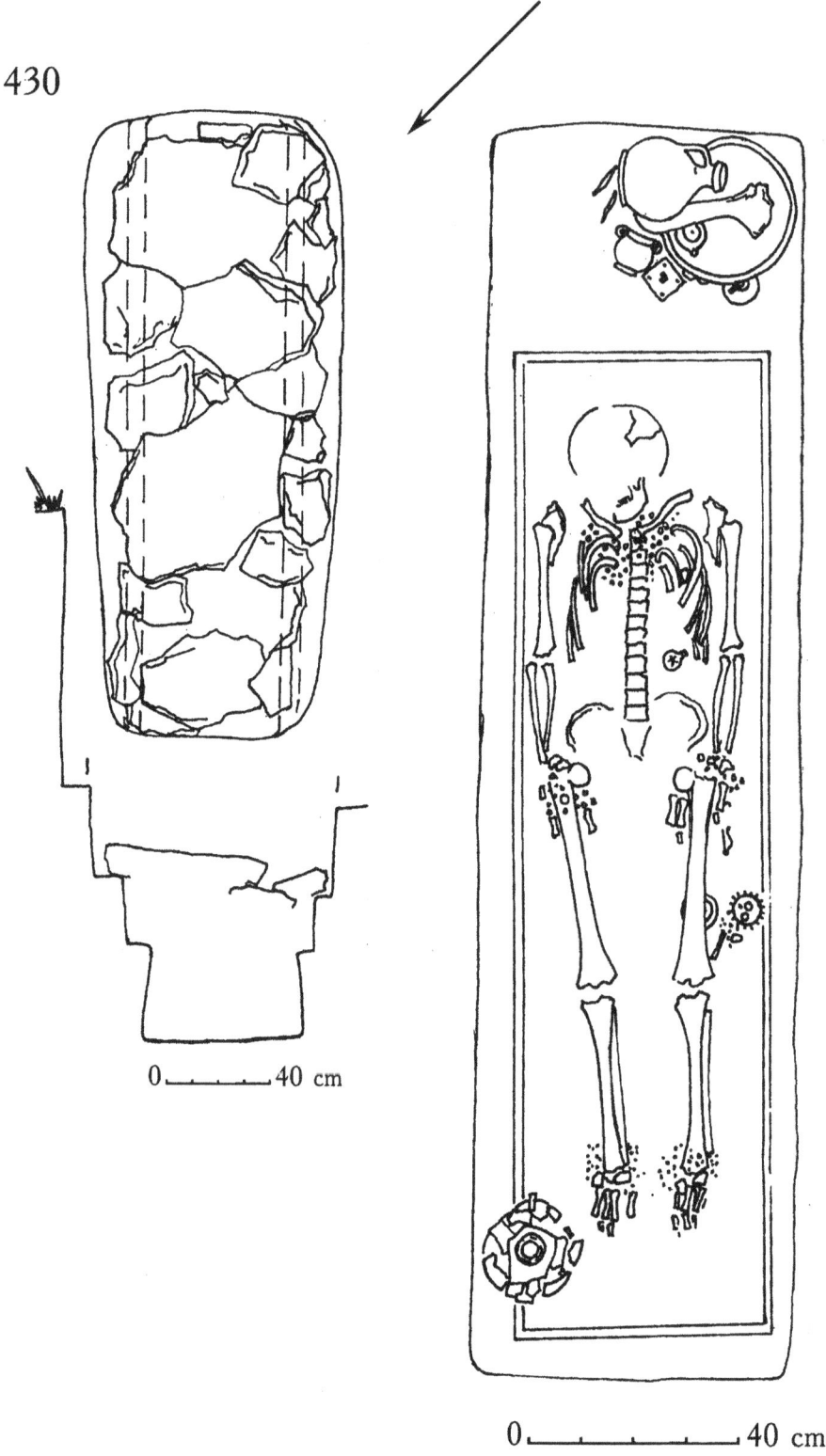

Fig. 2. Grave 430. Plan.

Yuriy Zaitsev: Imported Lamps and Candelabra from Ust'-Alma Necropolis (Crimea, Ukraine)

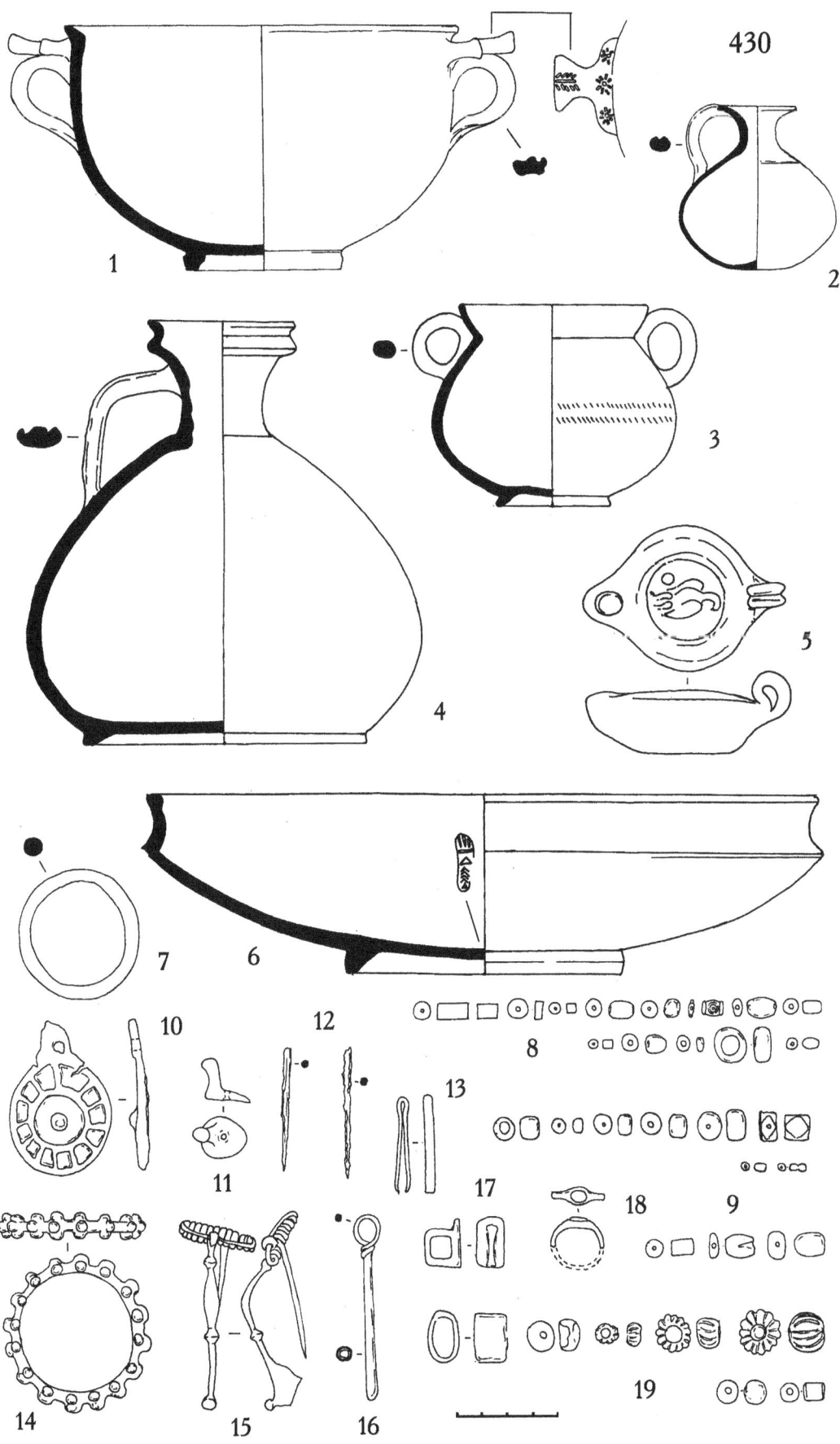

Fig. 3. Grave 430. Inventory.

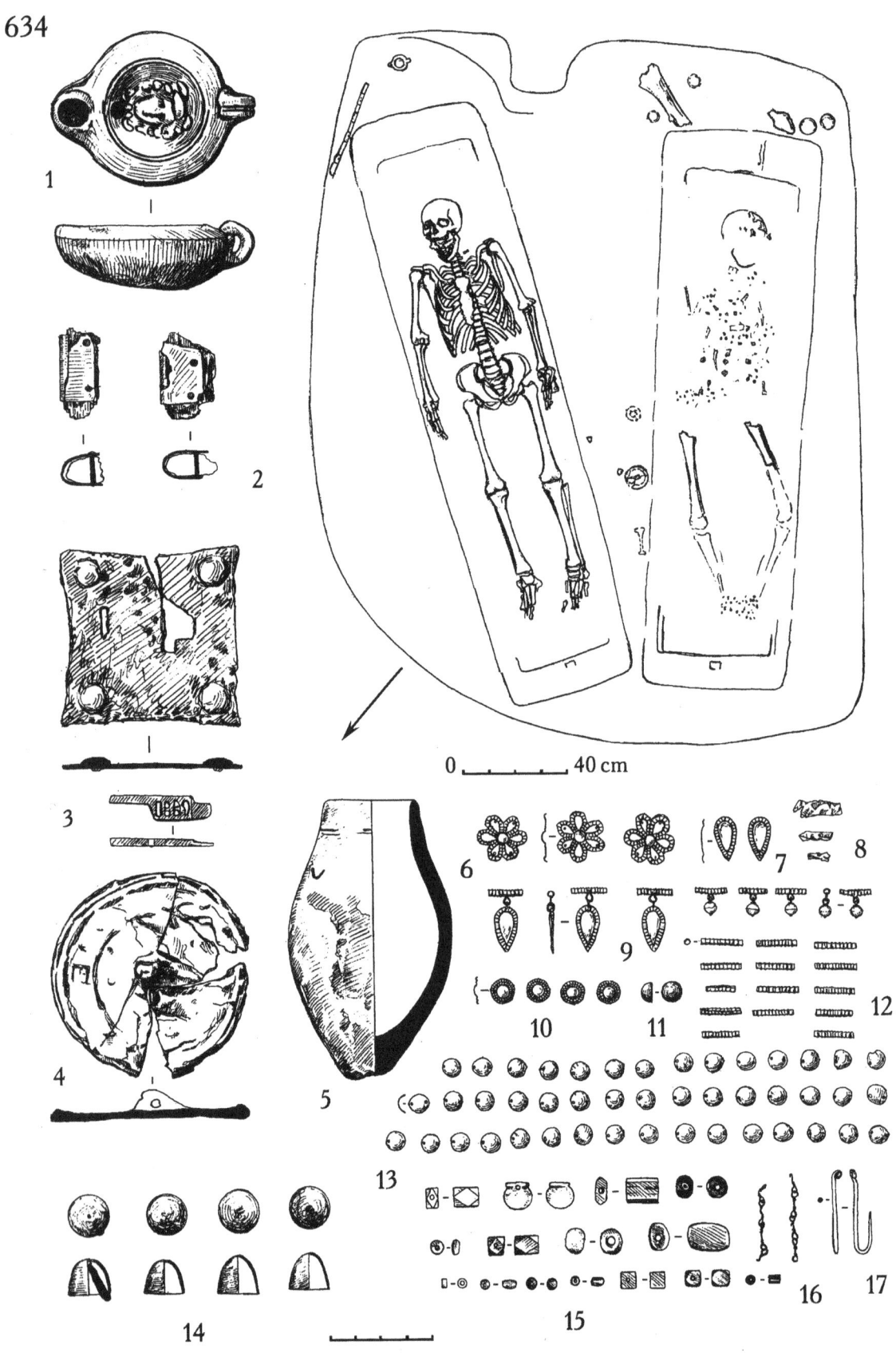

Fig. 4. Crypt 634: plan and inventory.

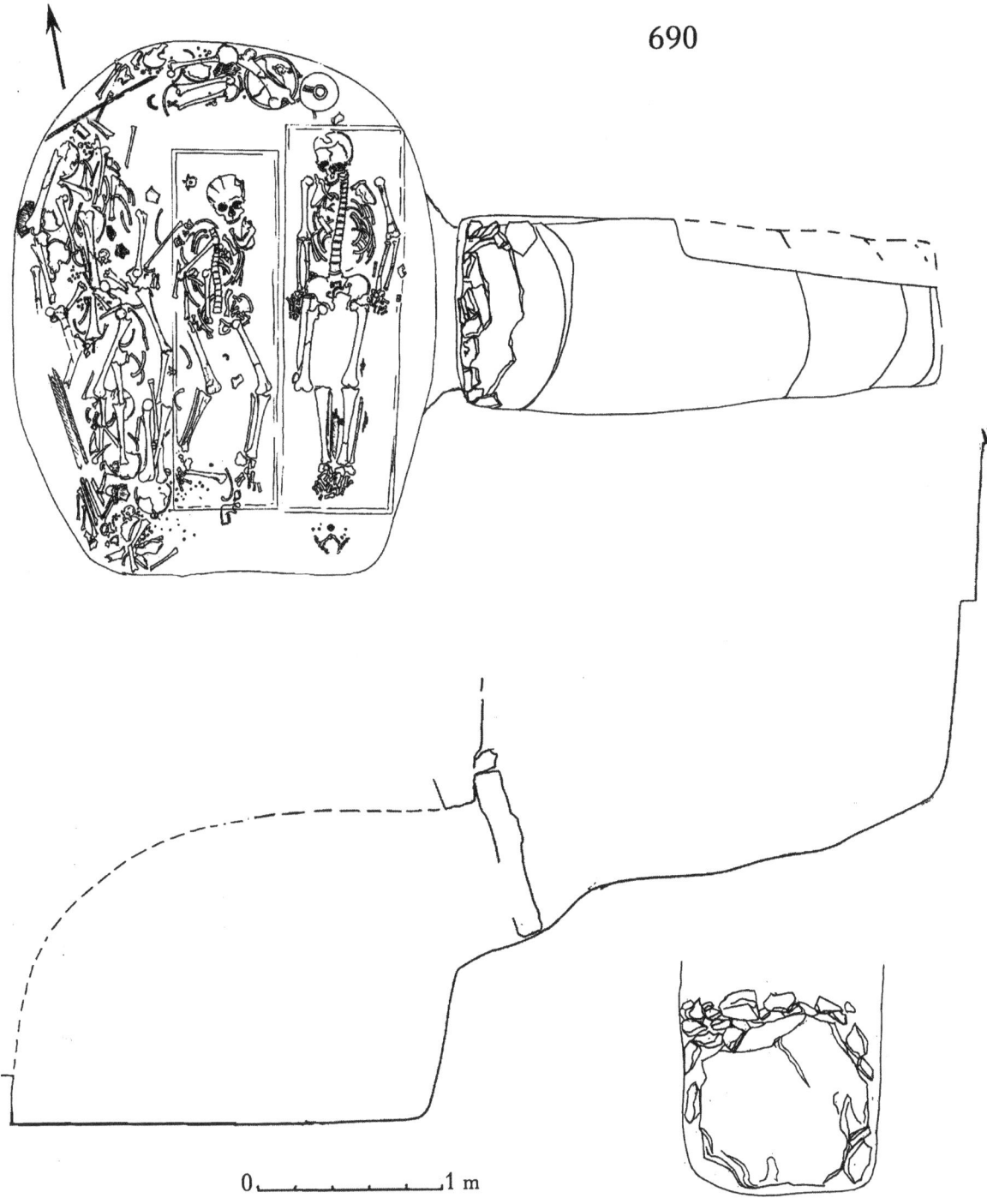

Fig. 5. Crypt 690. Plan.

Fire, Light and Light Equipment in the Graeco-Roman World

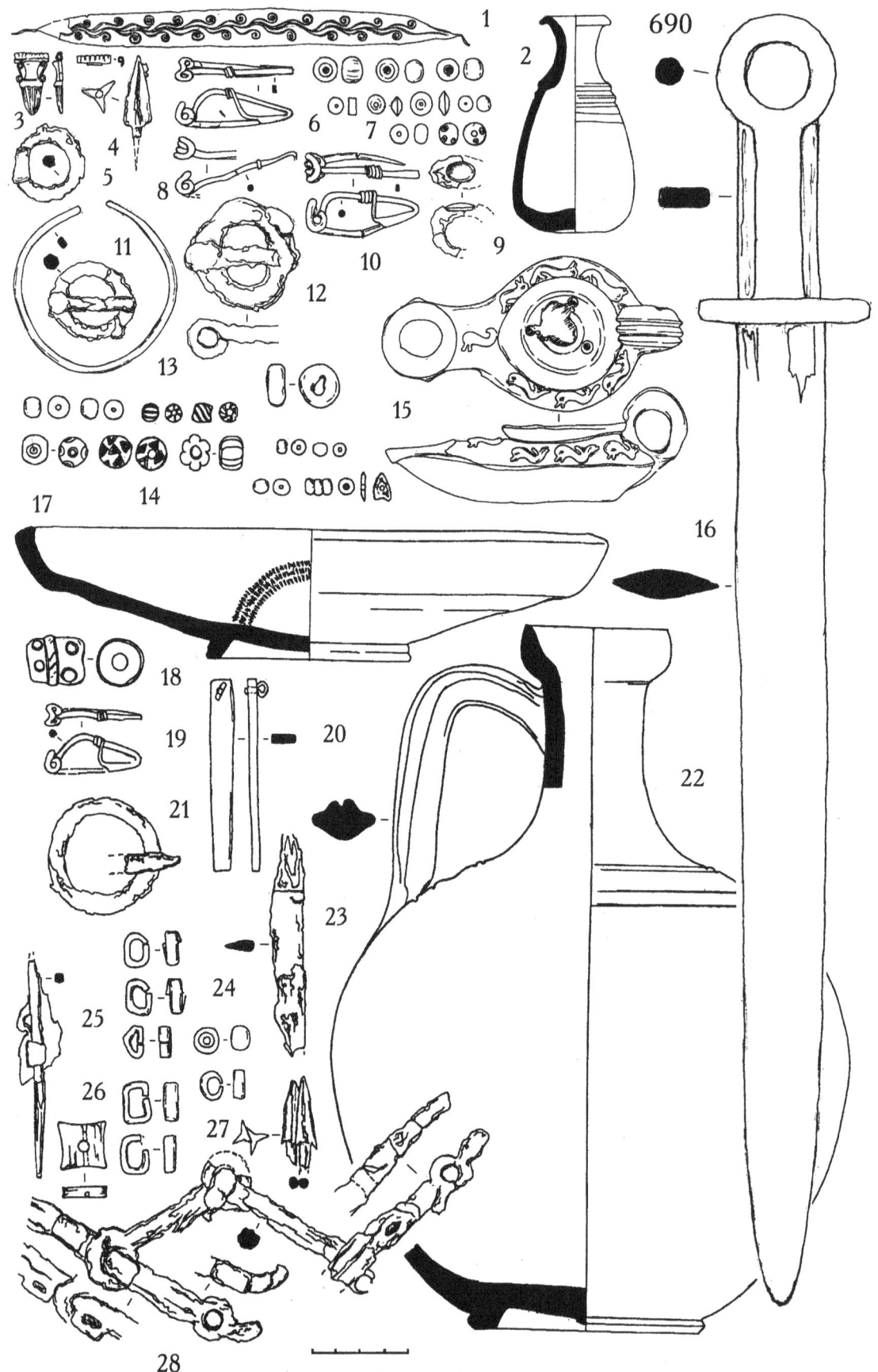

Fig. 6. Crypt 690. Inventory

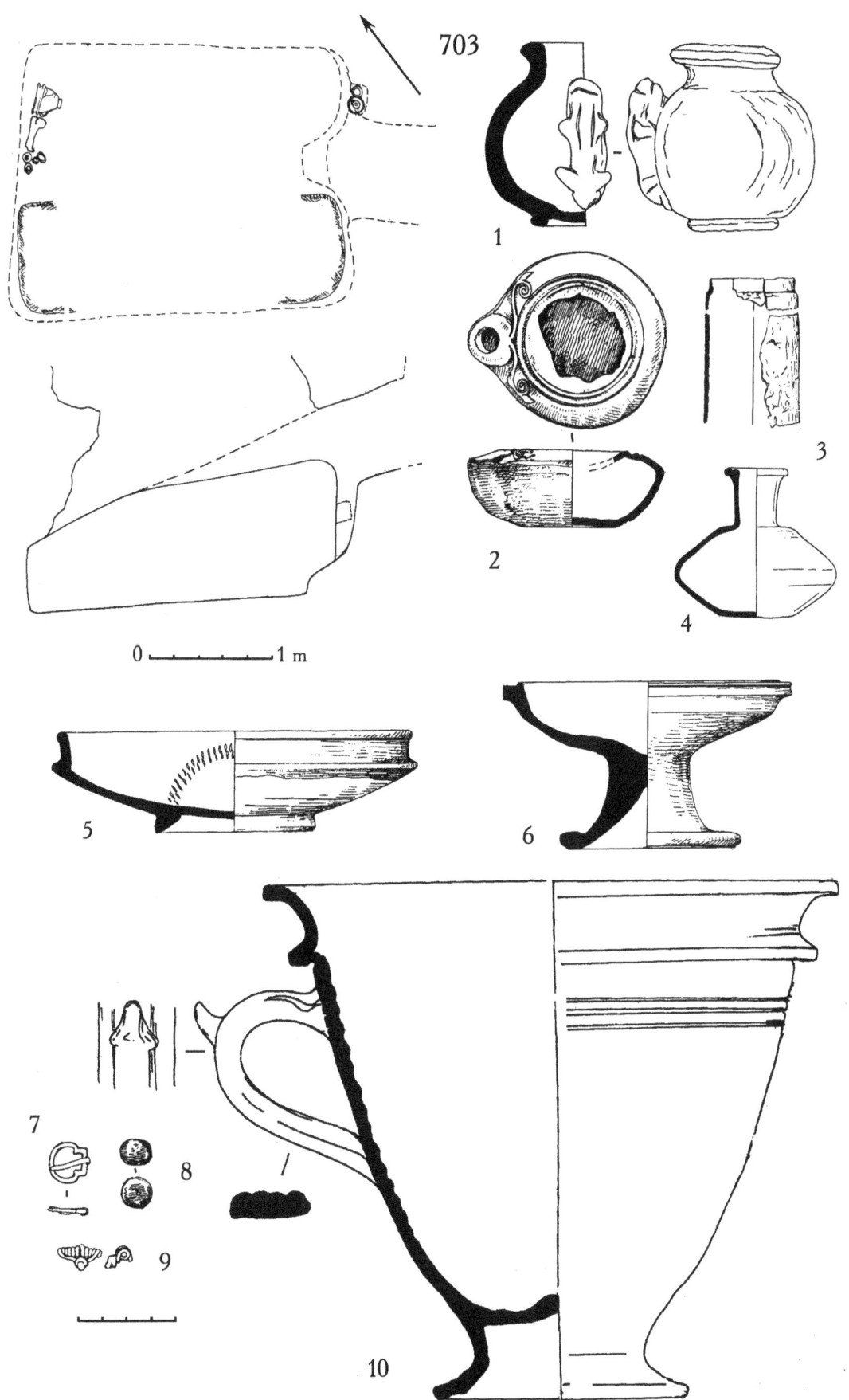

Fig. 7. Crypt 703: plan and inventory.

Fire, Light and Light Equipment in the Graeco-Roman World

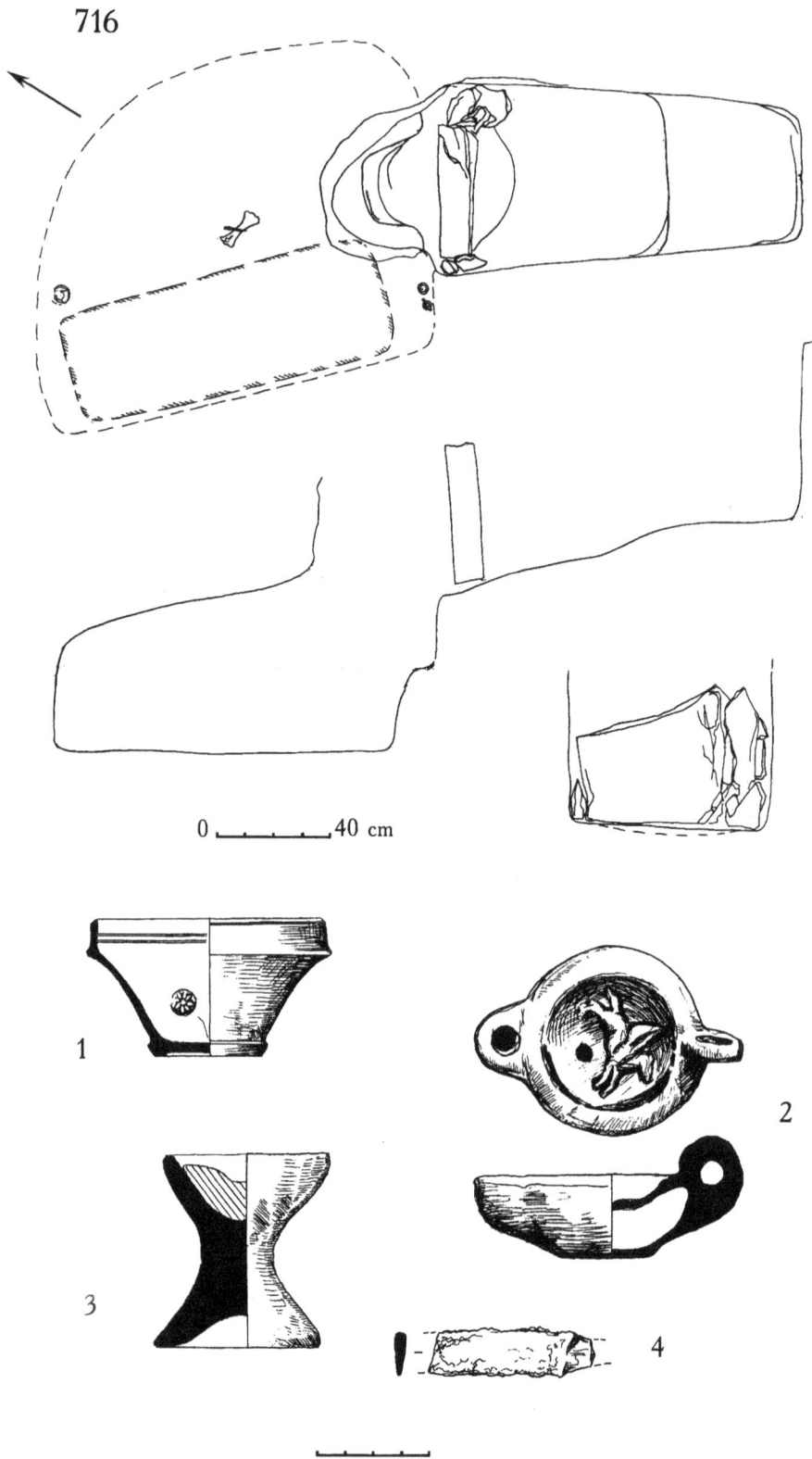

Fig. 8. Crypt 716: plan and inventory.

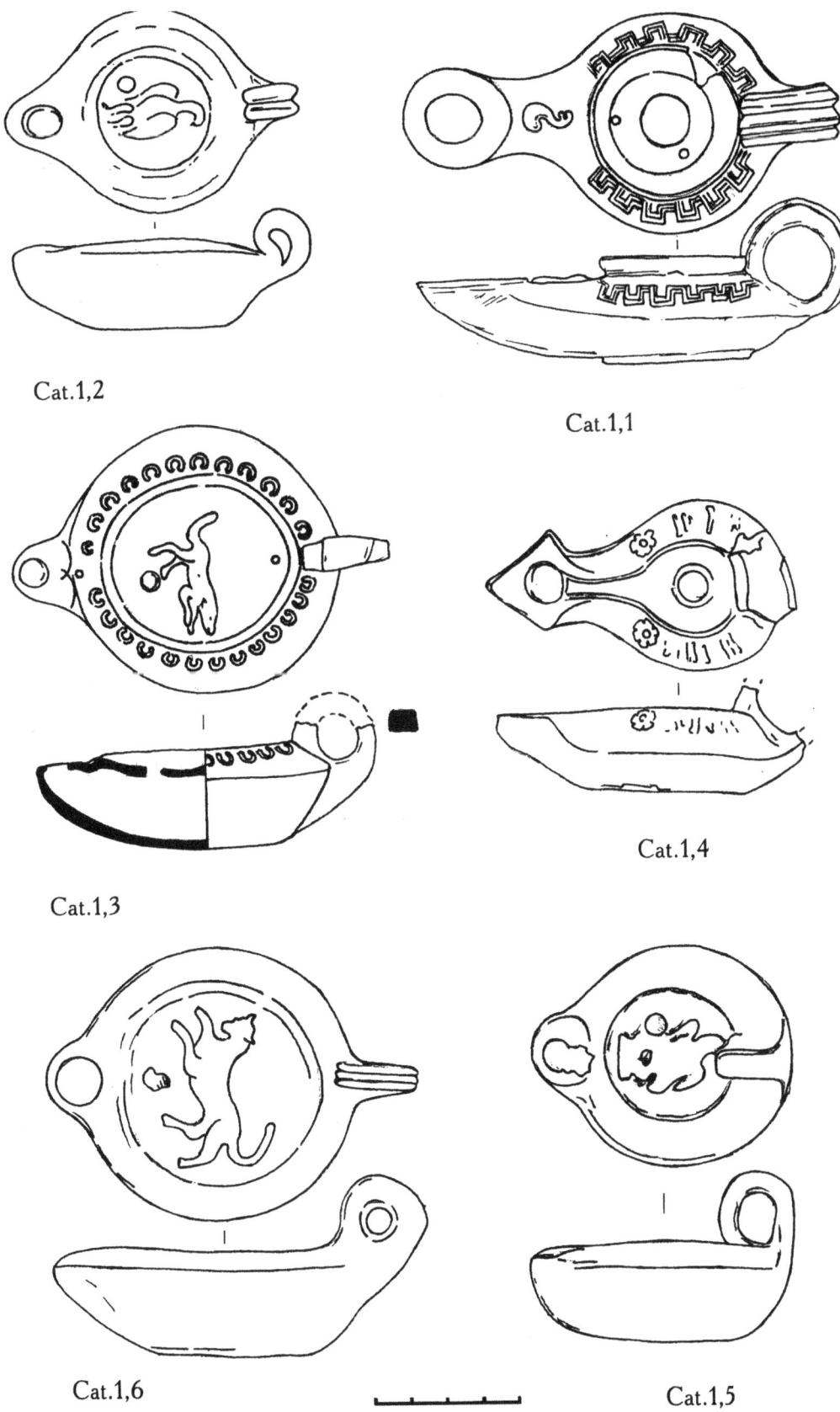

Fig. 9. Lamps (Cat. N. 1-6).

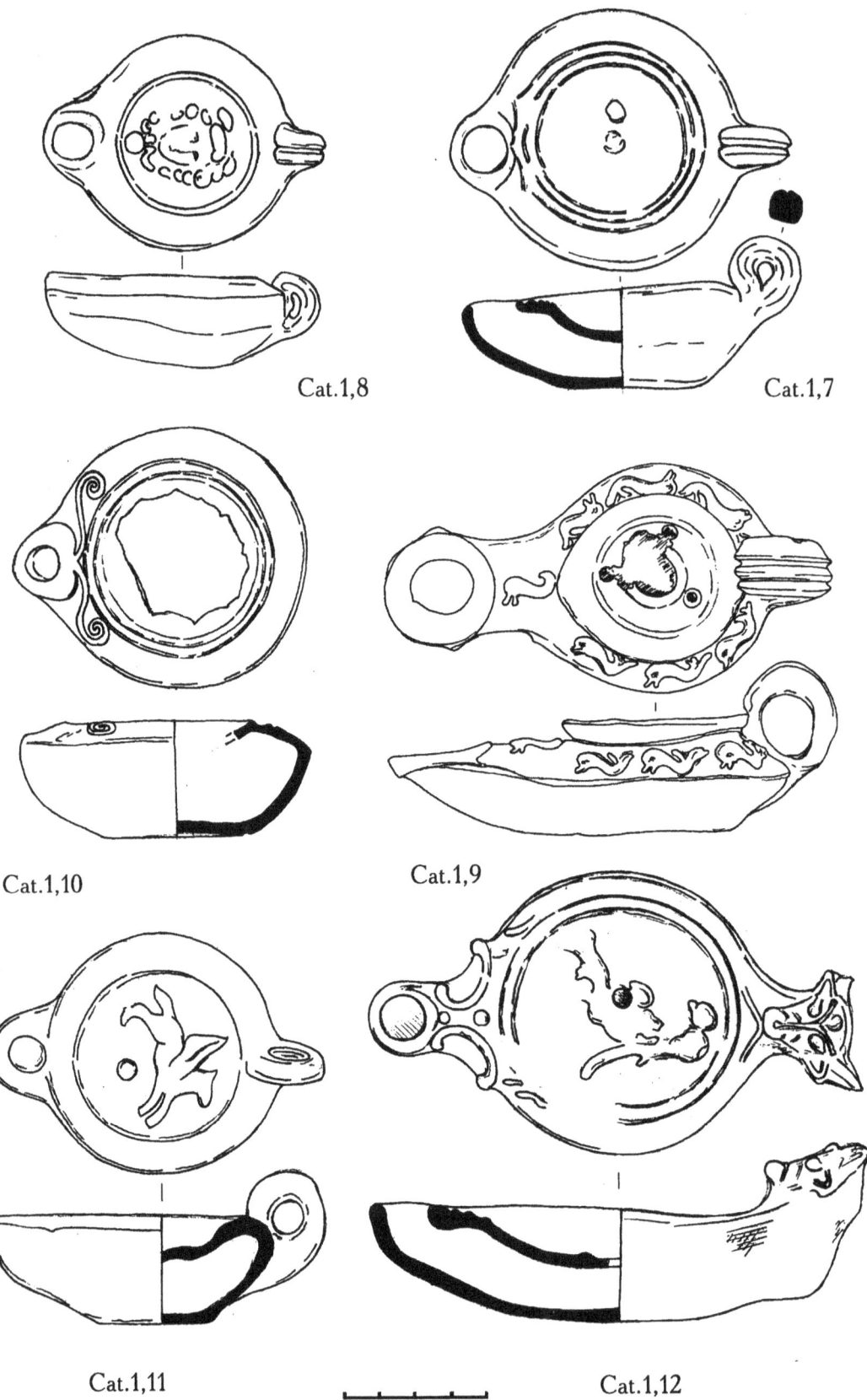

Fig. 10. Lamps (Cat. N 7-12).

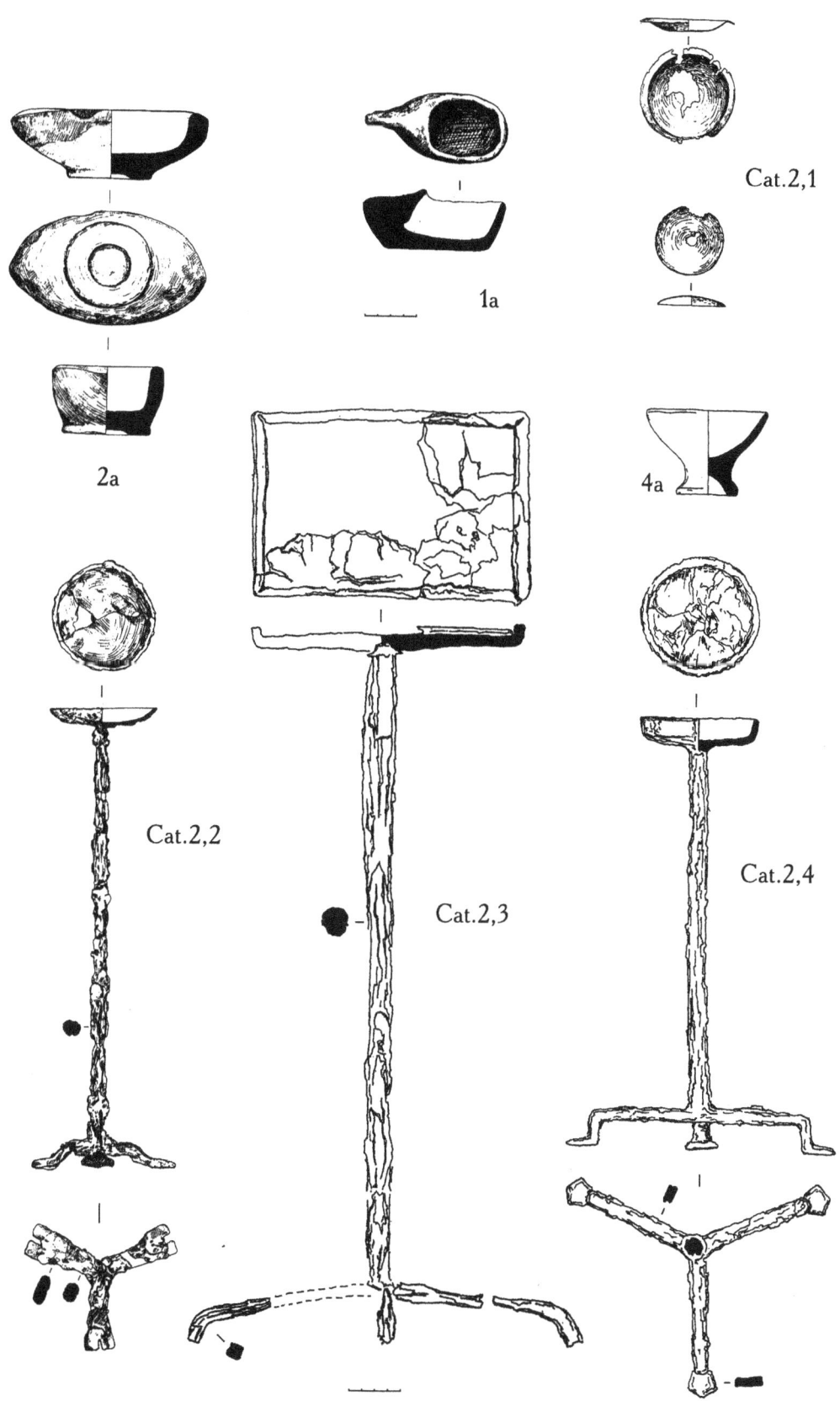

Fig. 11. Candelabra and lamps from the crypts 603 (Cat. 2,1; 1a), 620 (Cat. 2,2; 2a), 730 (Cat. 2,4; 4a) and grave 700 (Cat. 2,3)

Fig. 12. Lamp (Cat. 1,10) in situ in the grave.

Fig. 13. Lamps (Cat. 1,1; 1,2; 1,3; 1,6; 1,11; 1,12).

Fire, Light and Light Equipment in the Graeco-Roman World

Light and Fire in the Palace of Scythian King Skilur

Yuriy Zaitsev

(Simpheropol, Ukraine)

Neapolis Scythian is the largest and the most well known fortress in Crimea (fig.1). According to the recent researches it existed from the middle of the 2nd century B.C. until the middle of the 3rd century AD. During the years of excavations at Neapolis rich cemeteries, buildings and objects of art were discovered, and the great number of pottery and metal objects was found. For ancient history and archaeology of the North Black Sea coast and Mediterranean area Neapolis Scythian is one of the most important sites for the solution of the problem of relations between Greeks and Barbarians. In the 2nd century B.C. Neapolis was the fortress - capital of the famous Scythian King Skilur and the main military base in the struggle with the armies of Pontian King Mithridates the 6th Eupator (Vinogradov 1987; Zaitsev 1997; Zaitsev 1999; Zaitsev & Puzdrovski 1994; Koltukhov 1999.).

The main feature of the fortress at that time was the Southern Palace — sophisticated architectural complex with the area of about 2500 sq. m, which functioned as the king's residence as well as a ritual complex (fig.2). The central construction of the palace was a huge megaron with the area of 250 sq. m decorated with fresco paintings and sculpture. In front of it was a private courtyard surrounded by large Greek-type houses and fences. To the west of the megaron stood a ritual stone pool with paintings. The southern, ceremonial façade of the palace complex, facing the fortress gate, was built in Greek style. It was decorated with Dorian pilasters and marble statues. Between the façade of the palace and the gates, a large stone altar and a monument rising above the underground sepulchre of Argot, were located. The monument had the stepped base crowned with a bronze statue of a horseman on a high pedestal. The pedestal was decorated with reliefs and metric inscription. Skilur's Mausoleum was to the south of the sepulchre of King Argot, just behind the defensive wall (Zaitsev 1997).

The long-term excavations of the southern palace allowed us to accumulate plenty of material connected with various aspects of life and culture of Greek and Barbarian aristocracy.

The special place belonged to fire, which traditionally played a major role in daily life and in cult ceremonies.

Fire in daily life

1. Light. The excavations of the palace revealed more than thirty fragmented closed lamps (fig.3). Four of them were hand-made and only four were imported, coated with slip. Other lamps were made in potter's workshop situated in the palace and included several types. The largest lamp with three nozzles and the double-barrelled handle intended for intensive lighting is of the special interest (fig. 3,*1*). Such number of lamps would have been insignificantly small for any Greek monument, while in the ordinary Scythian life the use of clay oil lamps was an exception. For lighting the Barbarians used animal fat, and that required a special design of lamps (open, on a stand). Thus, according to Greek tradition, the palace premises were lit with oil, combustion of which gave less soot and smoke.

2. Food preparation. Food was prepared on the open hearths situated in the centre of premises. The hearths were made from clay in the shape of low rectangular platforms (fig.4, *4*). Their horizontal working surfaces and clay under them are always heavily burnt. The special research of these hearths makes it possible to assume that initially a strong fire which heated up the "body" of the hearth to a very high temperature, was lit. Then pieces of coal and ashes were removed from the working surface, on which the large frying pans were placed. Thus, at first energy was accumulated in the clay of the hearth, and was then given back through contact with the top plane and vessels with food. The special interest represents the hearth in the centre of the palace megaron (fig. 5). It was mounted as a two-step platform; its working surface was burnt up to the condition of gloss and covered the area of 2 sq. m (fig. 6). This hearth was regularly repaired together with the floor of the building. For this purpose all lateral sides were covered carefully with clay and were painted black. It is obvious that this hearth was used not only for cooking enormous amounts of food during feasts and other events in the palace. As the central hearth of the king's residence, it could also have been the main sacral altar during cult ceremonies of the palace.

3. The technological high-temperature processes, that required a lot of fuel and a rather complex organisation of production. Metalworking and potter's workshops are supposed to have been functioning at the palace. Their presence has been established by wasters, casting forms, and series of typical production made by small consignments. Thus the pottery workshops made tiles, jugs and cups, lamps, small altars, thymiaterions and rare terracotta figurines. The large part of these objects was intended for consumption inside the palace.

Use of fire for cult purposes

1. Fiery sacrifice (a ritual burning). A unique collection of diverse clay altars and thymiaterions was found during the excavations of the palace (figs.7, 8). More than sixty altars are known up to date. All of them were designed as profiled columns with a "cup" in the top. The smallest altar has the height of about 10 cm, the largest one is more than 40 cm high. The majority were made on potter's wheel, but many small altars were moulded in special forms. The large and middle - size examples were decorated with hand-made garlands, female busts, solar rosettes, and bucranians. Further, their surfaces and elements of decoration were painted in different colours (red, light blue, green, black, pink, and yellow) and some of them were gilt. The most beautiful altar on a two-step stand from the mausoleum of the King Skilur is of special interest (fig.9). It was decorated with the relief polychromic garlands, gilt bucranians and solar rosettae. Under the rim a garland of green leaves and red berries was drawn.

In the palace megaron the set of three similar altars decorated with polychrome drawings, gilding, moulded garlands, bucranians and solar rosettes have been found. They accompanied a large terracotta figure of the sitting man also covered with gilding and polychrome drawings. According to the archaeological context, all these objects were placed in a special niche (fig.10), which was arranged in the ceremonial western wall, on the background of the polychrome fresco. Another type of cult vessels is thymiaterion. About twenty thymiaterions were found. Their function was similar to that of the altars, but thymiatenions rest on a high conic stand. Among them only 3 were imported (one with paintings) and one is in the shape of a large female figure. This is probably the representation of Demeter or Cora; her face was painted pink, hair - red-brown, and coverlet - light blue.

2. Burning of aromatic substances. Special hand-moulded incense-burners in the shape of a ball on a massive base were used. Their rims had a pair of apertures for hanging. Two such incense-burners were found in the mausoleum of Skilur (fig.4, 2,3), and more than twentyduring the excavation of the palace. Many examples are decorated with solar symbols painted white and red and are supplied with apertures for smoke vent. Inside the intact incense-burners the grassy ashes were fixed a lot of times.

It is obvious that all these objects were used in the different cult ceremonies, in which worship of the Sun and lighting of fire was of main importance. It is no accident that their unusually high concentration is within the borders of the Southern Palace of Neapolis Scythian. For comparison, within all the territory of the Northern Black Sea area (except for Scythian Neapolis) only about one hundred finds of clay altars and thymiaterions of the 5th -1st centuries B.C. have been noted (Zaitseva 1998: 38). Together with many other facts the data allow the assumption that Skythian King Skilur, considered to be the son of the Sun, was the main figure in these ceremonies and the object of worship.

In the connection with such conclusions another feature unearthed on the territory of the palace is of great interest (fig.11). It is a monumental pool constructed of carefully worked slabs. In one of its walls a drain was arranged, through which the water that was flowing down from the roof of megaron during rain went down. The bottom of the pool was inclined and various symbols, including solar "wheel" were drawn with red paint on the slabs of its deepest part. It is obvious that rain water covered them first of all. But the most interesting is the fact that the top parts of the decorative slabs from inside were repeatedly burnt up to reddening and cracking of the stone. Thus, the object was probably also used for ritual actions with rain water and for recurrent lighting of strong fire. The use of the stone pool for mixing two basically opposite natural elements had, undoubtedly, a deep sacral sense, which is hardly possible to decipher nowadays. One can only assume with enough confidence the important role this pool played during the ritual events, the aim of which was to worship the basic forces of the nature.

Bibliography

Vinogradov Yu.G. 1987. Votivnaya nadpis docheri tsarya Skilura iz Pantikapeya i problemy istopii Skifii i Bospora vo 2 v. do n. e. In: *VDI, N 1*. (in Russian)

Zaitsev Yu.P. 1997. Yuzhnyi dvorets Neapolya skifskogo. In: *VDI, N 3*. (in Russian)

Zaitsev Yu.P. 1999. Skilur i ego tsarstvo: novye otkrytiya i novye problemy. In: *VDI. N 2*. (in Russian)

Zaitseva K.I. 1997. Kultovye chashi V-I vv. do n. e. iz Severnogo Prichernomorya. In: *Trudy gosudarstvennogo Ermitazha. XXVIII*. 38-53 (in Russian)

Zaitsev Yu.P., Puzdrovskii A.E. 1994. Neapol Skifskii v epochu Diofantovych voin. In: *Zapadnyi Krym v antichnuyu epochu*. Kiev. (in Russian)

Koltukhov S.G. 1999. *Ukrepleniya Krymskoi Skifii*. Simpheropol. (in Russian)

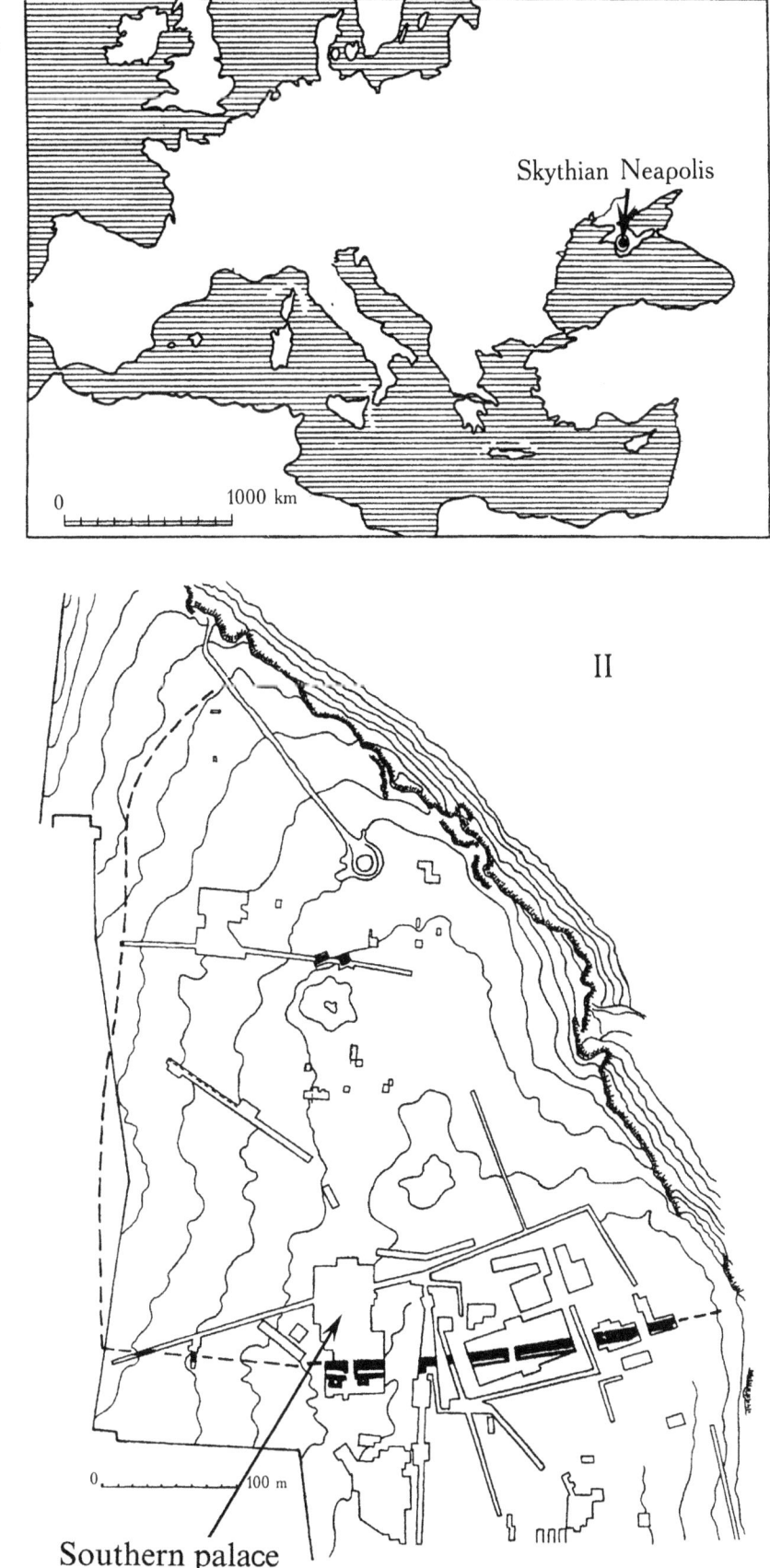

Fig. 1. Neapolis Skythian. General plan.

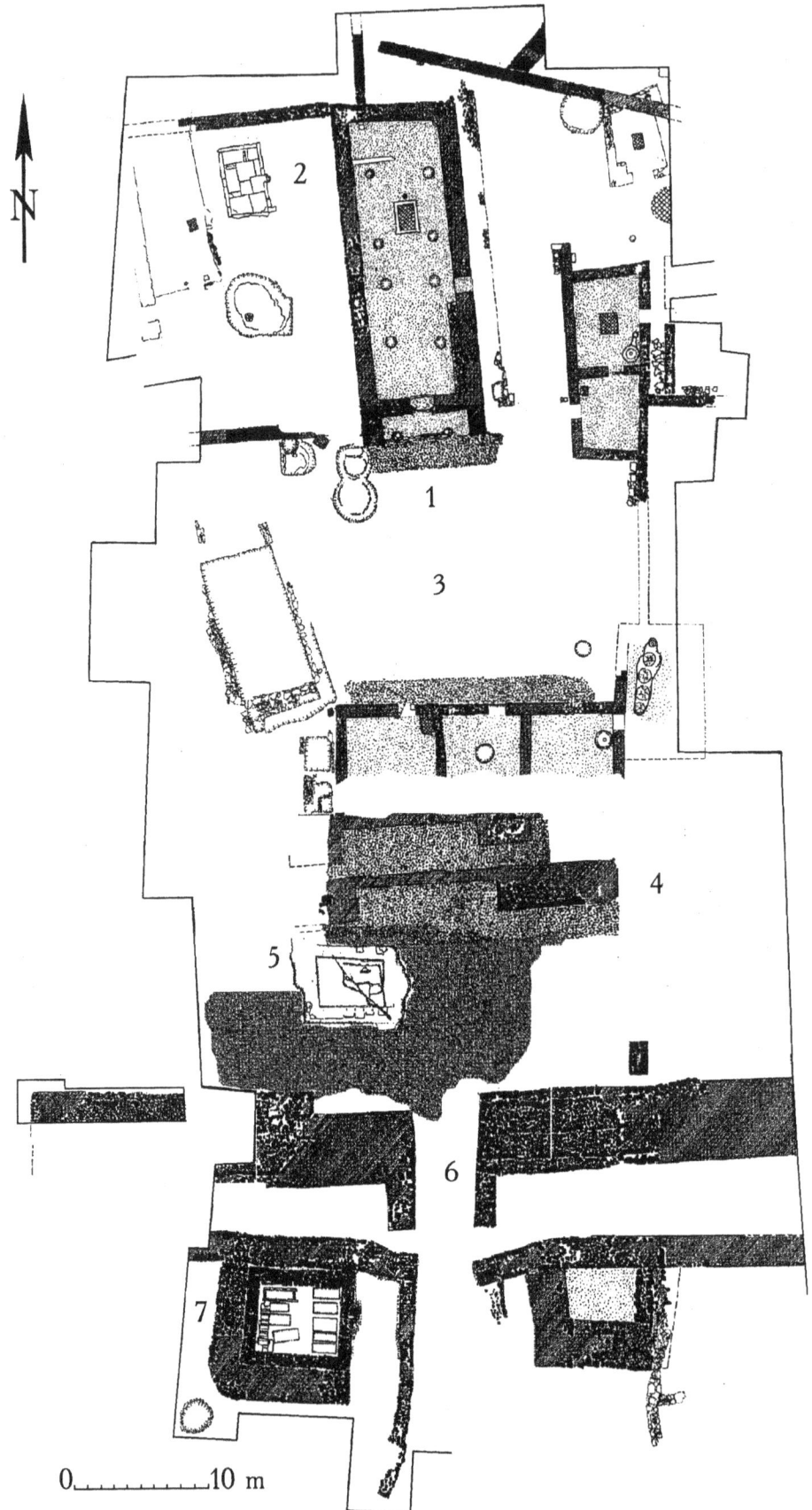

Fig. 2. Southern Palace. Plan.

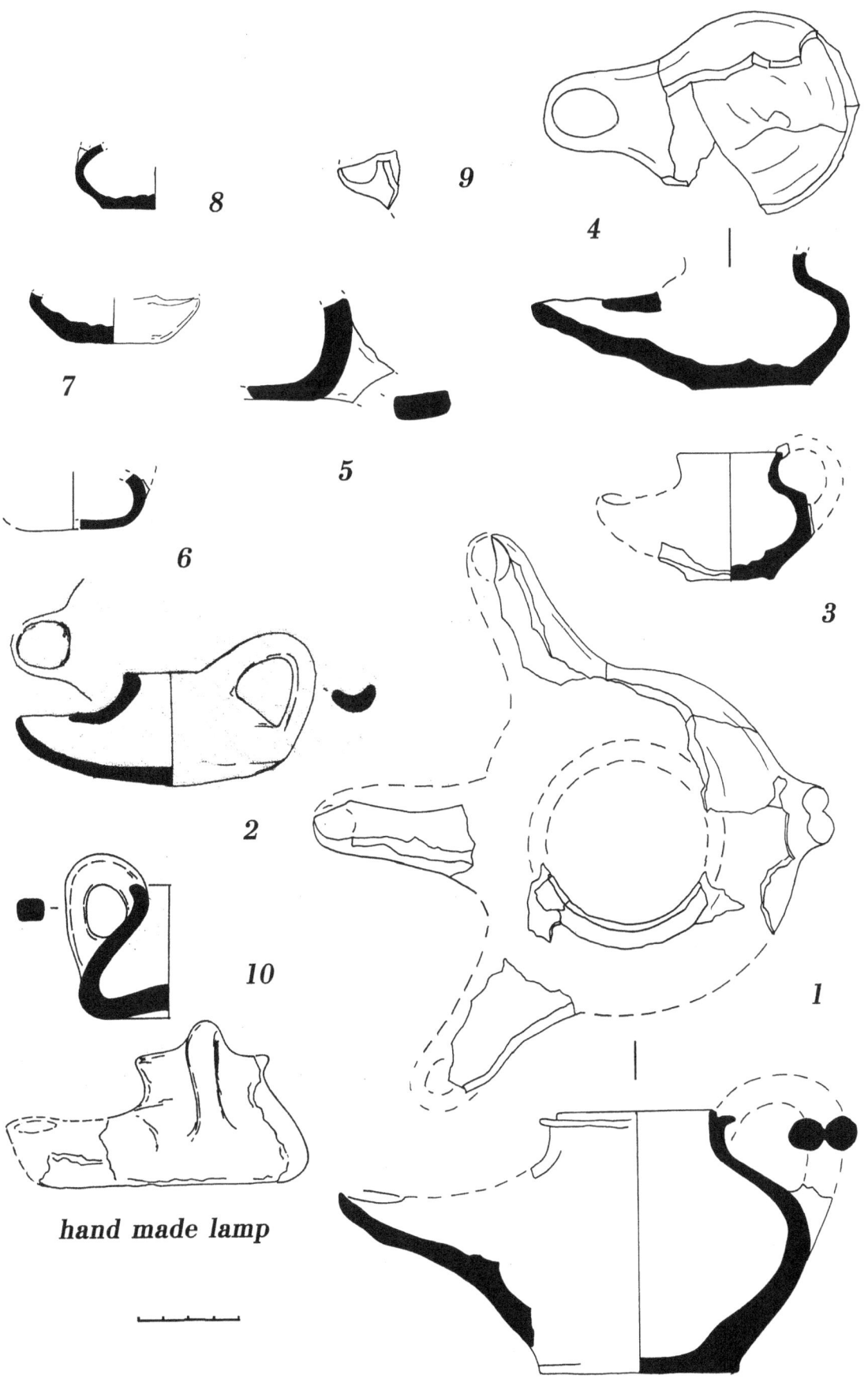

Fig. 3. Finds from the Southern Palace: lamps.

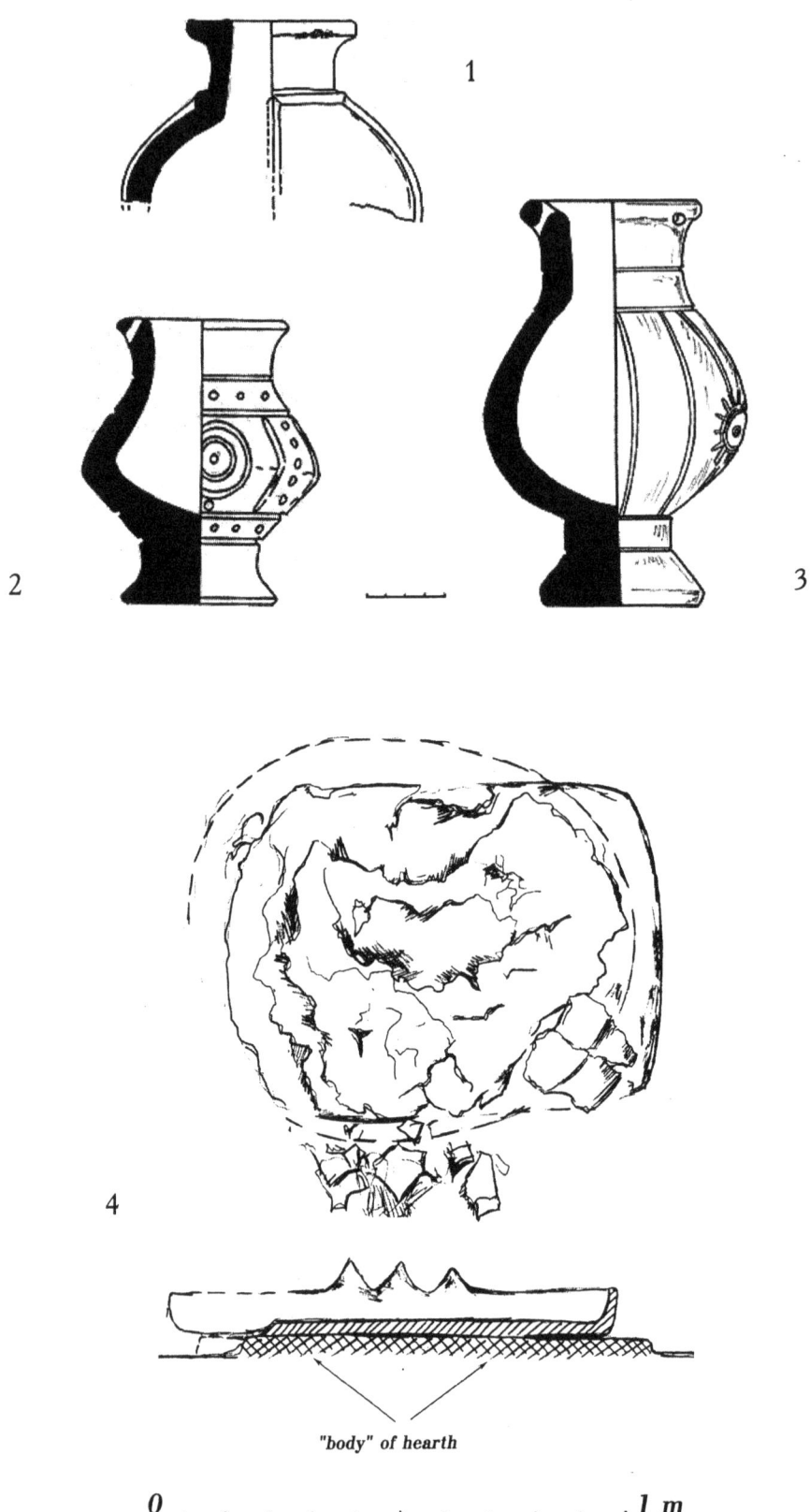

Fig. 4. Finds from the Southern Palace: incense - burners and hearth.

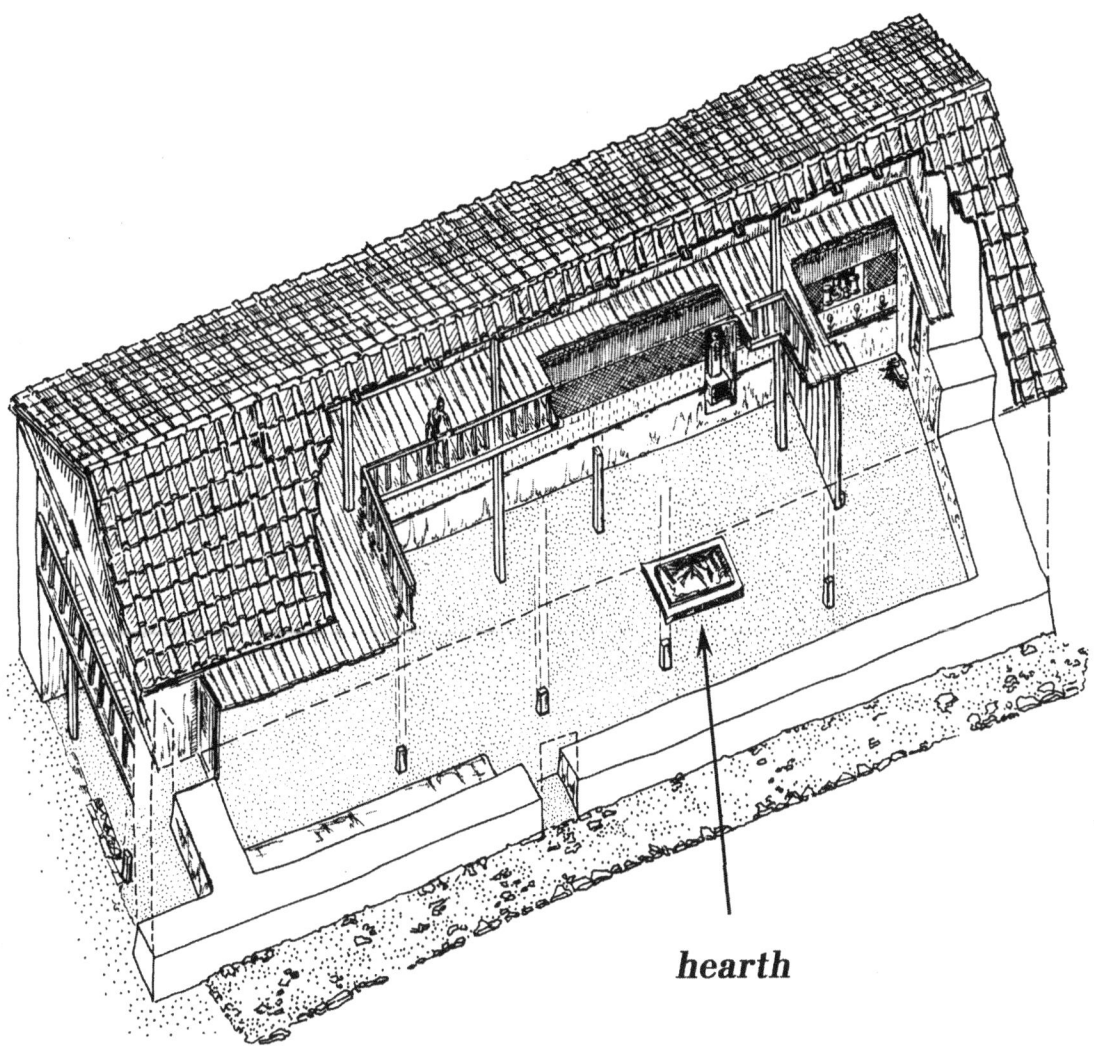

Fig. 5. Reconstruction of the building with the hearth.

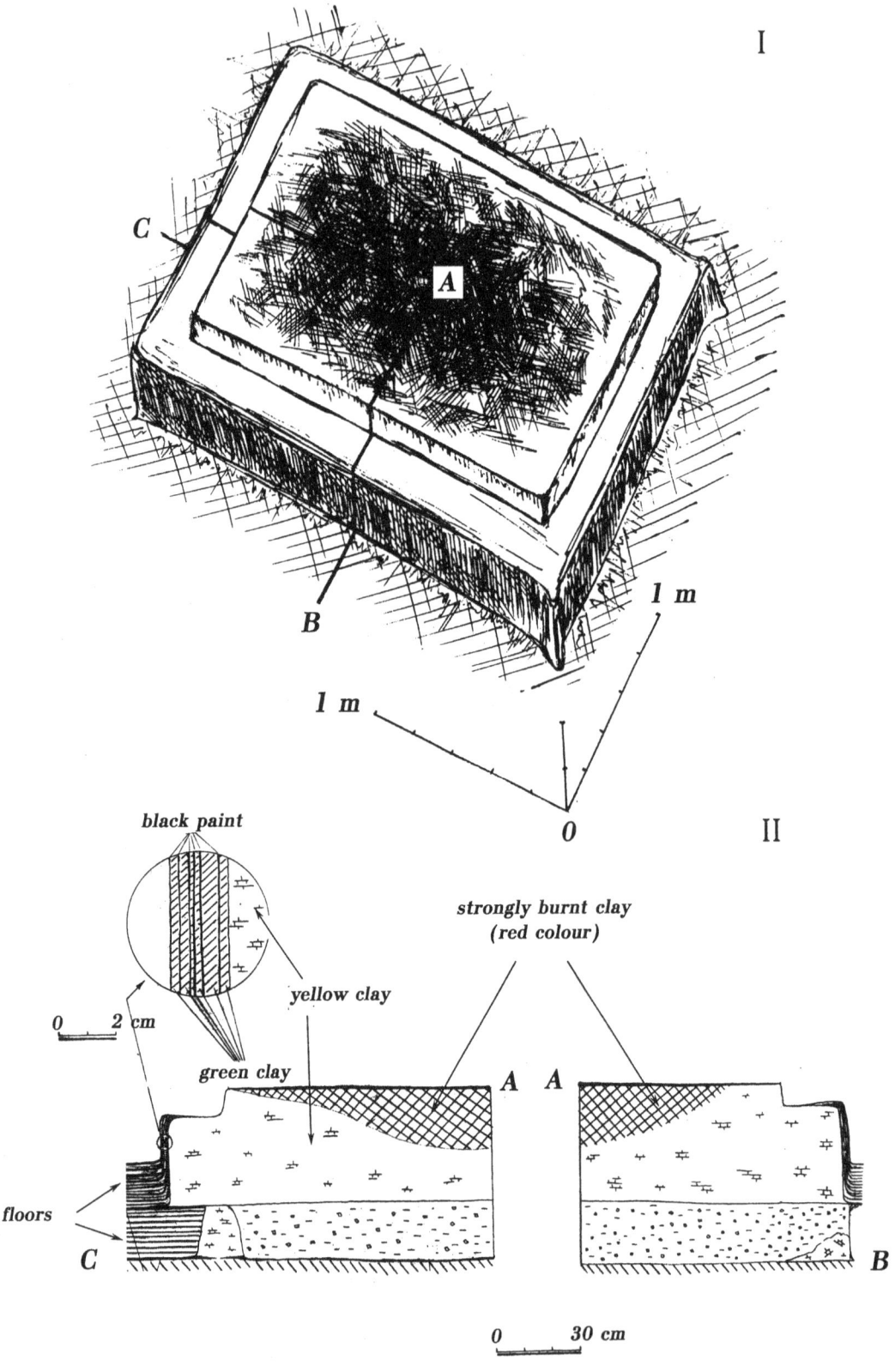

Fig. 6. Hearths.

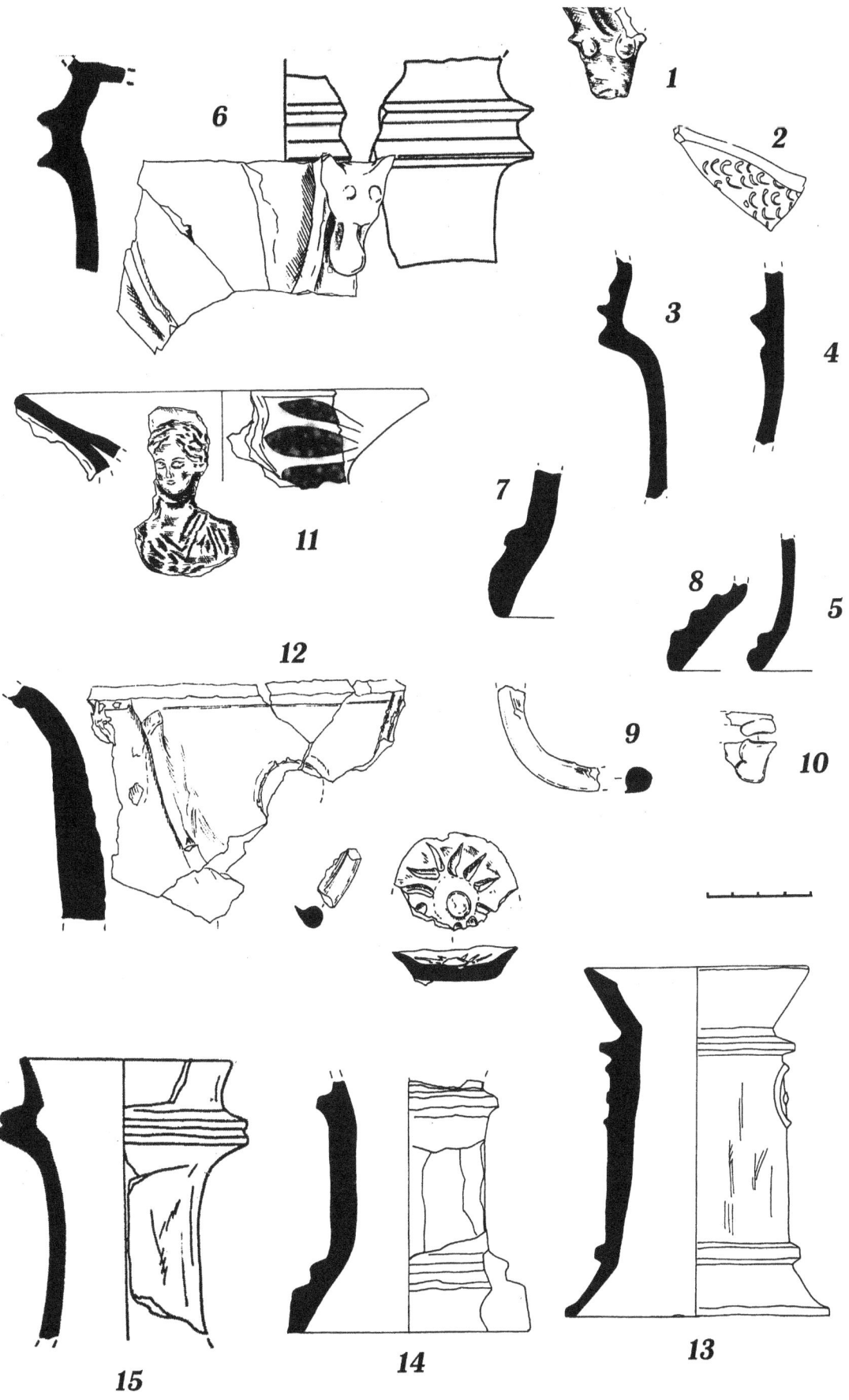

Fig. 7. Finds from the Southern Palace: clay altars.

Fire, Light and Light Equipment in the Graeco-Roman World

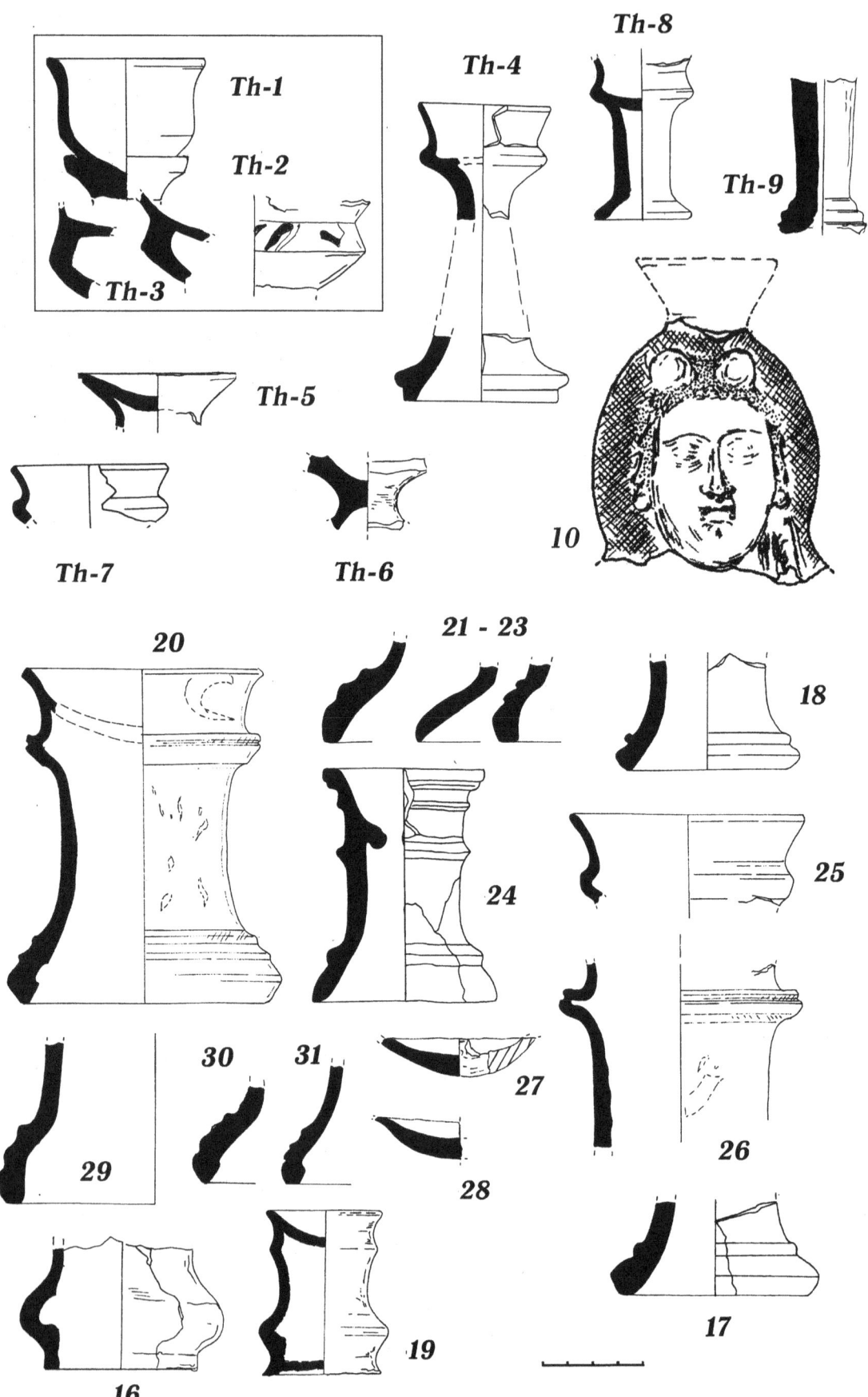

Fig. 8. Finds from the Southern Palace: clay altars.

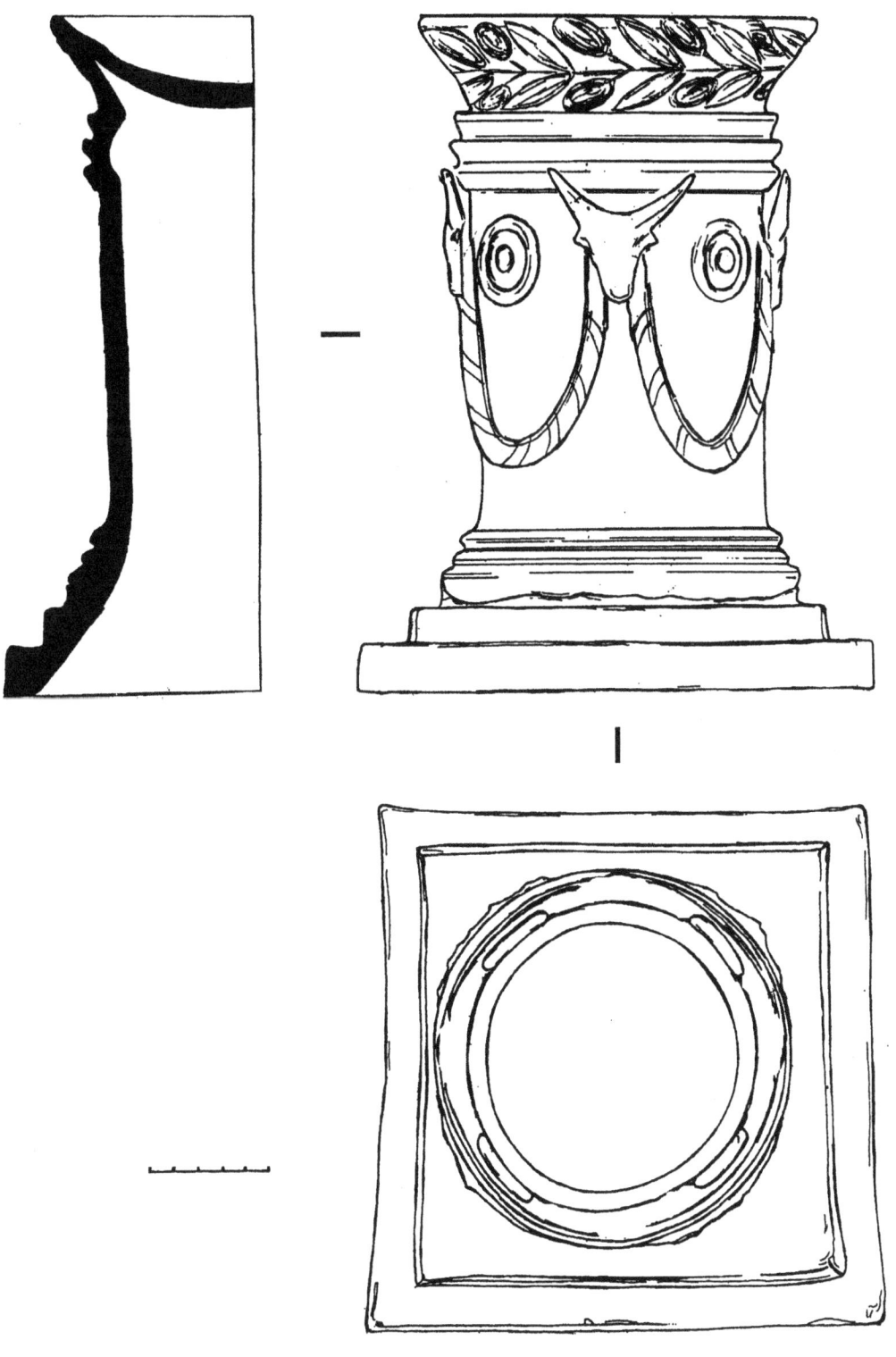

Fig. 9. Finds from the Southern Palace: altar.

Fig. 10. Reconstruction of the room with a niche for altar.

Yuriy Zaitsev: Light and Fire in the Palace of Scythian King Skilur

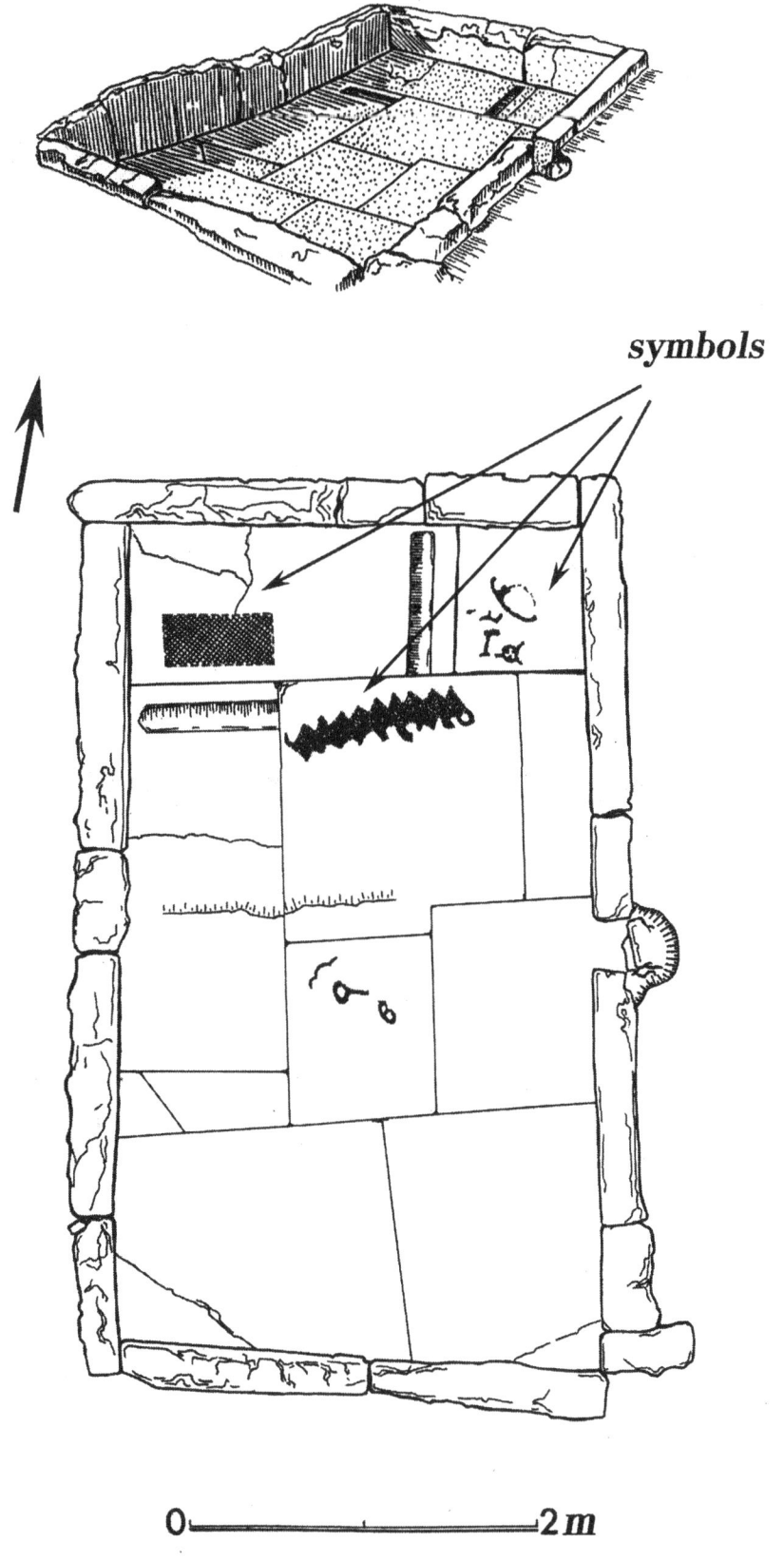

Fig. 11. Basin.

Fire, Light and Light Equipment in the Graeco-Roman World

Late Scythian Burial with a Lamp From Belbek IV Necropolis

Denis Zhuravlev
(Moscow, Russia)

In 1974 the Crimean expedition of the State Historical Museum excavated Grave N 131 on Belbek IV necropolis in south-west Crimea (Republic of Ukraine). The tomb contents did not differ in general from the objects usually found in burials of the Late Scythian culture (Dashevskaya 1991; Zhuravlev 1999), with the exception of a red slip lamp standing in a niche (fig.1). Lamps of Roman types are rather rare finds for Late Skythian burials; therefore I suppose that a special publication of the grave, where it came from, should be essential.[1]

Burial custom

The burial was made in a stepped-down chamber. The entrance pit (2 x 0.5 x 1.4 m) with its orientation from north-east to south-west had a stepped-down chamber partitioned off the entrance pit with three large vertically standing slabs, in the south-west wall. There was a badly preserved skeleton (female?) lying on its back with the head towards north-west on the bottom of the pit. Several objects (a glass jug with the high narrow cylindrical neck and the globe-shaped body; a blue alabaster bowl (completely destroyed) with a glass cup and an iron knife and a red slip lamp with an image of a bull on its discus) were placed near the head. A silver roundworm bracelet, a copper coin and a fibula were situated near the right arm and an animal bone was near the left arm. In the central part of the tomb (probably on a belt) there was a round bronze belt-buckle. According to its contents the burial was made in the first quarter of the 2nd century A.D. (100-125 A.D.). The finds of this grave were preliminary published (Guschina 1982, fig. 7, *11 - 17*). The general publication of all graves is forthcoming (Guschina & Zhuravlev, in print).

Grave Goods

Mouldmade lamp (fig.1, *12*; 2). Circular body with a short rounded nozzle. Two circular grooves define the concave discus, which is decorated with a standing bull facing right and occupying almost all the discus area. The ground is indicated by a line in relief. Under this line there is the small filling-hole. The shoulders are decorated with a row of ovules placed all around the discus rim, which is interrupted by the nozzle and at the level of the handle. A moulded, accurately pierced straight handle is situated at the rear. Discus is round, flat, with a stamp in *planta pedis* in the centre. The lamp is very well executed and of very good quality (Guschina 1982, fig. 7, *11*; Guschina & Zhuravlev 1996, fig. 2,*5*; Kadeev & Sorochan 1989: 82; Chrzanovski & Zhuravlev 1998, N 38).

Clay is light brown with some mica inclusions; slip is orange-red. Measurements: length 9,2cm; breadth 6,2cm; height 3,1cm (with the handle 4,2cm); diameter of the discus 2cm. This lamp belongs to type Loeschke VIII, but the nozzle-form is close to Loeschke H. On the basis of quality I can propose its imported origin (Asia Minor ?).

This lamp was published in the catalogue of lamps of the State Historical Museum, with a complete list of parallels (Chrzanovski & Zhuravlev: 1997: 87). I could note that this iconography is known on different types of lamps (OAK 1895:109, fig.265; Waldhauer 1914, N 197, Taf. XIX, N 319, Taf. XXXIV, N 368, Taf. XXXVII; Loeschke 1919, N 499, 500; S. 214 Taf. XII; Bruneau 1965, 4588, P. 125, Pl. 29; Iconomu 1967, 441, fig. 124; Deneauve 1972, pl. 52, 506; Heres 1972, 391, S. 68; Taf. 43; 326, S. 61, Taf. 37; Leibundgut 1977, 468, P. 250; Bailey 1985, N 952, 953, p. 136, fig. 10; Son & Sorochan 1988, fig. 5, *1*; Krapivina 1993, fig. 72, *13).*

The glass cup (fig.1, *2*) (height - 6.6 cm, neck diameter - 6.6 cm, base diameter - 4,2 cm). The cup's walls are rather straight; the body widens towards the bottom, grows round and turns into the foot-ring at its lower part. The base is concave, cone-shaped, and there is a trace of an empty tube of the diameter of 2cm on the bottom. The vessel was made from shining bluish glass with a green tint. It dates not later than the beginning of the 2nd century A.D.

The glass jug (fig. 1, *3*). Body is globe-shaped and slightly flat, base is concave in the centre, throat is tubular with the small rim. Height is 20.2cm, neck diameter - 5.8cm, base diameter - 6.3cm, and wall thickness - about 2mm. This shape is rather rare for west European sites (Isings 1957: 90, Form 70), but is found often enough in the Mediterranean and Pontic areas (Kunina 1997, NN 214-215 with many parallels). The vessel dates to the 1st century A.D. (Sorokina & Guschina, 1980: 96) and came probably from Anatolia (Sorokina 1997).

The silver bracelet (fig.1, *10*) was made from a round wire. Such finds are among the most common ones in Late Scythian burials and come both from male and female tombs (Dashevskaya 1991: 39).

The copper coin (fig.1, *5*; 3) is from Panticapaion; coinage time of Asandros (49/48 -20 B.C.). Avers: Apollo head towards right. Reverse: Drinking Pegasus towards left; two-lines Greek inscription ΠANTI / KAΠAIΩN. (See: Zograf 1951, Pl. XLIV,*9*). Badly preserved. Coined a century and a half before the time of the burial, it was doubtlessly put into the grave as an amulet. Such custom

---

[1] See recent publications on Late Skythians in special collection of articles: I.Guschina, D. Zhuravlev. 2001. In English see: Firsov, 1999; Zhuravlev, 1999 (with a complete bibliography).

was widespread among Late Scythians (Dashevskaya 1991: 21, Pl. 1). The rarity of coin finds proves the bad maturity of money circulation in the Late Scythian culture.

Fibula (fig.1, *4*). The well profiled, spring bronze fibula was made from round wire and had a bead at the bow. According to Ambroz's classification it is similar to fibulae of the 11 group, series I, variant II-1. (Ambroz 1966: 40, 42; Pl. 8,*6, 7, 9, 11, 14*). In general they date to a rather long period: from the 1st century A.D. to the beginning of the 3rd century A.D. They were widespread in the Pontic area (Romania, Crimea, the river Cuban basin, the north Caucasus) and in the Volga basin.

Belt-buckle (fig.1, *6*) was situated presumably on a belt. The similar belt-buckles are not rare in the Late Scythian burials (Dashevskaya 1991: 36).

Further, a common iron knife and parts of other bronze fibulae (fig.1, *7-9, 11*) were also found in the grave.

Conclusion

When it was placed in the tomb, the lamp must have been burning. It is rather difficult to explain why the lamp was found only in one of the 331 excavated burials. I can presume that a man buried there was one of a group of people among the Late Scythians who had close connections with Greeks. The unusual presence of glassware for this period for the Late Scythians also proves this supposition. Normally the Late Scythians in the 1st-early 2nd centuries used sigillata vessels (Zhuravlev 2000) with iron knives and ritual food in them. On the contrary meat in Grave N 131 was put into an alabaster bowl that also distinguish this burial from others.

In the 3rd-4th centuries A.D. the number of lamps in the burials of Chersonesos necropolis increases sharply as compared with their amount in ones of the 1st-2nd centuries A.D. (Zubar & Sorochan, 1984: 150). On the other hand the number of lamps in the Barbarian necropolises of south-west Crimea is not large: besides the lamp from Grave N 131, there is one more lamp from Belbek I necropolis (fig.4), situated nearby, dated to the 3rd century A.D. This lamp is of Athenian production of Elpidephoros workshop. A similar lamp is known in Chersonesos (see: Chrzanovski & Zhuravlev 1998: 125-126, N 68, with complete bibliography). The special article by Yuriy Zaitsev, published in this volume, is devoted to Greek light equipment (lamps and candelabra) from Late Skythian Ust'-Al'ma necropolis. I should also mention a "rubchatyi" (sunburst) lamp[2] from Late Scythian necropolis Mologa I situated not far from ancient Tyra (Gudkova, Fokeev 1982, fig 8,*5*). That is the exhaustive list of finds of the Roman type lamps from the graves of Late Skythians. A Greek custom to put lamps into tomb did not influence population of the Belbek valley a lot. The tradition of using open lamps with animal fat was the characteristic feature of Barbarians in the region. The Greek tradition of lighting burial chambers was not widespread between Late Skythians.

Bibliography

A.K. Ambroz 1966. *Fibuly yuga evropeiskoi tchasti SSSR. II v. do n.e. — IV v. n.e. SAI, Vol. D1-30*. Moscow (in Russian).

D. Bailey 1985. *Excavations at Sidi Khrebish Benghazi (Berenice), Vol. III, part 2: The Lamps*. Tripoli.

P. Bruneau 1965. *Délos 26, Les Lampes*, Paris.

L. Chrzanovski & D.Zhuravlev 1998. *Lamps from Chersonesos in the Collection of the State Historical Museum - Moscow*. Roma.

O.D. Dashevskaya 1991. *Pozdnie skify v Krymu. SAI. Vol. D1-7*. Moscow. (in Russian)

J.Deneauve 1974. *Lampes de Carthage, Paris*.

K.Firsov 1999. The Roman Period necropolis of Zavetnoe in southwest Crimea. Burial structures and mortuary ritual. In: M.Rundkvist (Ed.) *Grave Matters. Eight studies of First Millenium AD burials in Crimea, England and southern Scandinavia. Papers from a session held at the European Association of Archaeologists Fourth Annual Meeting in Göteborg 1998. BAR International Series 781*. 1-18.

A.V Gudkova. & M.M. Fokeev 1982. Poselenie i mogil'nik rimskogo vremeni Mologa II. In: *Pamyatniki rimskogo i srednevekovogo vremeni v Severo-Zapadnom Prichernomor'e*. Kiev. (in Russian).

I.I. Guschina 1982. O lokal'nykh osobennostyah kul'tury naselenia Belbekskoi doliny Kryma v pervye veka n.e. In: Talis D.L. *(Ed.). Arkheologicheskie issledovania na yuge Vostochnoy Evropy. Part 2. Trudy GIM., Vol. 54*. Moscow. 20-30. (in Russian).

I.I.Guschina & D.V. Zhuravlev 1996. Rimskiy import iz mogil'nika Belbek IV. In: *D.V. Zhuravlev, K.B. Firsov (Eds). Tezisy dokladov otchetnoi sessii Gosudarstvennogo Istoricheskogo muzeya po itogam polevykh archeologicheskih issledovaniy i novykh postupleniy v 1991-1995 gg*. Moscow.45-50 (in Russian).

I.I.Guschina & D.V.Zhuravlev (Eds). 2001. *Late Skythians of Crimea*. Papers of the State Historical Museum, Vol. 118. Moscow. 282 p.(in Russian and English).

I.I.Guschina & D.V.Zhuravlev (in print). *Pozdneskifskiy nekropol rimskogo vremeni Belbek IV v Yugo-Zapadnom Krymy*. Steppenvölker Eurasien. Moskau-Berlin.

G.Heres 1972. *Die römischen Bildlampen der Berliner Antiken- Sammlung*. Berlin.

C. Iconomu 1967. *Opaite greco-romane*. Bucuresti.

C. Isings 1957. *Roman Glass from dated Finds*. Groningen; Djacarta.

V.I. Kadeev & S.B. Sorochan 1989. *Ekonomicheskie svyazi antichnykh gorodov Severnogo Prichernomor'yav I v. do n.e. — V v.n.e. (na*

---

[2] See about this type of lamps: Chrzanovski & Zhuravlev 1998:133-139, with a complete bibliography.

materialakh Khersonesa). Khar'kov. (in Russian).

V.V. Krapivina 1993. *Olbia. Material'naya kul'tura I — IV vv. n.e.* Kiev. (in Russian).

N.Z. Kunina 1997. *Antichnoe steklo v sobranii Ermitazha.* Sankt-Peterburg. (in Russian).

A. Leibundgut 1977. *Die Römischen Lampen in der Schweiz.* Bern.

S. Loeschke 1919. *Lampen aus Vindonissa.* Zürich.

OAK — Otchet Arkheologicheskoi Komissii za 1895 g. Sankt Peterburg. (in Russian).

N.A. Son & S.B. Sorochan 1988. Antichnye svetil'niki iz Tyry. In: *Antichnye drevnosti Severnogo Prichernomor'ya.* Kiev. (in Russian).

N.P. Sorokina 1997. Anatoliyskie steklyannye sosudy I — II vv. n.e. iz Severnogo Prichernomor'ya. In: *Antichnyi mir. Vizantia.* Khar'kov. (in Russian).

N.P. Sorokina & I.I. Guschina 1980. Steklyannye izdelia iz mogil'nikov pervykh vekov n.e. Yugo-Zapadnogo Kryma. In: *Istoria i kul'tura Evrazii po arkheologicheskim dannym. Trudy GIM, Vol. 51.* Moscow (in Russian).

O. Waldhauer 1914. *Kaizerlische Ermitage. Die antike Tonlampen.* St. Peterburg.

D. Zhuravlev 1999. The Late Skythian Burial Rite in the Belbek Valley of southwest Crimea in Roman Period. In: M.Rundkvist (Ed.) *Grave Matters. Eight studies of First Millenium AD burials in Crimea, England and southern Scandinavia. Papers from a session held at the European Association of Archaeologists Fourth Annual Meeting in Göteborg 1998. BAR International Series 781.* 19 — 31

D.Zhuravlev 2000. Terra sigillata and red slip pottery from the late Skythian necropoleis of the South-Western Crimea (1st — 3rd centuries AD) In: *Rei Cretariae Romanae Favtorvm Acta 36.* Abingdon. 151 — 160.

A.N. Zograf 1951. *Antichnye monety. MIA, Vol. 16.* Moscow-Leningrad (in Russian)

V.M. Zubar' & S.B. Sorochan 1984. Svetil'niki v pogrebal'nom obryade antichnykh gorodov Severnogo Prichernomor'ya. In: *Antichnaya kul'tura Severnogo Prichernomor'ya.* Kiev. (in Russian).

Fire, Light and Light Equipment in the Graeco-Roman World

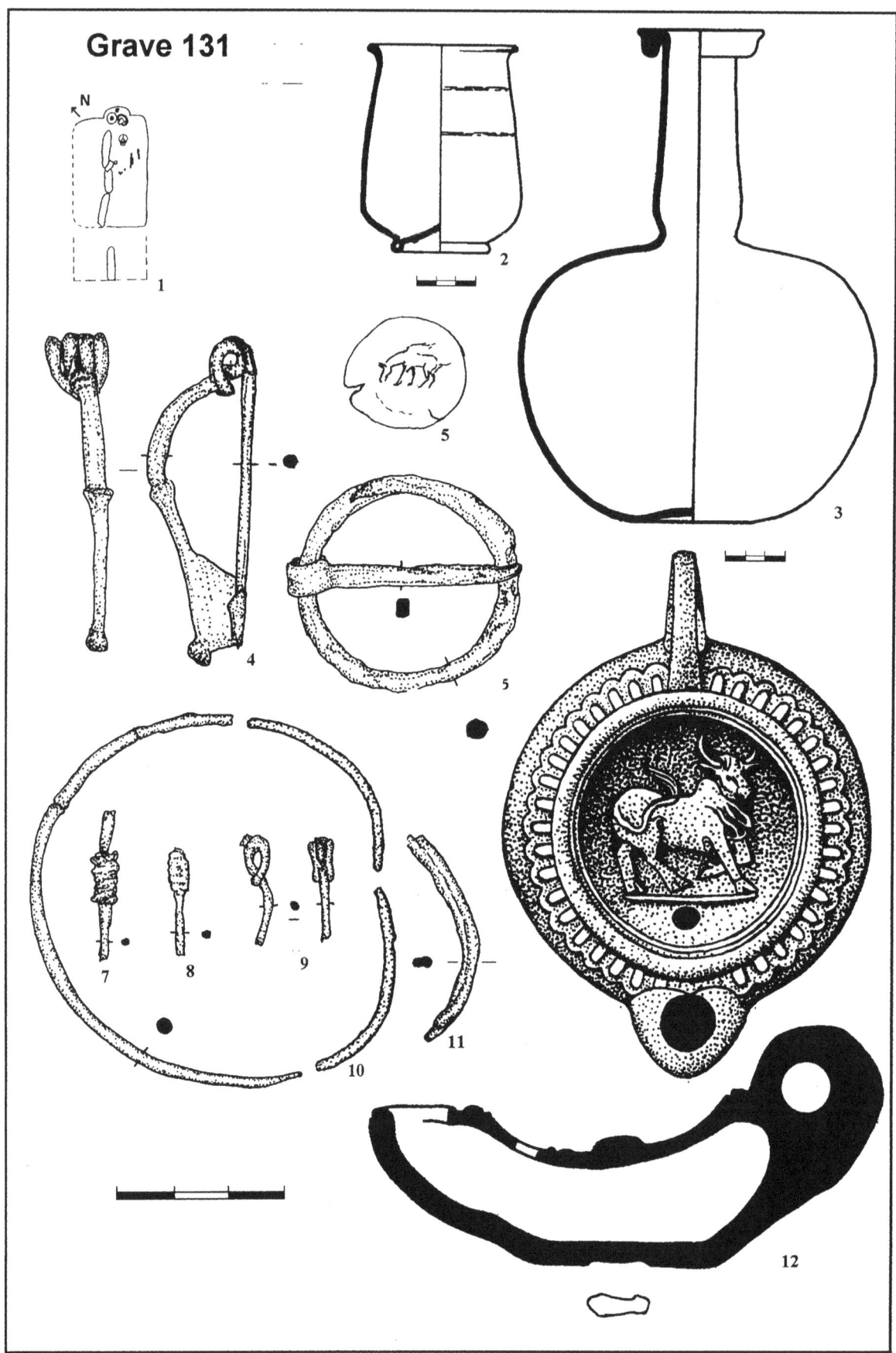

Fig. 1. Grave N 131. Plan and inventory.

Fig. 2. Clay lamp.

Fig. 3. Bosporan bronze coin.

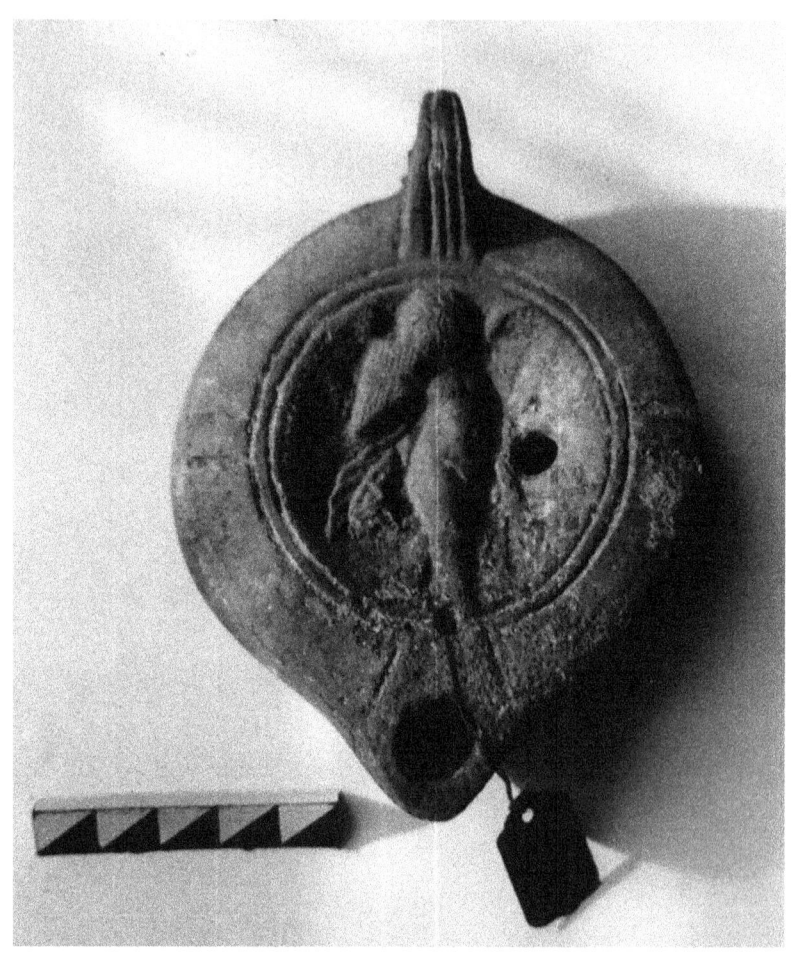

Fig. 4. Clay lamp from Belbek I necropolis

Scènes vetero-testamentaires sur les lampes à huile tardo-antiques

Corinne Sandoz
(Geneva, Suisse)

Introduction

1) LAMPES " CHRETIENNES " :

Les lampes sur lesquelles nous rencontrons, dans la majeure partie des cas, les scènes vetero-testamentaires sont les lampes dites "chrétiennes" ou plutôt de "type africain" qui ont une forme très homogène, caractérisée par un aspect oblong dû à la longueur du canal du bec. Par ailleurs, ces lampes sont plus longues que larges et plus larges que hautes (Ennabli 1976: 12).

Leur partie supérieure se compose d'une navette formée du disque et du canal, délimité par un bourrelet. Autour du disque, compris entre des bourrelets intérieur et extérieur, l'épaule est légèrement en creux et est décorée de motifs répétés dont le nombre varie de un à trois. Ceux-ci sont soit géométriques, soit possèdent un lien direct avec la scène représentée sur le disque (Béjaoui 1997: 13)[1].

Le disque, quant à lui, est légèrement concave et comprend un, ou plus souvent deux trous de remplissage, disposés différemment suivant la structure du décor, très varié.

L'anse, moulée, légèrement aplatie sur les côtés, s'attache de manière très homogène au sommet du disque; elle n'est jamais percée. Son inclinaison est variable (Ennabli 1976: 12).

"La partie inférieure comprend le réservoir. En forme de coupe, il repose sur une base aplatie toujours cernée d'un bourrelet qui en rehausse l'assise. Ce bourrelet est rejoint à l'arrière par un appendice du tenon qui descend en suivant la courbe du réservoir" (Ennabli 1976:12).

L'ensemble donne une structure harmonieuse et solide, le point faible se situant au niveau du bec, que l'on retrouve souvent brisé.

2) TECHNIQUE DE FABRICATION :

Le matériel utilisé pour la fabrication des lampes de type africain est spécifique (Ennabli 1976:13) : il se compose d'une argile rouge orangé variant du vif au clair lorsqu'elle est bien cuite et passant au marron et même au gris lorsqu'elle a subi des excès de cuissons.

La pâte, généralement homogène, présente plusieurs variétés en fonction de ses origines: siliceuse, granuleuse ou friable; en fonction de l'atelier qui l'a traitée, elle est plus ou moins bien épurée (Ennabli 1976:13).

Comme c'est le cas pour toutes les lampes moulées, les deux parties de la lampe sont jointes et ébarbées avant la cuisson (Hoff 1986: 77 et Béjaoui 1997:16). Plusieurs moules, surtout supérieurs, sont parvenus jusqu'à nous, comme le superbe exemplaire conservé au British Museum (Bailey 1988, lampe Q 1795) représentant les trois jeunes Hébreux devant Nabuchodonosor.

Le décor du disque, comme celui de l'épaule, est donc reproduit dans le moule (Ennabli 1976:13 et Béjaoui 1997:16) et non point rajouté par la suite, suivant la même technique que celle des coupes en sigillée C (Béjaoui 1997: 16). Quelquefois, ces lampes étaient aussi enduites d'un engobe ou d'un vernis (Hoff 1986: 77).

Par ailleurs, il est à remarquer que si, déjà depuis le Ier siècle, la production des lampes était devenue le plus souvent un travail en série, on remarque, durant l'antiquité tardive, de moins en moins d'ajouts personnels de la part des artisans (Graziani Abbiani 1969: 9).

3) LIEUX DE FABRICATION :

Ces lampes, dites aussi à "canal allongé" (Hoff 1986: 79), proviennent pour la plupart de Tunisie, raison pour laquelle on leur a collé l'étiquette de "type africain". Selon Béjaoui (1997:17), les lieux de production de cette classe de céramique restent limités à quelques ateliers: les uns dans le Nord du pays, notamment Carthage et Oudna (Ennabli 1976: 14)[2], les autres en Byzacène et en Tunisie centrale. Sidi Marzouk Tounsi, dans la région d'El Ala (au sud de Kairouan), qui semble avoir été le plus important, sinon du pays, du moins de la région, nous a livré nombre de sigillées "C" et "D", des moules de lampes, ainsi que des plats rectangulaires.

"Ce centre de production avait autour de lui et à un rayon de quelques kilomètres, d'autres petits ateliers de moindre importance et qui ont principalement produit de la sigillée "D", type de céramique que nous retrouverons produite en très grande quantité plus au sud, essentiellement dans la région de Sbeitla-Kasserine et Sbeitla-Jilma" (Béjaoui 1997:17).

Deux autres ateliers d'envergure sont également signalés à Mactar (Bourgeois 1980: 35); ils ont produit, entre le IVe et le VIe s., de la céramique fine et des lampes.

4) TYPES DE LAMPE :

Nous utiliserons ici la typologie d'Anselmino et Pavolini qui renvoie elle-même à toutes les propositions

---

1 Ces motifs sont illustrés sur la planche 1 du présent article.

2 L'atelier d'Oudna se trouvait dans les thermes de la maison des Laberii.

précédentes (Anselmino & Pavolini 1981)³.

On peut ainsi observer que les scènes vetero-testamentaires sont représentées presque exclusivement sur deux types: VIIIC1a et XA1a.

Le type VIIIC1a est caractérisé par un canal ouvert et une épaule plate (dépourvue de bourrelets); le décor de l'épaule est constitué de feuilles de palmes en relief, d'une série d'incisions, ou encore de simples motifs géométriques imprimés (comme des cercles) (Pavolini 1981:193)⁴. L'anse est décorée d'une rigole en son milieu.

Le type XA1a, qui est d'ailleurs le plus fréquent et le plus diffusé, représente le type dit "africain classique". C'est la première forme sur laquelle l'iconographie de l'épaule ne se limite pas à des décors végétaux, mais embrasse un nombre très vaste de motifs aussi bien végétaux que géométriques et même figuratifs, disposés de manière alignée ou encore alternés en série. L'anse pleine (Pavolini 1981:199) constitue l'autre caractéristique de cette forme.

Ce type débute avec des motifs figuratifs de style "naturaliste", semblables à ceux qu'on rencontre sur les sigillées C3 et C4; dès le milieu du Ve s., on peut le comparer à la sigillée D, avec des motifs en relief de style "linéaire".

Enfin, deux exemplaires de notre étude ne peuvent être classés dans aucun des deux types que nous venons de décrire: il s'agit des lampes 3 (DACL, II,2, 1910, col. 1802) et 18 (Garrucci 1875, pl. 475). Elles correspondraient à une dérivation tardive du type Loeschcke VIII (Loeschcke 1919). Il convient cependant d'observer la plus grande prudence, puisque ces lampes ne sont connues que par des dessins de la fin du XIXe s.- début XXe s.

5) DATATION:

Nous reprenons ici les datations proposées dans la typologie adoptée ci-dessus (Anselmino et Pavolini 1981: 1939), qui s'appuie sur les fouilles et les relevés stratigraphiques.

Pour le type VIIIC, il ne semble pas y avoir de repères chronologiques précis (Pavolini 1981: 193), mais Salomonson considère que le type "Navigius", prédécesseur des lampes "d'Henchir-es-Siron", comporte des motifs décoratifs qu'on retrouve sur les disques des lampes de type VIII et des vases "Navigius". Selon des critères typologiques, les lampes dites "d'Henchir-es-Siron" s'insèrent dans un laps de temps assez restreint (325-375 ap. J.-C.), précédant de peu l'apparition des lampes dites "africaines classiques" de type XA1a, que les fouilles permettent de dater entre la fin du IVe s. (nécropole de Raqqada) et la fin du VIe s. (fouilles de la mission italienne de Carthages).

La production du type VIII commence donc peu avant celle du type X, mais ce groupe VIII se développe en grande partie parallèlement à la production X (Anselmino & Pavolini 1981: 193). Cette fabrication connaît son apogée au Ve s. (Anselmino & Pavolini 1981: 199).

La datation de ce matériel est par ailleurs confirmée par les comparaisons iconographiques que l'on peut faire avec d'autres formes d'art, tels les sarcophages, le métal, l'ivoire, les fresques ou encore les mosaïques.

La datation peut également se vérifier grâce à la parenté qu'on observe entre ce type de lampes et les plats de sigillée africaine. En effet, selon les recherches de Bourgeois (Bourgeois, 1980, p. 85), cette parenté avec la céramique sigillée claire D estampillée a été depuis longtemps établie, grâce à la qualité de la pâte et de l'engobe, par des trouvailles conjointes (comme à Oudna), et également au regard des poinçons.

6) DIFFUSION:

Tout le matériel céramique que nous venons de citer a d'abord été diffusé à l'intérieur de sa région de production, puis à travers l'Afrique du Nord, mais, très rapidement, les lampes furent exportées en masse dans tout le bassin méditerranéen, ainsi qu'en Orient.

En ce qui concerne les lampes de type VIII, celles-ci étaient produites en quantité modeste et pour une diffusion limitée presqu'exclusivement à l'Afrique et en particulier à la Proconsulaire. Vers le milieu du IVe s., la fabrication de lampes en sigillée connut un essor inattendu, et ces produits commencèrent à s'affirmer et à prévaloir sur les marchés du monde méditerranéen.

Cette diffusion, cela est évident, s'est opérée en étroite relation avec la circulation de céramiques contemporaines en sigillée D africaine.

Ce type est également présent dans les contingents retrouvés en Italie, qui constituait une aire privilégiée pour le commerce de ce genre de produits (tous les types de lampes sont répertoriés (Anselmino & Pavolini 1981:193)).

Outre l'Italie, la diffusion du type VIII couvre une aire assez bien définie, comprenant toute la côte de l'Afrique septentrionale et les autres provinces de la Méditerranée occidentale, le Portugal, le *limes* rhénano-danubien, les confins du Danube et de l'ex-Yougoslavie, ainsi que toute la Méditerranée orientale (Anselmino & Pavolini 1981: 194).

Le type X est le plus fréquent et le plus diffusé. Il circule principalement avec les vases en sigillée africaine D qui étaient exportés en masse, et dont l'expansion a atteint son apogée entre 350 et 450 ap. J.-C. (Anselmino & Pavolini 1981: 199).

---

3 Dans les fiches, on indiquera également celles d'Hayes et d'Abbiani.
4 Voir les lampes 6, 14, 16 et 17 du présent article.

L'exportation diminua considérablement en Orient dans la seconde moitié du Ve s., mais reprit de plus belle avec la sigillée D au VIe s. et dura jusqu'au VIIe s. (Béjaoui 1997: 20).

La diffusion de ce type comprend toute la Méditerranée occidentale, la côte atlantique, les régions du confin rhénano-danubien, l'Istrie et la Dalmatie, l'Egypte, la Méditerranée orientale (Anselmino & Pavolini 1981: 221).

Certaines régions ont été plus privilégiées que d'autres, comme la Sicile, où l'on trouve du matériel africain en abondanc e (Béjaoui 1997: 20), ce qui est peut-être dû à la proximité des deux régions.

A part ces importations massives, certaines régions s'adonnaient aux imitations. Ainsi, Anne Bovon (Bovon 1966: 86-87) écrit à propos des lampes de type "nord-africain": "Quoiqu'il en soit de l'origine du type, il est connu en Grèce, puis imité dès la fin du IVe s. ap. J.-C. L'imitation attique a été importante aux Ve et VIe s. ap. J.-C.; les exemplaires étudiés ici, d'argile rose violacé, grossière et friable, prouvent qu'il en a été de même à Argos.

Les provenances de ces lampes invitent à dater du Ve s. ap. J.-C. la plus grande extension de la fabrication argienne. En effet, plusieurs exemplaires proviennent de la couche brûlée sur laquelle furent édifiées les parties nouvelles du théâtre, et se trouvaient associés à des monnaies du Ve s. ap. J.-C.".

7) REFLECTEURS:

Ceux qui nous intéressent sont ronds ou, plus souvent, de forme variable, et leur argile présente les mêmes caractéristiques que celles des lampes (Béjaoui 1997:13).

"Nous ne connaissons pas les moules dont se servaient les céramistes pour les décorer, mais il faudrait supposer la même technique de travail que celle des lampes" (Béjaoui 1997:16).

Aucune typologie n'a été établie pour ce matériel et l'on ignore presque tout de leur diffusion probable, qui devrait logiquement être semblable à celle des lampes et des plats en sigillée fine D. En ce cas, ces matériaux seraient à dater entre la fin du IVe et leVIe s.

8) LES SCENES VETERO-TESTAMENTAIRES:

Les représentations chrétiennes étaient très fréquentes sur les différents types de lampes, du IVe au VIIe s., mais il n'est pas exacte de prétendre, que seules les lampes du type X d'Anselmino et Pavolini s'ornaient de scènes de l'Ancien Testament (Hoff 1986: 79); nous avons observé en effet que de rares exemples nous les montrent sur d'autres types de lampes.

Mais, il est vrai que les scènes empruntées à l'Ancien Testament illustraient généralement des thèmes liés au salut de l'âme en vertu de la foi chrétienne (les Trois Hébreux, Daniel et Jonas) (Hoff 1986: 79).

Plutôt que chrétienne, cette iconographie devrait porter le nom de judéo-chrétienne; en effet, cette imagerie n'est-elle pas, comme le dit Réau (1956, préface), "due presqu'exclusivement à des artistes chrétiens qui ont choisi dans les Livres sacrés des Juifs ce qui pouvait se rapporter au Nouveau Testament"?. Mais il ajoute que, "toute juive qu'elle soit, l'Ancienne Loi est donc le prélude ou la préfigure de la religion chrétienne et les deux iconographies n'en font qu'une".

Parmi les thèmes empruntés à l'Ancien Testament, ceux que l'on retrouve sur les lampes sont les suivants: le sacrifice d'Isaac; Nabuchodonosor et les Trois Hébreux; Daniel; Jonas. Ces scènes ne sont pas l'apanage exclusif des lampes, car on les retrouve sur d'autres monuments de l'époque des premiers Chrétiens: sarcophages, fresques, mosaïques, verres, ivoires, gemmes, etc.

"La fréquence de pareils sujets, précisément choisis parmi tant d'autres dans l'Ancien Testament, implique un choix qui n'est nullement décoratif, mais religieux. Leur figuration sur les tombeaux confirme cette préoccupation et révèle les sentiments religieux de l'époque. Il ne s'agit donc pas de les considérer comme de simples scènes bibliques, mais comme des allégories dont il importe de comprendre le contenu et le sens mystique" (Ennabli 1976:27).

A côté de ces scènes, très fréquentes, d'autres apparaissent presqu'uniquement sur la céramique de la fin du IVe s.-Ve s. qui les a popularisées. Il s'agit en particulier des explorateurs de Canaan (Béjaoui 1997: 29).

Un autre point très intéressant de cette iconographie, et qui sera abordé systématiquement pour chaque scène dont il va être question, est l'utilisation de motifs païens en association avec les sujets chrétiens (Béjaoui 1997: 30).

LE SACRIFICE D'ISAAC

Genèse, XXII, 1-14.
Cet épisode a reçu un traitement très privilégiéde la part des premiers Chrétiens, comme l'atteste l'iconographie depuis le IIIe siècle ap. J.-C. (Bovon 1966)[5].

A. M. Smith (Smith 1922), distingue plusieurs types d'Abraham sacrifiant recensés sur les lampes. Le type le plus courant, et qui correspond à notre type 1, est celui qu'elle nomme "hellénistique": Abraham portant le

---
[5] Dans la chapelle des Sarments à Rome; mais il s'agit du moment précédent le sacrifice: la prière. Le sacrifice sera présenté pour la première fois à Dura-Europos, personnages vus de dos (244 ap. J.-C.) cf. Speyart Van Woerden 1961. Milieu du IIIe, peinture de la Cappella Greca, dans les catacombes de Priscille.

pallium ou la tunique *exomis* (sur les lampes, il s'agit toujours de l'*exomis*), tient le couteau de la main droite et saisit de la gauche Isaac agenouillé. L'autel, le bélier et la main de Dieu figurent le plus souvent.

Le type "hellénistico-asiatique", représenté par trois lampes d'Ephèse, montre Isaac déjà sur l'autel. Dans ce cas, Abraham porte toujours de longues draperies. La main de Dieu fait partie de la scène (Smith 1922:164)[6].

Sur le type suivant est le "copte-alexandrin", représenté par deux lampes d'Ephèse, Abraham, barbu, en position frontale, porte de longues draperies flottantes. Isaac est vêtu d'une tunique et porte une petite boîte (parfois Sarah est présente(Smith 1922:167). Ce type se caractérise par un autel à cornes.

Smith propose un quatrième type, "copte-palestinien" où Abraham est nimbé, eet où le bélier porte parfois un collier (Smith 1922: 167)[7]. Un cyprès s'ajoute dans quelques cas. C'est pourquoi Smith rattache à ce type 4 la lampe du Campo Santo (**lampe 3**), qui présente toutes les caractéristiques du type précédent. En effet, le cyprès semble avoir une origine syro-palestinienne. Mais il faut noter que sur le dessin conservé de cette lampe (DACL II, 2, col. 1802 & Speyart Van Woerden 1961: 247), Abraham ne semble pas être nimbé. La colonne à l'arrière peut avoir une signification locale (Smith 1922: 168-169).

Ces quatre types correspondent également à ce que l'on peut trouver sur les autres supports iconographiques, auxquels il faut ajouter un cinquième type (Smith 1922: 168), le "byzantin", qui correspond à peu près au type "asiatico-hellénistique"

La scène dépeinte le plus fréquemment sur les lampes montre Abraham dominant l'espace, en position frontale (barbu et portant une tunique courte) avec le visage légèrement tourné vers le haut. Son bras droit est levé, sa main tient une longue épée; de la main gauche, il saisit Isaac par les cheveux. Isaac, portant une tunique courte, est agenouillé, les mains nouées derrière le dos. A sa droite, nous pouvons observer des stries, interprétées comme un autel ou comme le fagot que portait l'enfant. A côté d'Abraham, un agneau s'avance vers la gauche, mais la tête tournée du côté droit. Au sommet du disque, au-dessus de l'agneau, apparaît la main de Dieu (Il est important de noter, que c'est seulement à partir du IVème s. que l'on peut observer la main divine sur ces représentations (Di Berardino 1990: 8). Sur le bord gauche, parfois un arbre est figuré. Ce type correspond à notre **lampe 1**.

On retrouve le même type de scène sur un réflecteur conservé au Musée de Carthage (**réflecteur 1**), à la différence près que dans ce cas, la scène est conçue de manière schématique et fortement ornementale. Le bûcher est figuré par un élément décoratif de type M2 que l'on retrouve dans le décor de bordure du réflecteur: preuve de la connaissance précise qu'on avait de la scène, car elle était presque illisible pour un novice.

Si l'on tente à présent d'analyser la lampe du Musée de Faverges (**lampe 2**), on se heurte à un problème: elle correspond au type 1, en raison de la tunique d'Abraham et de la position agenouillée d'Isaac. Cependant on ne trouve pas trace d'autel, ni de fagot ni de main de Dieu. De plus si l'on observe bien, on constate qu'Abraham ne tient pas le couteau en l'air, comme c'est le cas sur toutes les lampes de type 1, mais sur la gorge d'Isaac, comme c'est le cas sur la lampe du Campo Santo (**lampe 3**). L'arbre, sans être un cyprès, lui ressemble, comme si l'auteur de la lampe avait tenté de représenter quelquechose qu'il ne connaissait pas. De plus, l'animal ne s'apparente ni au bélier, ni à l'agneau, mais ressemble plutôt à une chèvre (animal que l'on ne retrouve dans aucune scène de sacrifice. De plus, il n'est jamais question de chèvre dans ce récit). Peut-on penser qu'il s'agit de l'âne portant les fagots plutôt que d'une chèvre? La scène offrirait alors un raccourci[8].

La dynamique de la scène diffère de ce que l'on trouve habituellement sur les autres lampes. Il est également intéressant de noter que le groupe Abraham-Isaac est très effacé, très usé, tandis que l'"âne" et l'arbre sont tout frais.

Nous sommes en droit de nous poser une question: ces éléments ont-ils été conçus originellement pour former un ensemble? Il faudrait disposer d'un autre exemple semblable pour en juger. En tout cas, il est tout-à-fait certain qu'il s'agit ici de deux poinçons différents.

La seule lampe sur laquelle nous trouvons un arbre plus ou moins similaire constitue également un exemple unique en l'état actuel des recherches. Elle est conservée au musée de Campo Santo à Rome et porte l'inscription TIMO (**lampe 3**). Abraham porte des vêtements syriens et tient le couteau sur la gorge d'Isaac qui regarde, en arrière, on y voit la main de Dieu, le même arbre que précédemment et un bélier; sur la droite se dresse une étrange colonne. La forme de la lampe est également rare.

Le thème d'Abraham est fréquent sur la céramique sigillée africaine (Béjaoui 1997: 38). Les coupes retrouvées en Tunisie illustrent toujours le type dit "hellénistique-asiatique" et sur certaines coupes, la main de Dieu est remplacée par le messager de Dieu (Béjaoui 1997: 21).

Comme l'écrit F. Béjaoui (Béjaoui 1997: 21), la scène du sacrifice est de loin la plus fréquente dans l'art chrétien. On la retrouve d'ailleurs sur d'autres supports comme les fresques (Cappella greca des catacombes de Priscillia), les sarcophages (Junius Bassus), les mosaïques (Tigzirt), les coupes en verre (Timgad), la pyxide du Museo Civico à

---

6 Cas de la fresque d'El-Bagawat.
7 Miniature d'Etschmiadzin.

8 En ce qui concerne les représentations de chèvres, elles sont rares dans l'art des premiers chrétiens, et ne figurent qu'en tant que décoration (DACL II, 1, col. 1320). Speake 1994: 76, nous dit que l'on peut rencontrer l'âne dans les représentations du sacrifice d'Isaac.

Rome, la glyptique, l'ivoire, etc.

Il faut encore signaler qu'outre les fresques et quelques rares coupes africaines, où figurent plusieurs étapes du récit, la scène est représentée dans les autres arts plastiques de manière assez constante (Di Berardino 1990: 10)[9].

INTERPRETATION:

Le sacrifice d'Isaac est une scène que les Chrétiens ont privilégiée et que l'on rencontre sur des supports iconographiques de tout genre.

"Dieu, pour éprouver Abraham, lui ordonne alors de sacrifier son fils Isaac, conformément à l'usage des tribus sémitiques de Palestine de consacrer à Dieu le premier-né. Abraham obéit, mais au dernier moment, un ange lui fait tomber le couteau des mains" (Réau 1956: 126). L. Réau (Réau 1956: 135), met en parallèle la substitution du bouc et celle de la biche dans la scène païenne du sacrifice d'Iphigénie (Grimal 1951: 235-236).

Cette scène du sacrifice d'Isaac est lourde de symboles pour les premiers Chrétiens; en effet Isaac est la préfiguration du Christ (Speyart Van Woerden 1961: 215 & Réau 1956: 135). Tout d'abord, Abraham sacrifiant son fils unique préfigure Dieu donnant son fils pour le salut des hommes; Isaac portant le bois du sacrifice (comme on le voit représenté sur les fresques des catacombes et sur les coupes africaines)[10] préfigure Jésus portant la croix. L'âne "porte-bagages" est l'image de la Synagogue recevant sans la comprendre la parole de Dieu. Le bélier immolé à la place d'Isaac représente le Christ crucifié; et enfin, le sacrifice d'Abraham est le type du sacrifice non-sanglant de l'Eucharistie (Réau 1956: 135).

Sur le plan moral, l'obéissance d'Abraham est un exemple pour les Chrétiens et c'est également une représentation du Salut de l'âme grâce à la volonté divine. C'est pour toutes ces raisons et pour se souvenir de la toute-puissance de Dieu, que les Chrétiens ont choisi ce motif pour décorer les lampes notamment.

LES DEUX EXPLORATEURS DE CANAAN

Livre des Nombres, XIII, 24.

La scène des deux Hébreux portant la grappe de raisin de Canaan est très fréquemment représentée sur les lampes, mais contrairement aux autres scènes de l'Ancien Testament, elle n'apparaît pas avant le IIIe siècle après Jésus-Christ et on la trouve d'abord sur les lampes Syropalestiniennes (Beit Natif) (Moderzewska 1988: 46); peut-être parce que la tradition vient de cette région.

Dans la plupart des cas, les deux explorateurs sont nus, debout et de face, cheveux courts. Ils portent une énorme grappe à l'aide d'un bâton posé horizontalement sur leurs épaules (**lampe 4**). A partir de ce schéma, de nombreuses variantes ont été créées, par exemple le lièvre placé à la verticale en-dessous de la grappe (**lampe 5**). D'autres montrent les deux explorateurs vêtus d'une tunique courte (DACL, VIII,1, col. 1158) ou encore ayant une coiffure radiée (Bailey 1988, lampe Q 18419). Mais l'élément central, la grappe, ne change pas. Elle est toujours énorme et la figuration de ses grains par de gros ronds, ne fait qu'ajouter à sa monumentalité. Les variantes concernant les deux porteurs s'expliquent par le fait que "l'adoption de la scène par les Chrétiens n'est pas due aux deux personnages eux-mêmes, mais à l'image de la grappe de raisin qui symbolise la crucifixion du Christ" (Béjaoui 1997: 22), comme nous le verrons par la suite.

On trouve, sur au moins quatre lampes, le chrisme représenté au-dessus de la grappe, et sur une de ces lampes, l'explorateur de droite regarde en direction de la grappe (**lampe 6**).

Il faut remarquer que cette imagerie est quasi inexistante dans les arts des premiers Chrétiens, mais curieusement, elle apparaît relativement fréquemment sur les lampes des IIIe et surtout IVe s. (DACL, III,1, col. 169-172). Sa diffusion massive ne se fera pas avant le XIIe s. (Réau 1956: 211).

Nous retrouvons le même schéma sur un fond de coupe conservé au musée Olivierano à Pesaro (daté du IIIe-IVe s.), l'explorateur de droite regardant la grappe. Les deux sont vêtus d'un *pallium*, et ,sur le pourtour, on peut lire l'inscription ANIMA DVLCIS PIE ZESES IN DEO (DACL, III,1, col. 169).

Il faut encore signaler trois autres témoignages antiques de ce récit. Tout d'abord, un réflecteur conservé au musée de Carthage, (**réflecteur 2**) montre les deux explorateurs de profil avançant vers la gauche et portant une tunique courte. Puis, il faut signaler deux bas-reliefs. L'un a été retrouvé dans la région d'Hébron (Vincent 1902: 600-601) et présente exactement le même schéma avec les explorateurs croulant sous le poids de la grappe dont la monumentalité est très marquée. L'autre relief (Ovadiah 1974: 210-3) provient de Carthage: il s'agit à nouveau du même schéma, à la différence près que l'explorateur tournant le dos à la grappe détourne la tête, non pas pour regarder la grappe, mais pour parler à son compagnon. Ce relief est daté de la fin du IVe-début du Ve s. et proviendrait du couvercle d'un sarcophage (Ovadiah 1974: 211), ce qui est très intéressant, car cela porterait à deux le nombre de sarcophages où cette imagerie apparaît[11].

Ces trois derniers témoignages diffèrent du schéma que l'on trouve sur les lampes et sur le verre, où les explorateurs sont statiques et ne dévoilent pas physiquement le poids de la grappe. Cependant, il faut

---

9 Dans ce cas, il s'agit toujours du moment du sacrifice.
10 Cubiculum "velatio", catacombes de Priscilla (début IIe s.).

11 L'autre serait conservé au musée de Marseille (Ovadiah 1974: 212).

remarquer que dans tous les cas de figure, l'élément principal et le plus régulièrement mis en évidence reste la grappe, ce qui ne laisse aucun doute quant à l'interprétation du sujet, même sans la présence du chrisme.

INTERPRETATION:

La Bible nous enseigne que pour calmer l'impatience des Israélites, Moïse envoya en Canaan deux émissaires: Josué et Caleb, qui rapportèrent d'Escol[12] une gigantesque grappe de raisin suspendue à une perche.

Les symbolistes ont vu dans cette grappe le corps de Jésus suspendu à la croix: car Jésus est la grappe percée dont le sang remplit le calice de l'Eglise (Réau 1956:211). Cette pensée se prolongera dans la littérature[13].

Réau (Réau 1956: 211) signale encore que "Josué et Caleb ont également un sens figuratif. Les deux porteurs, explique Saint Augustin, sont les deux Testaments. Le premier, qui tourne le dos à la grappe mystique et ne voit pas ce qu'il porte (*aversa facie*), symbolise le peuple juif qui ferme les yeux à la vérité. Le porteur placé à l'arrière, qui a le regard fixé sur la grappe, est l'image des Gentils qui se rallient au Christ".

Saint Bernard (Réau 1956: 211), quant à lui, explique que le premier porteur symbolise les Prophètes qui ont marché devant le Christ et le second les Apôtres qui l'on suivi.

Cette explication correspond exactement au réflecteur et aux deux bas-reliefs dont il a été question plus haut. Il explique également pourquoi parfois un des deux explorateurs tourne la tête en direction de la grappe comme c'est le cas sur le verre et sur au moins une des lampes conservées.

La présence du chrisme n'est pas obligatoire, car la grosseur de la grappe suffit à expliquer et identifier la scène avec certitude. C'est l'élément primordial.

Cette iconographie signifiait également pour le peuple du désert une terre promise pleine de richesses et donc l'espoir d'un avenir meilleur (Larese 1997: 371-372, N 656).

Enfin, ce schéma de porteur a été emprunté à l'art païen où figurent de nombreux exemples (enseigne de marchand de vin à Pompéi) (DACL, III,1, col. 169).

LES TROIS JEUNES HEBREUX

Livre de Daniel III, 1-30

Cette scène semble avoir énormément touché les premiers fidèles. Nous la trouvons dès le IIe siècle ap. J.-C. dans les peintures des catacombes et depuis le IVème s. a. p. J.-C. dans les autres formes d'art. Le sujet restera populaire jusqu'à la fin de l'antiquité tardive.

On retrouve sur les lampes deux épisodes de la vie des Trois jeunes Hébreux: 1) leur refus d'adorer le buste du roi Nabuchodonosor et 2) en oraison dans la fournaise.

Dans le premier épisode, Hananiah, Mishael et Azariah refusent d'adorer le buste en or de Nabuchodonosor. Ce thème fait son apparition dans l'art chrétien à la fin du IIIe s.-début du IVe s. (Di Berardino 1990: 815 & Carletti 1976: 64); on y voit les Trois Hébreux portant une longue tunique orientale blousante avec ceinture et un bonnet phrygien sur la tête, faisant un geste de recul. Devant eux Nabuchodonosor, barbu, vu de profil, est vêtu d'une riche tunique orientale et porte également un bonnet phrygien. Il est assis sur une *sedia curulis* et montre du doigt son buste (trait pour trait identique au roi) posé devant lui sur une colonne. Entre la colonne et les Trois Hébreux se tient un cinquième personnage barbu, debout, de face, la tête tournée vers le roi. Il est vêtu d'une tunique et tient quelque chose dans les mains; il s'agit soit d'un serviteur, soit d'un soldat (**lampe 7**). Ce type est très courant sur les lampes, comme sur les sarcophages (De Villefosse 1877: 157ss), mais on le retrouve plus rarement sur les fresques des catacombes[14].

Entre le milieu du IVe s. et le milieu du Ve s., nous observons trois formulations de cette scène (Carletti 1976: 88): la première est celle que nous venons de voir. Dans la seconde Nabuchodonosor et les Trois Hébreux sont nimbés, mais les vêtements ne changent pas. Le nimbe des Trois jeunes Hébreux s'explique sans nul doute par la sanctification des trois martyrs et le culte qui leur était rendu (Rassart-Debergh 1978: 451). Celui qui est au-dessus de la tête de Nabuchodonosor s'explique comme un "segno di regalità" (Carletti 1975: 91). Il n'y a plus de soldats et la colonne ressemble plus à un tronc d'arbre d'où sort le buste du roi qu'à autre chose (**lampe 8**). Enfin, l'évolution suivante transforme la colonne avec le buste en un palmier: le siège du roi n'est plus une *sedia curulis*, mais un trône (**lampe 9**); ce dernier point est déjà valable pour l'évolution précédente.

Béjaoui (1997: 23-30 & 110 N 55) interprète cette scène plutôt comme représentant les visiteurs venus voir Abraham, en pensant que l'artisan c'est inspiré de la scène précédente.

Pour M. Rassart-Debergh (1978: 452), il s'agirait d'une maladresse technique ou d'un défaut du moule; il s'agirait

---

12 Escol, signifie en hébreux: grappe de raisin (Réau 1956: 211).
13 Eucher de Lyon au Ve s., ainsi qu'Ambroise de Milan, *De Fide*, I, 20 et IV, 12, et Saint Augustin, *Contra Faustum*, XV, 42 et *In psalm*, VIII, 2: *Dictus est enim et Dominus Botrus uvae quem lingo suspensum de terra promissionis qui praemissi erant a populo Israel, tanquam crucifixum, attulerunt.*

---

14 Cependant quelques exemples existent: dans les catacombes de Priscillia (DACL, VI,2, col. 2111-2112).

donc bien d'une colonne et du buste. Le rond sous l'arbre figurerait un petit tabouret pour poser les pieds.

Nous pensons également, que l'on est ici devant une incompréhension du céramiste, qui aurait copié des lampes du deuxième type ou retravaillé un moule usé sans comprendre véritablement la scène. Ceci expliquerait pourquoi nous n'avons pratiquement aucun exemplaire de cette figuration, car il est fort possible que s'il s'agissait d'une nouvelle figuration, comme le pense Béjaoui, nous la retrouverions plus fréquemment (comme c'est le cas pour toutes les autres). Cependant, le petit tertre sous l'arbre serait plutôt une déformation du socle de la colonne que du tabouret que proposait Rassart-Debergh (n'apparaissant d'ailleurs pas sur les autres représentations).

La diffusion majeure de ce type s'est opérée durant les IVe-Ve s. (Carletti 1976: 95) pour les lampes et fut très fréquent, surtout pour le type de la **lampe 7**.

La représentation des trois Hébreux devant Nabuchodonosor n'est pas très commune sur les fresques. Néanmoins nous trouvons un exemple dans les catacombes de Priscilla; ce thème est par contre très fréquent sur les sarcophages (Aix-en-Provence).

En ce qui concerne le deuxième épisode, c'est-à-dire l'oraison dans les flammes, il apparaît dès le IIe s. ap. J.-C.[15] dans les catacombes d'abord, puis, dès la seconde moitié du IIIe-début IVe s., on le retrouve sur les autres formes d'art.

Sur les lampes à huile, deux schémas sont représentés: tout d'abord, les Trois Hébreux sont tête nue et habillés avec des caleçons et une tunique courte (comme les amazones). Il sont debout, de face, et serrés les uns contre les autres, peut-être liés ensemble comme le précise la Bible. La fournaise est alors représentée par trois petits ronds sous leurs pieds (**lampe 10**) ou par une croix (Lyon-Caen 1986, Lampe N 47).

L'autre schéma montre les Trois jeunes Hébreux en tunique orientale longue, bouffante, avec ceinture et un bonnet phrygien (en fait le costume qu'ils portent devant Nabuchodonosor).

Les flammes s'élèvent jusqu'à la taille des malheureux. Entre le premier et le deuxième Hébreux, se tient l'ange du Seigneur déployant ses ailes pour les protéger (**lampe 11**).

Ce schéma est celui qui se rapproche le plus des autres représentations du même thème. En effet, il fut très populaire dans l'art des premiers Chrétiens, beaucoup plus que le premier épisode. On trouve de nombreux exemples de cette imagerie dans les catacombes (le premier témoignage, datant du début du IIe s., se trouve dans la Cappella Greca des catacombes de Priscillia). Sur les fresques, la main de Dieu est parfois représentée. Les sarcophages (Latran, Saint Gilles, Agen), les mettent souvent en relation avec les Rois Mages, comme le fait remarquer Réau (Réau 1956: 400)[16]. On les retrouve également sur les coupes de céramique sigillée africaines (Béjaoui 1997, n.21) et les mosaïques (Tipasa), ainsi que sur les verres (disque de Podgoritza), etc...

A partir du IVe s., apparaissent parfois l'accusateur, l'ange ou le serviteur attisant le feu (Di Berardino 1990: 815). Ce dernier est bien visible sur une des coupes du catalogue de Béjaoui (1997, N 21), ainsi que sur de nombreux sarcophages, comme celui d'Agen.

Sur les sarcophages et les fresques des catacombes, le foyer devient une véritable structure[17].

Cette imagerie orne également, dès le IVe s., des objets d'usage liturgique, petites boîtes, ciboires ou reliquaires (Di Berardino 1990:815), comme la boîte en ivoire de Brescia.

INTERPRETATION:

L'épisode des Trois jeunes Hébreux devient populaire auprès des premiers Chrétiens dès le IIe s., en premier lieu à cause des persécutions. En effet, ils représentent l'image des morts que Dieu protège des flammes de l'Enfer (Réau 1956: 399).

Lorsqu'ils sont dans la fournaise, ils ont les paumes tournées vers le ciel en signe d'orant. Pour les premiers Chrétiens, ce sont trois âmes de persécutés, en oraison, protégés par Dieu intervenant pour les sauver (Réau 1956: 400). Le thème est donc celui du Salut de l'âme.

En ce qui concerne les représentations des Trois mêmes Hébreux devant Nabuchodonosor, on remarque leur représentation massive dès le IVe-Ve s., témoignant de l'importance du souvenir des persécutions, du refus de vénérer le culte impérial et des risques qu'encouraient les Chrétiens. Ce refus, né au cours de la dernière période de l'époque tétrarchique, manifestait l'attitude polémique de la communauté chrétienne à l'égard du culte impérial (Di Berardino 1990: 815).

Ceci est encore plus probant lorsque l'on considère que sur certains sarcophages (Cherchel notamment), cette scène sert de pendant à l'adoration des mages. Alors "la royauté du Christ est confirmée de façon encore plus explicite et en termes clairement polémiques; seul le Sauveur est digne de vénération et c'est donc à lui que revient l'adoration" (Di Berardino 1990: 815).

---

15 Catacombes de Priscillia (DACL, VI,2, col. 2111ss., Réau 1956: 400 & Di Berardino 1990: 815).

16 Ce dernier précise (p. 399) que le vêtement qu'ils portent sur la lampe 10 de cet article, (braies collantes = anaxyrides) les apparente également aux Rois Mages.

17 DACL, VI,2, col. 2110 pour la Cappella Greca et col. 2120 pour les sarcophages du Vatican et Rome.

La scène des Trois Hébreux était donc utilisée pour représenter le châtiment injuste infligé aux Chrétiens et le secours que Dieu, grâce à leur foi, leur accordait.

Comme l'ajoute Béjaoui (1997: 23), ce récit a été aussi popularisé dans l'Ecriture sainte (Saint Augustin). "Ainsi, dans le cas des trois Enfants dans la fournaise, seules l'iconographie et l'épigraphie reflètent le culte qui leur fut voué en Afrique. Ce thème a longtemps appartenu uniquement au répertoire des décors funéraires; mais à partir sans doute du Ve s., quand leurs reliques ont circulé, les trois Enfants ont été vénérés au rang de martyrs chrétiens, comme les Macchabées dont le culte en tant que martyrs est nettement plus ancien et mieux implanté en Occident" (Duval 1982: 620). Les premières reliques connues auraient circulé de Babylone vers Constantinople au milieu du Ve s. (Béjaoui 1997: 23).

DANIEL DANS LA FOSSE AUX LIONS

Livre de Daniel VI, 17 et addition XIV, 23-42

Les épisodes de la vie de Daniel ont été inlassablement représentés dans l'art chrétien. Ils apparaissent très tôt: dès le milieu du Ie s., sur les peintures des catacombes[18], et le thème restera en vogue jusqu'au VIIe s. (Réau 1956: II, 1, p. 405). Il devient très populaire dès le IIIe s. (Speake 1994: 40).

L'iconographie que des lampesse limit à un seul type. Il s'agit de l'illustration du deuxième épisode du récit de Daniel. En effet, ce dernier fut livré aux bêtes à deux reprises (Deonna 1949: 122 & Réau 1956: 401). La première fois, sous le règne de Darius, pour avoir prié son Dieu; il ne resta alors qu'une seule nuit dans la fosse scellée par une dalle. La deuxième fois, pour avoir empoisonné le dieu-serpent des Babyloniens avec une galette de poix, de suif et de cire. Il resta alors six jours dans la fosse aux lions scellée d'une dalle que le prophète Habacuc traversa pour le ravitailler. Habacuc avait été quéri par l'ange du Seigneur alors qu'il préparait le repas des moissonneurs en Judée et il fut ramené par l'ange le tenant par les cheveux, pour qu'il aille nourrir Daniel.

Réau (Réau 1956: 402) pense que "les deux légendes se ressemblent trop pour ne pas être des doublets: cette répétition est l'indice de deux rédactions indépendantes qui ont été fondues maladroitement", il est en effet rare de ne pas rencontrer Habacuc sur les représentations de Daniel parmi les lions.

Sur les lampes, le schéma est le suivant: Daniel est debout en position frontale, vêtu d'une tunique orientale, longue, blousante avec ceinture (la même que celle que portent les trois jeunes Hébreux); ses paumes sont tournées vers le ciel en geste de prière.

A ses pieds se tiennent deux lions, la tête dirigée vers le bas, celui de gauche courant et celui de droite marchant.

Disposés symétriquement aux côtés de sa tête, on trouve, à gauche, l'ange du Seigneur volant et, à droite, Habacuc portant un gros pain rond (**lampe 12**).

Sur certains exemplaires, comme la lampe conservée au Musée de Lausanne (Deonna 1949: 120), une croix est figurée sous les pieds de Daniel, tandis qu'une des lampes conservées au Musée du Bardo (Ennabli 1976, n. 42 & Béjaoui 1997, n. 63) présente trois petits ronds sous les pieds de Daniel, rappelant la figuration des flammes aux pieds des Trois Hébreux[19].

Ce schéma représentant Daniel parmi les lions, était le seul connu pour les lampes, jusqu'à la parution de l'ouvrage de Béjaoui (1997), où est publiée une lampe du Musée de Carthage (**lampe 13**).

Sur cet exemplaire, Daniel est toujours de face en position d'orant, les coudes bien détachés du corps. Il est vêtu d'une tunique courte avec ceinture placée très bas et semble porter un bonnet phrygien. Les lions l'entourant (toujours au nombre de deux) ne sont plus tête en bas, mais assis de profil, la tête de face. Ils ont l'air totalement inoffensifs.

Au sommet du disque, Habacuc portant le pain est cette fois-ci sur la gauche, tandis que l'ange presqu'invisible est à droite.

Cette représentation est très proche de la vignette 3581 du manuscrit de Cosmas (Deonna 1949, pl. Ib). Cette lampe illustre encore plus le geste apaisant et bénédictoire de Daniel avec les lions totalement soumis.

En effet, les représentations de Daniel—jeune, imberbe, rarement barbu, et nu sur les sarcophages dès le IIIe s. (Deonna 1949: 124)— sont souvent réduites à un homme en position d'orant entre deux lions, parfois plus (Deonna 1949: 125ss), placés symétriquement à ses pieds; elles dériveraient d'un motif oriental (Deonna 1949: 138ss). "Le sujet n'est plus la représentation d'un événement déterminé dans le temps et l'espace, mais il est devenu un symbole, dégagé des détails réalistes qui sont inutiles à sa compréhension, et figé en un groupement abstrait. C'est pourquoi la fosse est rarement représentée. Aussi le groupe de Daniel entre les lions est-il parfois monté sur un socle (sarcophage du Latran), qui l'isole, comme un ensemble statuaire, des autres représentations. Et, libéré des contingences historiques, un motif symbolique se prête facilement à revêtir des apparences traditionnelles, dont le sens seul sera changé et adapté aux besoins nouveaux" (Deonna 1949: 124).

Dans le monde antique et particulièrement en Orient, de nombreux thèmes présentent des divinités et des mortels

---

18 Catacombes de Domitilia. (Deonna 1949: 123).

19 Lampe n. 10 du présent article.

aux bras virtuellement levés, souvent accompagnés de lions, thèmes de signification ouranienne et solaire (Deonna 1949: 139). L'origine du groupe antithétique "héraldique" formé par Daniel et les lions serait à chercher en Mésopotamie avec le maître des animaux, Gilgamesh (Deonna 1949: 350); cependant, dans le cas de Daniel, les lions sont sagement assis ou debout, non agressifs. Cela rappelle plutôt la maîtresse des animaux de la Grèce archaïque: la *Potnia Thérôn* qui a le geste de protection et de bénédiction face aux animaux (Deonna 1949: 356).

Ce motif, très courant dans l'art antique, est attesté également chez les Egyptiens (Deonna 1949: 364ss).

Le fait que l'on voit parfois les lions la tête en bas manifesterait un signe de soumission, mais dans le cas des lampes, où l'un court et l'autre marche, ils auraient été inclinés faute de place (Deonna 1949: 369)!

Cette iconographie, très courante sur toute forme d'art, apparaît d'abord sur les fresques (catacombes de Domitilla, seconde moitié du Ier s. a. p. J.-C.). C'est seulement au IIIe s. que l'on retrouvera Daniel nu (Deonna 1949: 124), en particulier sur les sarcophages (Junius Bassus et sarcophage de la chaste Suzanne) et dans les catacombes, ainsi que sur les coupes en sigillée (Béjaoui 1997: 123). Cependant, la plupart du temps il est vêtu, mais de façons diverses (Deonna 1949: 124).

Cette imagerie est également très fréquente aux Ve et VIIe s. sur les plaques de ceinture (Deonna 1949:124), ainsi que sur les mosaïques (Henchir-el Msâ'âdin, Tunisie); une console sculptée en haut relief (Baouit, musée de Berlin, Vème-VIème s. a. p. J.-C.) avec Daniel en habits persans; tissus (Egypte); ivoires; peignes en bois; glyptique; terre cuite, pyxide de Brit, où Daniel est en habits orientaux avec un bonnet phrygien (Ve-début VI e s.) (DACL, IV,1, col. 233); ampoules; etc.

INTERPRETATION:

L'engouement que connaît cette imagerie parmi les premiers Chrétiens n'est pas seulement dû aux symboles que ce thème représente, mais également, comme le dit Réau (Réau 1956: 403), à son analogie avec l'antique thème oriental des lions affrontés.

A part cela, pour les premiers Chrétiens, la biographie de Daniel était avant tout l'illustration du juste persécuté, livré au mal, puis sauvé par Dieu (Réau 1956: 391; Speake 1994: 40; Di Berardino 1990: 624 & Deonna 1949: 122), l'âme qui a triomphé de la mort et qui jouit d'une vie éternelle (Deonna 1949: 122). Cette idée de résurrection et d'espoir explique aussi, comme c'est le cas pour Jonas, la présence de ce thème sur les sarcophages et dans les catacombes. Il faisait directement référence aux fidèles qui risquaient d'être jetés aux lions. D'ailleurs certaines représentations (Deonna 1949: 137) montrent les lions léchant les pieds de Daniel, rappel sans doute du miracle d'Androclès (Deonna 1949: 347)[20] ou encore de l'épisode de Saint Ménas avec les chameaux, qui utilisent exactement le même schéma et que l'on retrouve également sur les lampes (Delattre 1898:38, N 3 & Deonna 1949: 133).

Ces lions entourant Daniel "expriment les puissances du mal, de l'enfer, de la mort, dont le fidèle est protégé et délivré par Dieu" (Deonna 1949: 347); déjà dans l'art païen, le lion, tout comme la sirène et le griffon, apparaissent en tant que symboles apotropaïques.

D'ailleurs, Daniel entre les lions est une image, un emblème protecteur; "c'est ce qui explique sa fréquence sur les plaques de ceintures burgondes où les inscriptions appropriées confirment cette signification talismanique. Depuis les peintures des catacombes qui en donnent les plus anciens exemples dès la fin du premier siècle de notre ère, nombreux sont les monuments de tout genre qui illustrent ce thème, qu'affectionnent en particulier les plaques de ceintures burgondes des VIe-VIIe s." (Deonna 1949: 123).

Pour les Chrétiens, Daniel est également la préfiguration du triomphe du Christ (Oriogène (C. Cels 7, 57). Di Berardino 1990: 624); c'est l'image du Sauveur dans le Sépulcre (Réau 1956: 342), du Christ ressuscité. En effet, Daniel est enfermé dans la fosse scellée d'une dalle et il en ressortira vivant grâce à Dieu, celui-ci lui ayant envoyé Habacuc avec des vivres, ce qui symboliserait l'Eucharistie (Béjaoui 1997: 124 (Wilpert 1933)). Sur certains sarcophages comme celui de Jonas, l'allusion à la multiplication est également visible (pain et poissons); la nourriture d'Habacuc vient du ciel (par l'intermédiaire de l'ange). C'est la nourriture qui donne la vie, le triomphe du bien sur le mal (Deonna 1949: 373).

Le symbole de résurrection est encore plus clairement mis en lumière, lorsque l'on trouve l'imagerie de Daniel en relation avec celle de Jonas. C'est le cas sur le couvercle d'un sarcophage d'Hammam Lif (Duval 1982: 618), où Daniel avec les lions est entouré de deux scènes du cycle de Jonas: avalé par la baleine et couché sous les ricins.

Daniel dans la fosse aux lions est l'un des thèmes bibliques le plus souvent représenté dans l'iconographie africaine (Duval 1982: 618 & Béjaoui 1997: 24).

JONAS ET LE MONSTRE MARIN

Livre de Jonas I-II:

Cette scène est très populaire dans l'art des premiers Chrétiens: attestée dès le IIème siècle[21], elle est encore

---

20 Androclès, esclave jeté dans l'arène, que le lion n'a pas touché, car il avait reconnu la main qui l'avait soigné. Il vint alors lui lécher les pieds.
21 Catacombes de Priscillia. (Réau 1956: 410ss.).

utilisée au VIème siècle ap. J.-C.[22].

Dans le premier art chrétien, trois scènes de la vie de Jonas sont représentées: Jonas jeté du bateau (1,15) et avalé par le monstre (2,1), Jonas vomi par le monstre marin (2,11) et Jonas se reposant sous les ricins.

Les lampes à huile illustrent ces trois scènes de façon inégale. En effet, l'épisode de Jonas jeté du bateau n'est connu que par une seule lampe conservée au British Museum (**lampe 14**); l'on peut y voir le bateau avec les voiles carguées (symbolisées par les deux traits en diagonale) où se trouve un matelot, les yeux arrondis, peut-être de peur à cause de la tempête qui fait rage. De Jonas, seules les jambes sont encore visibles en dehors de la bouche du monstre qui ressemble plus à un dragon qu'à une baleine.

Cette représentation correspond tout-à-fait à ce que l'on peut trouver sur les murs des catacombes[23] et sur les sarcophages[24], où fréquemment le cycle est représenté en entier.

Les premiers Chrétiens représentaient souvent un dragon (Réau 1956: 414, ou bien un hippocampe) pour figurer le monstre marin; cela est peut-être dû à une influence de légendes païennes comme celle d'Andromède, de Jason ou encore d'Hercule (Grimal 1951: 36; 242 et 187sq.).

La deuxième scène du cycle représente Jonas rejeté par le monstre sur le rivage de Syrie pour qu'il accomplisse sa mission. Cependant, l'imagerie le présente déjà sous les ricins. Cette scène est la plus constante dans l'art chrétien primitif. En effet, lorsque le mythe n'est plus représenté en entier, c'est celle que l'on retrouve le plus fréquemment, ce qui est également valable pour les lampes où l'on observe le dragon regardant en arrière et Jonas couché sous les ricins (**lampe 15**). Cette représentation résume le mythe à merveille: en effet, le monstre fait allusion à la désobéissance de Jonas et à sa pénitence de trois jours dans le ventre de la "baleine", puis à sa libération sur la côte syrienne. Par ailleurs, l'image de Jonas se reposant sous les ricins ou cucurbites[25] signifie que ce dernier a accompli sa mission en annonçant aux habitants de Ninive la destruction prochaine de leur ville; ces derniers se repentirent et Dieu les épargna. Jonas, fâché et craignant qu'on ne le prenne plus au sérieux, se retira dans le désert où Dieu, bienfaisant, fit grandir une plante pour le protéger du soleil et sous laquelle il se reposa.

Les lampes représentent également deux moments précis de cette aventure, dont la lecture n'est pas aisée.

En effet, Jonas est précipité la tête la première dans le ventre du monstre (Réau 1956:415), comme on le voit sur toutes les représentations du mythe. De plus, Réau (1956: 415) précise que "Jonas entre vêtu et chevelu dans le ventre de la baleine; il en sort chauve et nu. Sa caractéristique la plus individuelle est une calvitie totale". Il est vrai que sur les représentations, Jonas est souvent nu lorsqu'il est englouti par le monstre et chevelu lorsqu'il repose sous les ricins. Cependant, deux lampes pourraient illustrer les propos de Réau (concernant surtout l'art post-VIe): il s'agit d'une lampe conservée à la Bibliothèque Nationale (**lampe 16**), où l'on voit un gros poisson, la bouche ouverte, d'où émerge le buste vêtu de Jonas chevelu[26] et une lampe conservée à Moscou (**lampe 17**), où est également représenté un gros poisson, la geule ouverte, d'où sort la tête uniquement de Jonas chauve! Les deux lampes représenteraient la sortie de Jonas, même si sur l'une d'elles il est vêtu. En effet, Jonas habillé sortant du monstre serait attesté par d'autres pièces bien plus tardives (Réau 1956: 415: graveurs allemands du XVIe s.); cependant il faut rester prudents, car l'écart chronologique est considérable. Il est cependant vrai que sur la plupart des représentations, notamment les sarcophages, on le voit chevelu (sarcophage du Forum Romanum). Par contre, il n'y a aucune représentation de Jonas avalé par les pieds!!

En ce qui concerne la lampe de Moscou, la question ne se pose pas: elle illustre parfaitement les textes juifs (Duval 1973: 29) parlant du prophète chauve. Cette dernière représentation est unique sur les lampes, mais on retrouve Jonas chauve ou avec une calvitie sur les plats en sigillée africaine (Béjaoui 1997: 25) et sur au moins une des lampes conservées au musée de Carthage (**lampe 15**).

Deux lampes présentent Jonas se reposant sous les ricins; elles ne sont connues que par des dessins du début du siècle (Garrucci 1876, tavole III pl. 471 et 475). L'une est en terre cuite (**lampe 18**) et l'autre en bronze; aujourd'hui, elles sont perdues.

Le thème de Jonas, fut un des plus représenté dans l'art chrétien primitif et on le trouve sur de nombreux supports, fresques (catacombes de Calliste), sarcophages (Latran, Forum Romanum), boucles de ceintures du VI-VIIe s. (Suisse), sur lesquels le cycle de Jonas est souvent représenté dans sa totalité avec l'allusion aux habitants de Ninive, mosaïques (Bardo), coupes, gemmes, etc.

Beaucoup de ces objets proviennent d'Afrique; en effet, comme le dit Béjaoui (1997: 25) dans son ouvrage, les Africains affectionnaient et connaissaient particulièrement bien ce mythe, puisque l'évêque d'Oea raconta "à Augustin (Epist 71, 3-5) comment il a utilisé dans la lecture liturgique, la traduction de Jérôme faite sur l'Hébreu. Le peuple, mécontent de ne pas entendre l'évêque évoquer sa cucurbitacée, mais le lierre, fit du tapage, ce qui l'a obligé à revenir à l'ancienne traduction;

---

22 Miniatures byzantines. (Réau 1956: 410ss.).
23 Comme, celle des catacombes de Calliste.
24 Comme, le sarcophage du Latran.
25 Sujet controversé suivant la version biblique et pas toujours dans l'iconographie. Dans la version grecque (Septante), il est question de cucurbite. Dans la version latine (Vulgate), on trouve le lierre et dans les versions moderne, il s'agit de ricin. (Réau 1956: 418).

---

26 Voir aussi lampe de Marseille (DACL VII,2, col. 2615 & Dögler 1910, t.1, p. 119 et fig. 5).

le livre fut relu entièrement car l'épisode se situe à la fin" (Duval 1973: 40).

INTERPRETATION :

Cet engouement des premiers Chrétiens pour le cycle de Jonas s'explique parfaitement; en effet, il illustre la mort, la résurrection et le repos au Paradis (Speake 1994: 81). Jonas est donc la préfiguration du Christ mort, resté trois jours et trois nuits au coeur de la terre et ressuscité (Di Berardino 1990: 1343). Ce parallélisme est confirmé par la parole du Seigneur: "De même, dit-il, que Jonas fut dans le ventre du monstre trois jours et trois nuits, ainsi le Fils de l'Homme sera dans les entrailles de la terre trois jours et trois nuits" (Evangile de saint Matthieu, 12).

Réau (1956: 413) souligne justement que l'art chrétien primitif ne représente jamais réellement Jonas en tant que prophète allant apporter la nouvelle tragique aux habitants de Ninive, mais presque uniquement en tant que symbole de résurrection. A partir du Xe s. environ, la conception changera, probablement et même sûrement, parce que le symbole de résurrection se manifestera directement par l'image du Christ mort sur la croix et revenu vivant parmi les hommes.

Cette promesse de résurrection, et de victoire sur la mort est valable pour les fidèles également, ce qui explique l'extraordinaire popularité du thème dans l'art des premiers Chrétiens, sujets aux persécutions. L'image de Jonas est alors plus fréquente que celle du Bon Pasteur (Réau 1956: 412). Ce symbole d'espérance est donc logiquement très fréquent dans les catacombes et sur les sarcophages, mais également sur les objets de la vie courante.

Si l'on reprend les trois scènes, Jonas jeté à la mer et englouti par le monstre préfigure la mise au tombeau (Réau 1956: 415). Jonas rejeté par le monstre sur le rivage préfigure la résurrection et le salut éternel. C'est pourquoi elle est devenue la scène prépondérante dans la légende de Jonas (Réau 1956: 417). Enfin, Jonas à l'ombre des ricins préfigure le repos éternel, le Paradis (Béjaoui 1997: 25). Cette dernière scène, comme nous l'avons vu, fait bloc avec la précédente dans l'art.

Mais les scènes non représentées, auxquelles les autres font allusion, montraient également la clémence de Dieu à l'égard de tous. Si l'on reprend le récit, il pardonne à Jonas comme il pardonne aux habitants de Ninive; c'est le message du salut divin étendu à toutes les nations.

Cette imagerie ne visait "qu'à illustrer une seule foi et une seule espérance, dût-elle évoluer dans son contenu ou sa précision. Celle d'échapper indemne à la mort et au naufrage de cette vie, pour entrer dans une autre vie. Dissociés de leur contexte, l'engloutissement de Jonas et sa sauvegarde miraculeuse montraient la bienveillance divine pour l'homme, telle qu'elle s'exprime dans l'Ancienne et la Nouvelle Alliance" (Duval 1973: 31).

Les représentations iconographiques et idéologiques sont fortement influencées par l'art païen; en effet, la mythologie grecque nous présente Héraclès sautant dans la gueule du monstre et combattant avec lui pendant trois jours. Jason aurait passé trois nuits dans les entrailles d'un dragon qu'il tua ensuite. Persée tue le dragon qui allait dévorer Andromède. "Jonas serait la réplique juive du dieu-poisson des Assyriens Oannès, des héros grecs Héraclès, Jason et Persée" (Réau 1956: 411) et bibliquement "Jonas dort à l'ombre d'un ricin comme Elie à l'ombre d'un genévrier. Ezéchiel annonce la destruction de Tyr comme Jonas celle de Ninive" (Réau 1956: 411). Un conte du Moyen-Empire égyptien, "le Naufragé", montre un homme sauvé par un serpent géant qui le dépose à l'ombre d'un buisson.

Pour conclure, il est intéressant de remarquer que "l'attitude de Jonas endormi sous la treille rappelle celle de l'Endymion païen ou des dieux fluviaux. Il a la tête appuyée dans la main et les jambes croisées" (Réau 1956: 418). Dans l'imagerie antique, Jonas est toujours imberbe, jeune et nu ou vêtu d'une tunique et d'un *pallium* (Di Berardino 1990: 1343).

HOMME PORTANT UNE GRAPPE

Il reste encore à signaler une scène qui a été amalgamée par la majeure partie des archéologues avec celle que nous avons étudiée plus haut, à savoir les deux explorateurs de Canaan, très fréquente sur les lampes.

Il s'agit d'un homme nu courant vers la droite portant une grappe de raisin assez grosse, mais pas monumentale (**lampe 19**). Le schéma est invariablement le même et est interprété comme celui d'un explorateur seul.

Sur une lampe conservée au musée du Bardo, on retrouve cet homme, le même, en compagnie d'un lion (**lampe 20**). Parfois, le décor est très stylisé (Trévise).

Un problème se pose: selon les textes, il y a toujours deux explorateurs, jamais un seul; de plus, comme nous venons de le voir, toute la symbolique de cette scène s'efface, si l'on ne voit le bâton horizontal supportant la grappe. Cette dernière doit être gigantesque et parfois (comme sur les bas reliefs) les explorateurs plient sous son poids, ce qui n'est absolument pas le cas ici, puisque l'"explorateur" court en portant cette grappe pratiquement du bout des doigts! De plus, la grappe, qui est l'élément central, est parfois cachée par le trou de remplissage (**lampe 19**): il est donc clair que sur ce type de lampe l'élément principal est l'homme et non plus le fruit de la vigne.

Il est vrai que la présence du lion sur la **lampe 20** n'est pas un facteur suffisant pour affirmer que cette représentation ne fait pas partie de l'imagerie des explorateurs de Canaan, car une même figure peut être employée dans un autre contexte, comme c'est souvent le cas (Béjaoui 1997: 29) pour les céramiques. Elle pourrait même faire allusion au pays hostile dont parlent d'autres explorateurs (Livre des Nombres, XIII, 24). Nous ne pensons pas cependant que cette iconographie représente la scène dont il a été question aux pages précédentes.

Peut-être s'agit-il d'un vendangeur, la grosseur de la grappe signifiant une récolte abondante. La question reste ouverte à toute autre proposition. Il est cependant tentant d'adopter l'interprétation des vendanges. En effet, ce thème est représenté sur un assez grand nombre de monuments chrétiens (Tourret 1884: 201). On retrouve sur plusieurs lampes (dont une conservée au Musée du Bardo) un vase d'où sortent des pampres de vigne, dans les volutes desquels on distingue deux personnages accroupis, cueillant du raisin. Le thème de vendanges se retrouve également sur les sarcophages (musée Sainte Irène, Constantinople; Sainte Constance, Rome), sur les fresques des catacombes (cubiculum du cimetière de Calliste), sur les mosaïques (Ancône), etc...

Cependant, comme le remarque Tourret (1884: 202), ce sujet ne constitue pas un symbole exclusivement chrétien. On le retrouve très abondamment dans l'art païen (Amours vendangeurs de la maison des Vetii à Pompéi ou encore toutes les iconographies dionysiaques). Aussi, si l'on adopte cette hypothèse, la grappe de la **lampe 19,** sacrifiée par le trou de remplissage, pourrait s'expliquer comme simple valeur décorative.

EVE

Les scènes d'Adam et Eve cachant leur nudité sont très fréquentes dans l'art antique, comme on peut le voir sur les sarcophages notamment (Junius Bassus) et sur toutes autres formes d'art. Cela n'exclut pas les lampes à huiles où le couple n'est cependant pas souvent représenté (Béjaoui 1997: 108, lampe N 53, de Trieste). Par contre, on le trouve sur un réflecteur (**réflecteur 3**) et sur de nombreuses coupes en sigillée africaine (Béjaoui 1997:21), ce qui a incité certains chercheurs à interpréter la scène de quelques lampes, figurant une jeune femme debout et tentant de cacher sa nudité avec ses mains et ses jambes contorsionnés, (**lampe 21**) comme une représentation d'Eve.

Dans ce cas, comme précédemment pour l'homme portant la grappe, il faut se méfier des schémas et des généralisations. Il est clair que les représentations d'Eve pudique s'inspirent directement du thème de l'Aphrodite pudique, on ne peut plus populaire dans l'art antique, et que l'on retrouve dans toutes les formes d'art.

Ces représentations, comme celle du Bon Pasteur, pouvaient être chargées de deux significations: elles pouvaient représenter Eve pour les Chrétiens, avec peut-être une lampe lui faisant pendant et figurant Adam (mais prudence, aucune n'a été retrouvée!); pour les païens, elles représentaient tout simplement Aphrodite, selon une typologie courante depuis la plus haute antiquité.

Nous pouvons être assurés qu'il s'agit bien d'Eve, lorsqu'elle se trouve en compagnie d'Adam, comme c'est le cas sur la lampe conservée au Musée de Trieste (Béjaoui 1997, N 53), par ailleurs le seul exemple connu.

Il est assez courant de retrouver ce personnage féminin en train de se mirer, et le lien avec Aphrodite ne fait alors plus aucun doute; il suffit de comparer cette image avec les nombreuses statuettes en bronze de la déesse ou les représentations retrouvées dans certains laraires de Pompéi, pour en être convaincu.

Conclusion

Pour conclure, nous signalerons que le Dictionnaire d'Archéologie Chrétienne et Liturgique (DACL) mentionne encore trois types iconographiques, qui seraient tirés de l'Ancien Testament et représentés sur les lampes (DACL VIII,1, col. 1160-1):

1) Abel portant un agneau aux oreilles de lièvres.
2) Le Buisson Ardent
3) Joseph

Les deux premiers sujets ne sont illustrés dans aucun des ouvrages que nous avons consultés et sont de ce fait invérifiables. Cependant, nous pouvons signaler qu'ils n'ont été mentionnés dans aucun des ouvrages spécialisés, comme le livre d'Ennabli ou celui de Béjaoui.

Pour le premier sujet, Delattre (1892: 133, N 662-664) ne parle pas de lièvre, mais de brebis ou d'agneau. Il pourrait donc s'agir de n'importe quel croyant faisant une offrande ou même d'un païen sacrifiant à l'un de ses dieux; rien n'indique qu'il s'agit d'Abel plutôt que de quelqu'un d'autre.

Le deuxième sujet a été mentionné pour la première fois par L. Hautecoeur (Hautecoeur 1897, N 507) qui le décrit ainsi: "Lampe à queue pleine. Dieu dans le buisson ardent (?)", mais le point d'interrogation ne sera pas conservé par la suite. Il semble qu'une deuxième lampe porte cette iconographie (Hautecoeur 1907: 240, N 1395 avec mention: (Carthage 1899), celle que mentionne le DACL; il est fort possible que l'identification se soit faite par analogie avec la première. Malheureusement, aucun dessin ni numéro d'inventaire n'existent pour ces lampes. Nous sommes donc dans l'impossibilité de trancher.

Quant au troisième sujet, Joseph, on le connaît par un dessin du DACL (VII,1, col. 1157-8); il est clair qu'il s'agit ici d'une erreur d'interprétation (d'ailleurs le commentateur émet une réserve dans son analyse). En effet, l'image représentée est très fréquente sur les lampes: il s'agit de la figure de Sérapis avec la coiffe conique (*kalathos*), les cheveux longs et ondulés, et le bâton passant derrière sa tête.

Ce dernier point nous amène à parler des fausses

interprétations. En effet, souvent les chercheurs voient ce qu'ils désireraient voir et non pas la réalité! Il faut cependant être prudent: durant l'antiquité tardive, une même représentation revêtait fréquemment deux significations totalement différentes suivant le destinataire. D'ailleurs, n'a-t-on pas vu que la plupart de ces scènes chrétiennes tirent leurs schémas directement de l'art païen? Le Christ assis sur son trône n'est-il pas représenté à l'image de l'empereur Constantin, tel que le figure l'un des reliefs de son arc à Rome?!

Cette ambivalence affecte la dernière scène étudiée: Eve ou Aphrodite, cela dépend de la religion du consommateur! Ce même phénomène s'observe également sur les sarcophages avec le Bon Pasteur par exemple.

Il n'en reste pas moins que toute cette iconographie n'a qu'un seul but: "les images utilisées par les Pères présentent l'Eglise comme une Mère qui fait naître le baptisé à une vie nouvelle et le prépare tout au long de son existence à la procession définitive de cette vie paradisiaque" (Testini 1978: 484-485); "ces mêmes images décorent les lieux où les Chrétiens entrent dans l'Eglise et ceux où ils attendent la résurrection. Les images paléochrétiennes n'apparaissent plus seulement comme le reflet d'une lecture scripturaire, mais elles portent en elles le contenu d'une vision de Loi perçue par l'âme du fidèle" (Testini 1978: 484-485).

Il faut, bien entendu, adapter ces citations à notre contexte et substituer à église catacombe, ou encore sarcophages, lampe et tout autre support de l'antiquité tardive! Il est intéressant de voir que certains épisodes d'un cycle ou d'une geste sont séparés et figurent sur plusieurs lampes (Béjaoui 1997: 30): c'est le cas pour Jonas et pour les Trois jeunes Hébreux.

Des personnages peuvent figurer dans des scènes totalement différentes: ainsi (Béjaoui 1997: 29), l'homme à la grappe, accompagné ou non du lion; ou encore Eve-Aphrodite, avec ou sans Adam, ce qui montre une fois de plus que les artistes se servaient de schémas (poinçons) qu'ils appliquaient dans leur moules en créant des récits différents.

Cela explique aussi la très grande diversité des thèmes iconographiques que l'on trouve sur les lampes. Nos scènes vétéro-testamentaires, dont la diffusion, grâce aussi au type de lampe sur lesquelles elles étaient représentées, fut très importante dans tout l'Empire depuis l'époque de Constantin, en apportent un éloquent témoignage.

Les scènes de l'Ancien Testament figurées sur les lampes se répartissent en six types, sans compter les variantes. Mise à part celle des explorateurs de Canaan, elle se retrouvent également très fréquemment dans les autres catégories d'art. Sur ce point, il est intéressant de remarquer, comme le fait Duval (Duval 1973: 32), la grande fréquence des représentations de Jonas, de Daniel ou encore des Trois Hébreux ensemble, que se soit dans les catacombes, ou sur les sarcophages. "Dans les textes du milieu du IIe s. et du tout début du IIIe s., l'exemple de Jonas est associé à celui de Daniel, des Trois Hébreux et d'Elie pour prouver que la résurrection de la chair ou, plus précisément, pour montrer que la chair peut échapper à la corruption de la mort. Dans cette perspective, les scènes de Daniel, de Jonas et des Trois enfants, que l'on commence à peindre dans les catacombes ou graver sur les sarcophages, deviennent très évocatrices pour les Chrétiens comme pour les païens. Elles tendent en effet à montrer que le corps humain peut, par la puissance divine, échapper à la destruction des fauves -Daniel-, du feu-les Trois enfants-, de la mer et des monstres marins-Jonas" (Duval 1973: 32). Il n'est donc pas étonnant de retrouver ces trois imageries sur les lampes, objets utilisés communément et faisant partie de la vie de tout les jours et de ce fait rappelant à chaque instant ces préceptes aux premiers chrétiens qui étaient sujets aux persécutions. Ces trois thèmes, ainsi que la figure d'Isaac, dépeignent le Salut de l'Ame sauvée par la grâce divine et la Résurrection.

La désobéissance du fidèle et la colère de Dieu apparaissent dans les scènes d'Adam et Eve et de Jonas. La miséricorde de Dieu est illustrée par le thème de Jonas. L'obéissance aveugle est montrée par Abraham, tandis qu'Isaac préfigure le Christ qui sera sacrifié pour les hommes et enfin le Christ sur la croix est représenté par l'image de la grappe de Canaan portée par les deux explorateurs.

Toutes ces scènes représentaient les préceptes et les idéologies des premiers Chrétiens, comme un livre sans texte; les lampes servaient à diffuser ces idées, complétées par les sermons et les lectures d'hommes d'Eglise tel Saint Augustin.

Ce dernier poussa l'interprétation jusqu'à l'extrême. En effet, comme le remarque Abbiani (Abbiani 1969: 2), la lampe en tant qu'objet, a acquis une signification symbolique de renaissance et de résurrection. Saint Augustin (De Dedicatione Ecclesiae, ser. 17: *Lucerna est enim homo qui bene operatur*) voit dans les lampes les hommes justes. D'autres diront que la lampe est l'homme juste qui marche vers le Christ et est le Christ même, la lumière (Ugone de S. Victor, Annotations in quosdam Psalmos David, chap. 79); ou encore: la parole de Jésus est la lampe qui, comme sa splendeur, doit dissiper les ténèbres de l'ignorance et de l'erreur (Evangile selon Luc 8, 16).

Il n'est d'ailleurs pas étonnant que ces imageries se soient développées sur les lampes de type africain et dans les ateliers africains à partir du IVe s. C'est durant ces mêmes siècles que la religion chrétienne se développa de manière fulgurante en Afrique, pays qui donna naissance à de nombreux grands hommes d'Eglise, le principal étant Saint Augustin, dont les écrits se propagèrent vite dans tout le reste de l'Empire.

Notes

Ce travail a bénéficié de l'appui et des conseils de nombreuses personnes que nous tenons ici à remercier chaleureusement: M. Habib Ben Younès (directeur du Musée du Bardo, Tunis); M. Fathi Béjaoui (Institut National du Patrimoine, Tunis); M. Abdelmajd Ennabli (directeur des musées et site de Carthage); MM. Alain Piccamiglio et Michel Duret (Musée archéologique de Viuz-Faverges); M. Jacques Chamay (Musée d'Art et d'Histoire, Genève); M. Denis Zhuravlev, (Musée Historique d'Etat de Moscou); les professeurs Yves Christe (Université de Genève); Jean-Marc Moret (Université de Lyon II-Lumière); et Daniel Paunier (Université de Lausanne); ainsi que M. Laurent Chrzanovski (Université de Genève).

Fiches

Lampe 1 (fig. 4): *Inv. n.:*   IMC 46 (Musée de Carthage)
Origine: Tunisie
Date: IVe-VIe s. ap. J.-C.
Type de lampe :   Anselmino et Pavolini XA1a; Hayes II; Graziani Abbiani Ia; Dressel 31
Disque: Abraham sacrifiant Isaac
Mesures: l.: 11,2 L.: 7,9 h.: 3,2 h. a: 4,3
Bibliographie: Delattre 1892, n. 665 et 1928, p. 28; Stuhlfauth 1899, pl. X, *10*; Smith 1922, n. 31; DACL, lampes, col. 1160, n. 924; DHGE, Carthage, col. 1166; Salomonson 1969: 74, fig. 106; Ennabli 1976, n. 14; Anselmino & Pavolini, 1981: 202 et Béjaoui 1997: 112, n. 56.

Description: Bec brisé. Terre cuite brûlée à pâte grise à l'intérieur. Forme régulière.
Disque représentant Abraham barbu en tunique *exomis* de face tenant Isaac par les cheveux de la main gauche et brandissant le glaive de la main droite. Isaac est de profil tourné en direction d'Abraham, il est agenouillé, les mains liées derrière le dos. En arrière-plan, le bûcher et le tas de fagots représenté par des stries. A droite le bélier avec au-dessus la main de Dieu dans des nuages stylisés.
Epaule: motifs de chrisme inscrits dans un cercle alterné avec un losange inscrit dans un cercle (Ennabli F3 et F5).
Le rendu est soigné et l'état du moule frais.
Deux trous de remplissages, un au-dessus de la tête d'Isaac et l'autre placé sous le bélier.
Anse moulée non percée placée au sommet du disque.
Lieu de production: Tunisie.
Parallèles: Athènes (Palzweig 1961, n. 2385); S. Priscia, Rome (Ramieri 1978: 312, n. 3); cf Bovon 1966: 88 et Béjaoui 1997: 112.

Lampe 2 (fig.5): *Inv. n.:* AVF n. 154 (Musée de Viuz, Faverges)
Origine: Carthage
Date: IVe-VIe s. ap. J.-C.
Type de lampe: Anselmino et Pavolini XA1a; Hayes II; Abianni Ia; Dressel 31
Disque: Abraham sacrifiant Isaac
Mesures: l.: 14,1; L.: 8,15; h.: 5,64
Bibliographie: Inédite

Description: Lampe intacte. terre cuite rouge-orange.
Disque avec à droite Abraham en tunique *exomis*, de face, tenant de la main droite le glaive dirigé vers la gorge d'Isaac, agenouillé les mains liées derrière le dos, et qu'Abraham tient par les cheveux de sa main gauche. Isaac est de 3/4 face, la tête semble regarder le spectateur.
Sur la moitié gauche de la lampe, un arbre dont le tronc semble être celui d'un palmier et les feuilles celles d'un cyprès. Derrière l'arbre, se tient de profil en direction de la scène de sacrifice, un animal dont l'interprétation est peu sûre, chèvre ou âne.
Le rendu du groupe de gauche est soigné et semble sortie d'un moule frais, ce qui contraste avec le groupe de droite (qui devrait être le plus important) très arasé et dont on ne lit que le contour.
Epaule: motifs de cinq cercles concentriques alternés avec un motif végétal et losange inscrit dans un cercle (Ennabli E5, S2 et F5).
Deux trous de remplissage, l'un placé sous la tête de l'animal et l'autre au-dessus de la main droite d'Abraham tenant le glaive.
Anse moulée non percée placée au sommet du disque.
Lieu de production: Tunisie.
Parallèles: Aucuns.

Lampe 3 (fig.6): *Inv. n.:* Inconnu
Origine: Jérusalem
Date: IIIe-Ve s. ap. J.-C.
Type de lampe: Loeschcke VIII
Disque: Abraham sacrifiant Isaac
Mesures: Inconnues
Bibliographie: Roemische Quartalschrift 1904, t. XVIII, p. 21–34; DACL, II, 2, 1910, col. 1802; Speyart Van Woerden 1961: 229; Smith 1922: 167–8.

Description: D'après un dessin du DACL. Lampe intacte. Aucune indication concernant l'argile et l'engobe.
Disque où l'on voit représenté Abraham en tunique et *pallium* debout de 3/4, la tête tournée vers la main de Dieu (en haut à gauche). Il est barbu, les cheveux longs et porte une sorte de mitre assyrienne. De la main droite, il tient le couteau abaissé vers la tête d'Isaac qui est maintenu agenouillé (Abraham le tenant de la main gauche par les cheveux) les mains liées derrière le dos. Isaac est nu le corps tourné vers la droite face à un autel à cornes où brûle un feu, sa tête nous regarde. Derrière l'autel, une colonne. A la droite d'Abraham le bélier du sacrifice et derrière un cyprès.
Le rendu semble soigné et la lampe sortie d'un moule frais.
Deux trous de remplissage, l'un au-dessus du bélier et l'autre sur la gauche de la colonne.
Pas d'anse.
Lieu de production: Inconnu.

Parallèles: Aucun.

Lampe 4 (fig.7): *Inv. n.:* F 8388 (BNF, Paris)
Origine: Don Le Blant 1897
Date: IVe-VIe s. ap. J.-C.
Type de lampe: Anselmino et Pavolini XA1a; Hayes II; Graziani Abbiani Ia; Dressel 31
Disque: Les deux Explorateurs de Canaan portant la grappe d'Escol
Mesures: l.: 12,1; diam.: 8,2; h.: 1,9
Bibliographie: Trost, 1996, p. 79 et pl. VII.

Description: Bec et une partie du disque à droite brisés. Aucune indication concernant l'argile et l'engobe.
Disque avec les deux explorateurs de face nus portant sur leurs épaules un bâton horizontal d'où pend une énorme grappe de raisin occupant tout le centre de la lampe. Les grains sont figurés par de gros ronds.
Epaule: motifs de pampres (Hayes X1).
Décor assez simple, mais soigné, moule frais.
Deux trous de remplissage, un de chaque côté de la taille des explorateurs.
Anse moulée non percée, placée au sommet du disque.
Lieu de production: Tunisie probablement.
Parallèles: Très nombreux: Sophia (Kuzmanov 1992, n. 300); Kircheriano, (Barbera 1993: 196, n. 156); Hippone (Marec 1958: 236); Carthage (Delattre 1892: 133, n. 670-73 et Hautecoeur 1897, n. 512; 1907 n. 1399); Haïdra (Coll. Farges 1900: 18, n. 349); cf Béjaoui 1997: 114 et Trost 1996: 79.
Variantes: Boscoreale, tunique courte (DACL, VIII, 1, col. 1158, n. 12); Carthage, coiffure radiée, motifs d'épaule oiseaux alternés avec coeurs (Ennabli U1 et M1) (Bailey 1988: 202, n. Q1841; provenance inconnue personnages vêtus, motifs d'épaule losanges inscrits dans un deux cercles concentriques alternés avec carreaux (Ennabli F5 et A10) (Schäfer 1990: 59, n. 62).

Lampe 5 (fig.8): *Inv. n.:* IMC 22 (Musée de Carthage)
Origine: Carthage
Date: IVe-VIe s. ap. J.-C.
Type de lampe: Anselmino et Pavolini XA1a; Hayes II; Graziani Abbiani Ia; Dressel 31
Disque: Les deux Explorateurs de Canaan portant la grappe d'Escol
Mesures: l.: 14,4; diam.: 8,5; h.: 4,8
Bibliographie: Delattre 1892: 140, n. 674 et 1899: 33, pl. VIII, 3; Stuhlfauth 1898, pl. X, 16; Bauer 1907: 20 et 21; DACL, lampes, col. 1162, n. 997; DHGE, Carthage, col. 1166; Leonardi 1947: 178, n. 5; Ennabli 1976, n. 46; Anselmino & Pavolini 1982: 202 et Béjaoui 1997: 114, n. 57.

Description: Légère cassure sur le bec et le fond du réservoir. Terre rouge brunâtre, pâte rugueuse.
Disque: les deux explorateurs de Canaan de face, nus, portant un bâton posé horizontalement sur leurs épaules d'où pend une énorme grappe remplissant tout le centre de la lampe jusqu'au canal sur lequel est figuré un animal la tête dirigée à la verticale de la grappe, comme pour la manger.
Epaule: motifs de quatre cercles concentriques alternés avec chrismes inscrits dans un cercle et carrés (Ennabli E4, F3 et A9).
Anse non percée placée à la verticale du disque.
Bonne facture, mais le moule est déjà un peu usé.
Lieu de manufacture: Afrique du Nord
Parallèles: A part les deux exemplaires identiques cités par Delattre (Delattre 1892: 140, n. 674) trouvés également dans le cimetière des religieuses Carmélites, aucun parallèle n'est connu à ce jour.
Sans l'animal, les parallèles sont les mêmes que pour la lampe 4.

Lampe 6 (fig.9): *Inv. n.:* Inconnu
Origine: Achetée à Rome
Date: Ve s. ap. J.-C.
Type de lampe: Anselmino et Pavolini VIIIC1a; Hayes II; Graziani Abbiani IIa; Dressel 31
Disque: Les deux Explorateurs de Canaan portant la grappe d'Escol
Mesures: Inconnues
Bibliographie: Le Blant 1886, vol. VI, p. 238 et pl. IV.

Description: Bec et partie de l'épaule gauche brisés.
Disque avec les deux explorateurs de face vêtus d'une tunique courte. Celui de droite regarde en direction de l'énorme grappe pendant du bâton posé à l'horizontale sur leurs épaules. Au-dessus de la grappe, un cercle dans lequel est inscrit un chrisme. Sous leurs pieds trois ronds avec un point au centre. Les grains de la grappe sont figuré par des traits ondulés inscrits dans une forme oblongue.
Epaule: motifs de deux cercles concentriques.
Deux gros trous de remplissage placés de chaque côté de la taille des deux explorateurs.
Anse moulée non percée placée au-dessus du chrisme.
Facture mauvaise, dessin grossier et très schématique. Moule en bon état.
Lieu de production:
Parallèles: Pas d'exemplaire exactement identiques.
Variantes: Narbonne, le personnage de gauche regarde la grappe, ils sont nus (Garrucci 1876, pl. 476, n. 4); Don LeBlant, identique à la lampe 6, mais les explorateurs ont les deux la tête de face (Trost 1996: 121, n. 170).

Forme Anselmino et Pavolini XA1a: collection Zurla, les deux regardent de face, ils sont nus. Epaule: motif de rond inscrit dans trois losanges superposés alternés avec roue décorative (Ennabli C5 et F10) (DACL, III, 1, col. 170, n. 2457); Kircheriano, les deux regardent de face et sont nus. Epaule: motif de volutes alternées avec rosettes (Ennabli P2 et J1) (Barbera 1993: 336, n. 294).

Lampe 7 (fig.10): *Inv. n. :* CMA 1401 (Musée du Bardo)
Origine: Carthage, île de l'Amirauté 1908
Date: IVe-VIe s. ap. J.-C.
Type de lampe: Anselmino et Pavolini XA1a; Hayes II; Graziani Abbiani Ia; Dressel 31
Disque: Les Trois Hébreux et Nabuchodonosor
Mesures: l. 12,1; L.: 8,5; h.: 3,5; h. a.: 4,5
Bibliographie: Hautecoeur 1907, n. 1401; Merlin 1912: 285; DACL, lampes, col. 1164, n. 1015; Carletti 1975, n. 163, Ennabli 1976, n. 27 et Béjaoui 1997: 117, n. 59.

Description: Extrémité de l'anse et du bec brisés. Fracture nette. Terre cuite rouge, à pâte lisse.
Disque avec les Trois Hébreux habillés d'une tunique longue bouffante orientale avec ceinture et portant un bonnet phrygien. Ils sont debout, de face et ont un mouvement de recul. Ils sont imberbes et ont le bras droit replié sur la poitrine.
A leur droite, Nabuchodonosor barbu, de profil, est assis sur une *sedia cuvulis* et vêtu d'une riche tunique orientale; il porte également un bonnet phrygien. Nabuchodonosor désigne du doigt son buste posé sur le chapiteau d'une colonne. Ce dernier est la réplique exacte du roi. Il est également de profil, la face en direction des Trois Hébreux. Entre la colonne et les Trois enfants, un personnage barbu debout, de face, tournant sa tête nue en direction du roi. Il tient quelque chose dans la main droite, peut-être une arme. Il s'agit d'un serviteur ou d'un soldat.
Epaule: motif en coeur alterné tête bêche avec motif de palmes. (Ennabli M9 et N1).
Deux trous de remplissage, l'un au-dessus de la tête du premier Hébreu et l'autre sous ses pieds.
Anse moulée non percée, placée au sommet du disque.
Bonne qualité du moule et bon traitement des figures avec beaucoup de détails, travail soigné.
Lieu de production: Tunisie.
Parallèles: Musée Kircheriano (Barbera 1993: 299 et 308, n. 257 et 267); El Djem (Bailey 1988, Q1795) Bagaï (DACL, vol. VIII, 1, col. 1158, n. 1009); Colisée (DACL, VI, 2, col. 2123, n. 5612); Sulmona (DACL, VI, 2, col. 2124, n. 5613); Egnazia (Lattanzi 1972, fig. 28); Calgari (Pani Ermini 1981: 132, n. 218); cf. Béjaoui 1997: 117.

Lampe 8 (fig.11): *Inv. n.:* IMC 18 (Musée de Carthage)
Origine: Carthage, cimetière des Carmélites.
Date: IVe-VIe s. ap. J.-C.
Type de lampe: Anselmino et Pavolini XA1a; Hayes II; Graziani Abbiani Ia; Dressel 31
Disque: Les Trois Hébreux et Nabuchodonosor nimbés
Mesures: l.: 13,4; diam.: 8,1; h.: 3,8
Bibliographie: Delattre 1899, pl. VIII, 8 et 1928: 29; Toulotte 1900: 113; Bauer 1907: 49; DACL, Hébreux (les trois jeunes), col. 2123; Carletti 1975: 90 n. 146; Ennabli 1976, n. 30; Anselmino & Pavolini 1981: 203 et Béjaoui 1997: 119, n. 60.

Description: Bec légèrement brisé. Terre cuite rouge.
Disque comme lampe 11, mais les personnages sont tous nimbés. Le buste, qui ne reprend plus les traits du roi, semble posé sur un tronc d'arbre plutôt que sur une colonne et il n'y a plus de serviteur ou soldat. Le siège du roi semble correspondre à un trône, non à une *sedia cuvulis* comme on le voyait sur la lampe 11. Cette observation est possible grâce à un fragment représentant exactement la même scène.
Epaule: motifs de trois cercles concentriques alternés avec des cartouches et trois triangles superposés placés contre le canal du bec. (Ennabli E6 et D3).
Deux trous de remplissage, l'un placé sous le bras gauche du troisième Hébreu et l'autre sous le siège du roi.
Anse moulée non percée et placée au sommet du disque.
Le moule est frais et le motif de bonne facture.
Lieu de production: Tunisie.
Parallèles: Carthage (Ennabli 1976: 45, n. 31); provenance inconnue (Barbera 1993, n. 258).

Lampe 9 (fig.12): *Inv. n.:* 1934, 52 (Musée Kestner, Hannover)
Origine: Jérusalem
Date: Environ 400–500 ap. J.-C.
Type de lampe: Anselmino et Pavolini XA1a; Hayes II; Graziani Abbiani Ia; Dressel 31
Disque: Les Trois Hébreux et nabuchodonosor nimbés et arbre
Mesures: l.: 11,6; L.: 6,7; h.: 4,6
Bibliographie: Mlasowsky 1993: 398–9, n. 384.

Description: Lampe intacte. Aucune indication concernant l'argile et l'engobe.
Disque avec les Trois Hébreux nimbés en longue tunique orientale ceinturée, debout de face, le bras droit replié sur le ventre. A gauche du disque, le roi Nabuchodonosor assis sur un siège en forme de trône Il est nimbé, nous regardant et levant le bras doit vers l'arbre. Il est vêtu d'une longue tunique. L'arbre est un palmier posé sur un petit tertre.
Epaule: motifs de losanges inscrits dans un cercle et de

carreaux (Ennabli F5 et A9).
Deux trous de remplissage, l'un au-dessus de la tête du premier Hébreu et l'autre sous ses pieds.
Anse moulée non percée, placée au sommet du disque et semblant légèrement décentrée sur la gauche.
Bonne facture, moule très frais, mais peu de détails.
Lieu de production: Tunisie.
Parallèles: Alexandrie (Menzel 1969: 91-91, n. 596); cf. Béjaoui 1997: 110 n. 55).

Lampe 10 (fig.13): *Inv. n.:* CMA 511 (Musée du Bardo)
Origine: Carthage
Date: IVe-VIe s. ap. J.-C.
Type de lampe: Anselmino et Pavolini XA1a; Hayes II; Graziani Abbiani Ia; Dressel 31
Disque: Les Trois Hébreux dans la fournaise
Mesures: l.: 10,7; diam.: 9,9; h.: 3,3
Bibliographie: Delattre 1892, n. 666; Stuhlfauth 1898, pl. X, 14; DACL, lampe, col. 1161, n. 986; Carletti 1975, n. 147; Ennabli 1976, n. 17, Rassart Debergh 1978: 453, fig. 6 et Béjaoui 1997: 122, n. 62.

Description: Extrémité du bec brisée. terre rouge foncée.
Disque avec les Trois Hébreux vêtus d'une riche tunique courte et de chausses décorées de ronds. Ils sont tête nue et se tiennent de manière très serrée. Mouvement dynamique des jambes. Sous leurs pieds, trois ronds symbolisant les flammes.
Epaule: motifs de rosettes alternés avec coeurs (Ennabli J1 et M6).
Deux trous de remplissages situés au niveau de la taille du premier et du dernier Hébreux.
Anse moulée non percée située au sommet du disque.
Bonne facture, soignée avec détails. Moule assez frais, mais somme toute un peu usé au niveau des visages.
Lieu de production: Tunisie.
Parallèles: Carthage (Hautecoeur 1897, n. 511; 1907, n. 1397 et Bailey 1988: 198, n. Q1796); cf. Béjaoui 1997: 122.
Variante: Croix sous les pieds des Trois Hébreux à la place des flammes: Carthage (Lyon-Caen 1986: 102, n. 47), motif d'épaule alors différent: rosette inscrite dans un cercle, triangle orné, coeur, cinq cercles concentriques, carré orné et losange orné (Ennabli F9, D6, M1, E3, A12 et C5).

Lampe 11 (fig.14): *Inv. n.:* IMC 48 (Musée de Carthage)
Origine: Carthage
Date: IVe-VIe s. ap. J.-C.
Type de lampe: Anselmino et Pavolini XA1a; Hayes II; Graziani Abbiani Ia; Dressel 31
Disque: Les Trois Hébreux dans la fournaise et l'ange
Mesures: l.: 13,6; diam.: 7,9; h.: 3,5
Bibliographie: Delattre 1892, n. 667 et 1928, p. 29; DACL, Hébreux (les trois jeunes), col. 2124, n. 6 et lampes, col. 2731, fig. 3259; Carletti 1975, n. 148; Ennabli 1976, n. 25, Gallina 1985, n. 157, pl. XIX) et Béjaoui 1997: 120, n. 61.

Description: Lampe intacte. Terre rouge à pâte dure. Le bec comporte des traces de combustion.
Disque avec les Trois Hébreux debout de face, en longue tunique orientale bouffante et ceinturée avec un bonnet phrygien de face et les paumes levées vers le ciel. Les flammes nombreuses, semblant sortir du sol, montent jusqu'aux tailles des trois jeunes gens.
Entre le premier et le deuxième Hébreux se trouve un ange nimbé aux ailes déployées et vêtu de la même manière que les jeunes.
Epaule: motifs de volutes alternés avec rosettes et cinq cercles concentriques, aux extrémités quatre triangles superposés (Ennabli P4, E2, I1 et D5).
Deux trous de remplissage, l'un sous la main droite du premier Hébreu et l'autre sur l'épaule et une partie du visage du troisième Hébreu.
Anse moulée et non percée placée au sommet du disque.
Bonne facture avec détails, moule frais.
Lieu de production: Tunisie.
Parallèles: Constantine (DACL, III,1, col. 2731, n. 1010); Afrique du Nord (Trost 1996: 78, n. 43); cf. Béjaoui 1997: 120.

Lampe 12 (fig.15): *Inv. n.:* 3714 (Musée d'art et d'Histoire de Genève)
Origine: Lambèse, Algérie
Date: Ve s. ap. J.-C.
Type de lampe: Anselmino et Pavolini XA1a; Hayes II; Graziani Abbiani Ia; Dressel 31
Disque: Daniel dans la fosse aux lions
Mesures: l.: 14; diam.: 8,3
Bibliographie: Deonna 1949: 119, n. 1

Description: L'extrémité du bec est brisée. Terre ?
Disque avec Daniel debout de face, vêtu d'une tunique orientale, blousante et ceinturée aux plis en éventails. Ses paumes sont écartées et levées vers le ciel en geste de prière.
A ses pieds deux lions disposés obliquement la tête en bas, celui de gauche court et celui de droite marche.
A la hauteur de sa tête, on voit à droite, Habacuc, debout tenant un pain rond strié en rayons, et à gauche l'ange du Seigneur.
Daniel occupe tout le centre du disque, les quatre autres figures étant placées sur les bords.
Le rendu est assez soigné, mais le moule est usé à certains endroits, notamment sur la tête de Daniel.
Epaule: motifs de cercle inscrit dans deux carrés alterné avec losange inscrit dans un cercle (Ennabli A4 et F5).
Au revers deux cercles concentriques.
Deux trous de remplissage, l'un sous le coude gauche de Daniel et l'autre sur les pattes postérieures du lion de

gauche.
Anse moulée non percée, placée au-dessus du disque.
Lieu de production: Algérie ou Carthage (?).
Parallèles: Carthage (Hautecoeur 1897, n. 504-506; 1907, n. 1391-1394; Delattre 1892: 141, n. 676-80; Ennabli 1976: 45-47, n. 32, 41 et 42; Bailey 1988: 197, Q1793); Tunisie (Lyon-Caen 1986: 101, n. 45); cf Deonna 1946: "Ce sujet apparaît sur plusieurs lampes de même forme et de même époque. La plupart ont été trouvées en Afrique du Nord, à Carthage; étant donné l'identité de leurs détails, elles sortent assurément d'un même atelier, peut-être établi à Carthage." (p.119-120). Il faut cependant être prudent, car les moules ou les poinçons, pouvaient, comme la sigillée, voyager.

Lampe 13 (fig.16): *Inv. n.:* IMC 836 (Musée de Carthage)
Origine: Carthage
Date: IVe-VIe s. ap. J.-C.
Type de lampe: Anselmino et Pavolini VIIIA1a; Hayes II; Graziani Abbiani IIa; Dressel 31
Disque: Daniel dans la fosse aux lions
Mesures: l.: 12; diam.: 6,5; h.: 3,5
Bibliographie: Béjaoui, 1997, p. 125, n. 64.

Description: Lampe dont le bout du bec est brisé. Terre jaune-foncée, légèrement granulée.
Disque avec Daniel debout de face en position d'orant, vêtu d'une tunique avec ceinture basse et portant vraisemblablement un bonnet phrygien.
A ses pieds deux lions assis nous regardant, on peut voir nettement la crinière de celui de gauche.
En haut du disque, à gauche, Habaccuc, debout tenant un pain rond et à droite nous distinguons l'ange du Seigneur. Il est intéressant de voir qu'ici les deux personnages venus secourir Daniel sont inversés par rapport au schéma habituel (voir lampe 9).
Epaule: motif de chevrons terminés par de petits cercles.
Deux trous de remplissage situés de chaque côté de la taille de Daniel, au-dessus de la croupe des lions.
Anse moulée non percée séparée décorée par un sillon et placée au-dessus du disque.
Dessin stylisé, mais avec des détails biens marqués, le décor est effacé, le moule ne devant plus être très frais.
Lieu de production: Tunisie.
Parallèles: Aucun.

Lampe 14 (fig.17): *Inv. n.:* MLA 1936.11–12.1 (British Museum)
Origine: Grèce de l'Est
Date: Deuxième moitié Ve–VIe s. ap. J.-C.
Type de lampe: Anselmino et Pavolini VIIIC1a; Hayes II; Graziani Abbiani IIa; Dressel 31
Disque: Jonas jeté par les marins dans la gueule du monstre marin.
Mesures: l.: 15,2; L.: 9,1
Bibliographie: Bailey 1988, Q3323

Description: Lampe intacte. Terre cuite rose, engobe rouge-brun.
Disque avec bateau contenant un personnage dont on ne voit que la tête aux yeux arrondis et Jonas englouti par le monstre. On ne voit plus que les jambes du malheureux s'échappant du bateau. Le monstre remplit tout le bas de la lampe, il a la gueule ouverte vers le bateau qui remplit le haut du disque.
Epaule: motifs de trois cercles concentriques décroissants. Entre chaque cercle un point.
Deux trous de remplissage, de chaque côté du bateau juste en dessous de la quille.
Fond: cercle avec un *Alpha* incisé.
Anse moulée non percée au-dessus du disque.
Le rendu est soigné et le moule très frais.
Lieu de production: Grèce probablement ou Tunisie.
Parallèles: Aucuns.

Lampe 15 (fig.18): *Inv. n.:* IMC 54 (Musée de Carthage)
Origine: Carthage probablement.
Date: IVe-VIe s. ap. J.-C.
Type de lampe: Anselmino et Pavolini XA1a; Hayes II; Graziani Abbiani Ia; Dressel 31
Disque: Jonas rejeté par le monstre sous les ricins
Mesures: l.: 12,8; L.: 8; h.:3,3; h. a.: 4,4
Bibliographie: Ennabli 1976, n. 56.

Description: Anse brisée. Terre cuite rouge recouverte d'un engobe détérioré. Forme régulière. Modèle estompé. Patère à deux cercles.
Disque où l'on voit le monstre marin dont le corps est rond, sa tête portée sur un long cou regardant en arrière Jonas qui se repose sous les ricins stylisés par des bandes larges verticales. Jonas est couché jambes croisées, le bras derrière le tête comme Endémion. Sous lui est figuré en ondulé la colline, que Béjaoui (Béjaoui 1997: 126) interprète comme la queue du monstre, ce qui nous semble moins logique, car il n'y a pas de connexion entre le monstre et cette ligne ondulée. De plus l'arrière du monstre se termine par des nageoires représentées également à l'avant de son corps.
Le monstre est très détaillé: oeil droit grand ouvert et bouche aux dents acérées, son corps est décoré de petits points. Par contre Jonas et le cucurbite sont comme effacés.
Le monstre occupe la majeure partie de la lampe obligeant Jonas à empiéter légèrement sur le canal, sous sa tête est figuré un rond.
Au-dessus du bec est incisé une croix.
Epaule: motif de dauphins alternés avec coeurs (Ennabli V1 et M9). Béjaoui ajoute de façon pertinente que les "dauphins sont le complément pour créer une vraie scène marine. Ces dauphins pourraient être l'équivalent des vagues figurées sur les carreaux de terre cuite et les

sarcophages" (Béjaoui 1997: 126).
Le motif est soigné pour le monstre et un peu schématisé pour le reste. Le décor est fortement estompé, le moule devait être en mauvais état.
Deux trous de remplissage, l'un vers les nageoires avant du monstre et le deuxième au bout de sa gueule.
Lieu de production: Tunisie.
Parallèles: Cette scène se retrouve très fréquemment sur les lampes dont on ne compte plus les parallèles: Carthage (Hautecoeur 1907, n. 1400 et Delattre 1892: 140, n. 675. Il mentionne également trois autres exemplaires identiques); Zagouhan (Hautecoeur 1897, n. 516); Sloan (Bailey 1988: 198, n. Q1798); Afrique du Nord (Lyon-Caen 1986: 102, n. 46; Rosenthal 1978: 71, n. 292); cf Béjaoui 1997: 126. Les lampes comme celle du British Museum ont l'épaule décorée de dauphins et feuilles de lierres alternés (peut-être allusion à la Vulgate).

Lampe 16 (fig.19): *Inv. n.:* F. 8394 (BNF, Paris)
Origine: Afrique de Nord (Don Le Blant 1897)
Date: fin IVe-début Ve s. ap. J.-C.
Type de lampe: Anselmino et Pavolini VIIIC1a; Hayes II; Graziani Abbiani IIa; Dressel 31
Disque: Jonas sortant de la bouche du poisson
Mesures: l.: 11; diam.: 6,8; h.: 2,8
Bibliographie: Trost 1996: 65, n. 2.

Description: Lampe intacte. Aucune indication concernant l'argile et l'engobe.
Motif s'étendant du canal jusqu'à l'anse.
Disque avec au centre un gros poisson, tête dirigée vers l'anse. Il a la bouche ouverte d'où sort le buste d'un personnage aux cheveux longs vêtu d'une tunique. Ce personnage a été interprété d'abord comme une femme, puis comme représentant Jonas (Dölger 1928: 120).
Le motif est très détaillé et la lampe semble sortie d'un moule frais.
Epaule: motif en "arrête de poisson" fait de trais incisés.
Deux trous de remplissage, un de chaque côté du poisson.
Anse moulée décorée d'un sillon, placée au sommet du disque.
Lieu de production: Afrique du Nord
Parallèles: Marseille (DACL, vol. VII, 2, col. 2615, n. 6306), il s'agit d'une lampe de type Anselmino et Pavolini XA1a, avec décor d'épaule différent. Cette lampe illustrée dans plusieurs ouvrages, n'est connue que par des dessins.

Lampe 17 (fig.20): *Inv. n.:* 53151, OBIT, IT 281 (Musée Historique d'Etat de Moscou).
Origine: Chersonèse
Date: Ve s. ap. J.-C.
Type de lampe: Anselmino et Pavolini VIIIC1a; Hayes II; Graziani Abbiani IIh; Dressel 31
Disque: Jonas recraché par le monstre
Mesures: l.: 9,7; L.: 6,3; h.: 3,3
Bibliographie: Rumyantsevskiy Museumkatalog n. 3431; Chrzanovski & Zhuravlev 1997, pl. I n. 7 et 1998 n. 94

Description: Lampe intacte. Argile rouge-brun clair. Engobe rouge brun foncé, parfois brun foncé.
Le motif s'étend depuis le canal jusqu'à l'anse.
Disque avec au centre un gros poisson tête dirigée vers l'anse, la gueule ouverte avec des dents pointues d'où sort la tête chauve de Jonas ouvrant de grands yeux ronds. Le rendu du poisson est extrêmement fin avec mention d'écailles et nageoires. On voit également l'oeil gauche du poisson. La tête de Jonas est aussi très nette.
Epaule: motif en "arrêtes de poissons" incisé.
Deux trous de remplissage, un de chaque côté du poisson.
Anse moulée décorée d'un sillon, placée au sommet du disque.
Lieu de production: Afrique ou Italie.
Parallèles: Aucun.

Lampe 18 (fig.21): *Inv. n.:* Sans inv. (Musée du Vatican)
Origine: Inconnue
Date: IIIe-Ve s. ap. J.-C.
Type de lampe: Loeschcke VIII
Disque: Jonas sous les ricins
Mesures: Inconnues
Bibliographie: Garrucci 1876, pl. 475.

Description: D'après le dessin de Garrucci. Lampe fendue et recollée un peu plus haut que le bec. Aucune indication concernant l'argile et l'engobe.
Disque où l'on voit représenté Jonas nu couché sous les ricins ou plutôt les cucurbites. Il a les jambes croisées et le bras gauche sous la tête, le droit plié contre la poitrine, selon le schéma habituel (cf. lampe 5). Le plant de cucurbite est figuré, comme sur les sarcophages (Caillet 1990: 44-45), par un petit tronc d'où pendent les fruits et sur le dessus des feuilles. Le sol est figuré par des gros traits.
Le pourtour de la lampe est décoré de petits cercles.
Deux trous de remplissage, l'un au niveau du sol et l'autre au niveau des feuilles de la plante.
La facture semble bonne et le moule frais.
Anse moulée non percée placée au sommet du disque et fendue en son milieu.
Lieu de production: Inconnu
Parallèles: Aucun. Tourret (Tourret 1884), parle d'une lampe au motif identique, est-ce la même?

Lampe 19 (fig.22): *Inv. n.:* 25139 (Musée de Vérone)
Origine: Collection privée (Muselli)
Date: IVe-VIe s. ap. J.-C.
Type de lampe: Anselmino et Pavolini XA1a; Hayes

Disque:	II; Graziani Abbiani Ia; Dressel 31 Homme portant une grappe de raisin
Mesures:	l.: 9,5; l. a.: 10,7; L.: 6,4; h.: 2,7; h. a.: 3,8.
Bibliographie:	Muselli 1756: 47, ppl. 123; Graziani Abbiani 1969: 168, n. 554; Larese et Sgreva 1996: 371-2, n. 656a.

Description: Lampe intacte.
Disque avec homme vêtu d'une tunique courte courant vers la droite. Il porte à bout de bras dans la main gauche une grappe de raisin assez grosse. L'autre main est tendue devant lui.
Le personnage remplit tout le disque.
Epaule: motifs de rosettes alternées avec quatre triangles superposés et coeurs (Ennabli P1, D1 et M3).
Deux trous de remplissage, l'un placé derrière son dos et l'autre sur le haut de la grappe.
Anse moulée non trouée, placée au sommet du disque.
Personnage assez schématisé, mais de bonne facture, moule frais.

Lieu de production:	
Parallèles:	Nombreux: Athènes (Cahn-Klaiber 1977: 396, n. 368); Alexandrie (Cahn-Klaiber 1977: 397, n. 369); Corinthe (Broneer 1930: 287, n. 1471); Italie (Barbera 1993: 209-10, n. 170 et 197). Le motif d'épaule change fréquemment.
Variantes:	Trévise (Zaccaria Ruggiu 1980: 119, n. 216): très ornementale et stylisée. Carthage (Hautecoeur 1921: 266, n. 2490), le personnage court et est vêtu d'un manteau flottant derrière son dos, sur l'épaule décor de rinceaux.

Il est intéressant de remarquer que la plupart de ces lampes n'ont pas été trouvées en Afrique.

Lampe 20: *Inv. n.:* CMA 2485 (Musée du Bardo)
Origine:	EL Jem 1916
Date:	IVe-VIe s. ap. J.-C.
Type de lampe:	Anselmino et Pavolini XA1a; Hayes II; Graziani Abbiani Ia; Dressel 31
Disque:	Homme portant une grappe de raisin et lion
Mesures:	l.: 14,1; L.: 8,4; h.: 3,7; h. a.: 4,6
Bibliographie:	Hautecoeur 1921: 266, n. 2485 et Ennabli 1976, n. 245.

Description: Lampe intacte. Terre cuite rouge.
Disque avec personnage nu courant vers la droite et portant à bout de bras une grappe de raisin assez grosse, le droit tendu devant lui (identique à lampe 19).
En face sur la droite du disque, un lion assis de profil et rugissant. On distingue bien sa crinière.
Epaule: motifs de quatre cercles concentriques alternés avec quatre losanges superposés et rosettes (Ennabli E5, C3 et I5).
Deux trous de remplissage, l'un entre les jambes du personnage et l'autre sous la queue du lion.
Anse moulée non percée, placée au sommet du disque.
Bonne facture, dessin assez schématisé, mais avec des détails. Moule frais.
Lieu de production: Tunisie.
Parallèles: Aucun.

Lampe 21 (fig.24): *Inv. n.:* CMA 2480 (Musée du Bardo)
Origine:	Carthage
Date:	IVe-VIe s. ap. J.-C.
Type de lampe:	Pavolini XA1a; Hayes II; Graziani Abbiani Ia; Dressel 31
Disque:	Eve (?)
Mesures:	l.: 13,7; L.: 8; h.: 3,4; h. a.: 4,7
Bibliographie:	Ennabli 1976, n. 120.

Description: Lampe brisée sur le haut de l'épaule côté droit. Terre cuite rouge, à pâte rugueuse.
Disque avec femme nue debout, de face, bras droit essayant de cacher son pubis et bras gauche replié sur sa poitrine. La jambe gauche a le genou plié vers l'intérieur pour cacher sa nudité. Elle porte une coiffure radiée.
Epaule: motifs de rectangles décorés de treillis.
Deux trous de remplissage, un de chaque côté de la taille du personnage.
Anse moulée non percée, placée au sommet du disque.
Facture assez grossière, décor très effacé, moule passablement usé.
Lieu de production: Tunisie.
Parallèles: Il n'en existe aucun avec la même coiffure. De très nombreux parallèle existe avec une coiffure constituée d'un chignon, certaines tiennent un miroir (Ennabli 1976, n. 153). Souvent le décor d'épaule diffère.

Réflecteur 1 (fig.1): *Inv. n.:* (Musée de Carthage)
Origine:	Carthage, probablement
Date:	IVe -VIe s.
Disque:	Abraham sacrifiant Isaac
Mesures:	diam.: 9
Bibliographie:	Béjaoui 1982: 142. fig. 5 et 1997: 157, n. 90

Description: En deux fragments collés, il manque une partie à gauche, et le bord inférieur. Terre rouge brique lisse.
Disque: Abraham debout, de face, vêtu d'une tunique courte ceinturée. Il a les cheveux courts et ne porte pas de barbe, les yeux ronds. Il devait tenir de la main droite le couteau. De la main gauche il tient le sommet de la tête d'Isaac agenouillé de profil vers lui. Les mains liées derrière le dos et également vêtu d'une tunique courte. A la droite d'Abraham, le bélier tourné vers la scène centrale. A la gauche d'Isaac un motif de type M2 à la place du bûcher (peut-être le représente-t-il).
Le disque est rond avec un décor denteté sur le bord, mais uniquement dans la moitié supérieur. Les coins portent alors de petits motifs circulaires. Sur le haut une bande décorée de motifs M2 et E3 alternés.
Facture assez bonne, mais dessin simplifié et schématique

avec rendu ornemental.
Lieu de production: Tunisie
Parallèles: Aucun.

Réflecteur 2 (fig.2): *Inv. n.:* (Musée de Carthage)
Origine: Carthage, probablement
Date: IVe-VIe s.
Disque: Les deux Explorateurs de Canaan portant la grappe d'Eschol
Mesures: diam.: 6
Bibliographie: Béjaoui 1982: 143. fig. 8 et 1997: 158, n. 91

Description: Disque brisé en diagonale sur le côté gauche. Terre jaunâtre granulée.
Disque avec les deux explorateurs, ils sont de profil et vêtus d'une tunique courte. Ils avancent vers la gauche. Sur leurs épaules un bâton horizontal d'où pend une énorme grappe de raisin.
Le réflecteur est de forme circulaire simple, sans décor sur le pourtour.
Décor simple et stylisé, moule assez frais.
Lieu de production: Tunisie
Parallèles: Aucun.

Réflecteur 3 (fig.3): *Inv. n.:* (Musée de Carthage)
Origine: Carthage, probablement
Date: IVe-VIe s.
Disque: Adam et Eve
Mesures: diam.: 9
Bibliographie: Béjaoui 1982: 141, fig. 1 et 1997: 156, n. 89.

Description: Bas du disque cassé horizontalement. Terre rouge-orangé, légèrement granulée.
Disque avec homme debout, nu, de face, avec feuille sur son sexe, la main droite sur son bas ventre et la gauche en l'air; il a les jambes écartées. Sa tête est tournée vers la droite, il regarde la figure féminine qui se tient à ces côtés, également nue avec une feuille de vigne sur le pubis, les deux bras croisés sur le bas ventre. Elle semble tenir quelque chose de long, dans la main gauche. Elle a les jambes serrées.
Le réflecteur est de forme circulaire à bord mouluré et dentelé.
Facture assez grossière, moule un peu vieux.
Lieu de production: Tunisie.
Parallèles: Aucun parallèle exact, mais proche la lampe de Trieste (Béjaoui 1997: 108, n. 53).

Bibliographie

L. Anselmino & C. Pavolini, 1981. *Terra sigillata: lucerne,* in Enciclopedia dell'Arte Antica. Atlante delle forme ceramiche I, Roma, pp. 184-207 et pl. CLV-CLXII.

D. M. Bailey, 1988. *Catalogue of the Lamps in the British Museum, vol. III*, London.

Barbera et Petriaggi, 1993. *Le lucerne tardo-antiche di produzione africana,* Museo Nazionale Romano, Nuova Serie, n. 5, Roma.

M. Bauer, 1907. *Der Bilderschmuck früchristlichen Tonlampen,* Greifswald,

F. Béjaoui, 1982.*Les thèmes bibliques sur quatre réflecteurs de lampes du Musée de Carthage,* dans Africa IX.

F. Béjaoui, 1997.*Céranmique et religion chrétienne. Les thèmes bibliques sur la sigillée africaine,* Tunis.

A. Bourgeois, 1980. *Les lampes en céramique de Mactar,* dans Karthago 19, p. 33ss.

A. Bovon, 1966. *Lampes d'Argos,* EFRA, Etudes Péloponnésiennes 5, Paris-Vrin.

G. M. Bravar, 1946. Lucerne paleocristiane della villa romana di Desenano, in *Sibrium 8,* pp. 113-120.

O. Broneer, 1930.*Corinth, vol. IV, part. II: Terracotta Lamps,* Cambridge.

E. M. Cahn-Klaiber, 1977. *Die Antiken tonlampen des archäologischen Institut der Universität Tübingen,* Tübingen.

J.-P. Caillet, 1990. *La vie d'éternité, la sculpture funéraire dans l'Antiquité Chrétienne,* Paris-Genève.

C. Carletti, 1976. *I tre giovani ebrei di Babilonia,* in Quaderni di Vetera Christianorum IX.

L. Chrzanovski et D. Zhuravlev, 1998. *Lamps from Chersonesos in the State Historical Museum — Moscow,* Studia archeologica 94. Roma.

Catalogue de la collection Farges, 1900.

F. E. Day, 1942. Early Islamic and Christian Lamps, in *Berytus 7,* pp. 65-75.

H. De Villefosse, 1877. *Sarcophage Chrétien de Syracuse,* dans Gazette archéologique.

A. L. Delattre, 1880. *Lampes chrétiennes de Carthage,* Lyon.

A. L. Delattre, 1892. *Lampes chrétiennes de Carthage,* dans Revue de l'Art chrétien, t. III, p. 133-41.

A. L. Delattre, 1899. *Lampes,* dans Catalogue du musée Lavigerie de St Louis de Carthage, III, p. 33ss.

J. Deneauve, 1969. *Lampes de Carthage,* Paris.

W. Deonna, 1949. *Daniel le "Maître des Fauves" à propos d'une lampe chrétienne du musée de Genève.*

A. Di Berardino (dir.), 1990. *Dictionnaire encyclopédique du christianisme ancien,* 2 vol.,

Dictionnaire d'Archéologie chrétienne et liturgique (DACL), Paris, (1924-1953).

Dictionnaire d'histoire et de géographie éclésiastique (DHGE), Paris, (1932).

F. J. Dölger, 1910-28. *Das Fish-Symbol in früh christlicher Zeit,* 4 vol.

Y. M. Duval, 1973. *Le livre de Jonas dans la littérature grecque et latine.*

Y. Duval, 1982. *Locra sanctorum Africae. Le culte des martyrs en Afrique du IVe au VIIe siècle,* t. II.

A. Ennabli, 1976. *Lampes chrétiennes de Tunisie (musée du Bardo et de Carthages),* Paris.

M. A. Gallina, 1985. *Le lucerne fittili di Dertona,* Dertona.

P. R. Garrucci, 1876. *Storia dell'arte cristiana.,* vol. III-IV et tav. III.

M. Graziani Abbiani, 1969. *Lucerne fittili paleocristiani*, in Studi di Antichità Cristiane 6, Bologne.

P. Grimal, 1951. *Dictionnaire de la mythologie grecque et romaine.*

L. Hautecoeur, 1897, Lampes, dans *Catalogue du musée Alaouï*, p. 194-207.

L. Hautecoeur, 1907. Lampes, dans *Catalogue du musée Alaouï, Suppl. 1*, p. 173-217.

L. Hautecoeur, 1921. Lampes, dans *Catalogue du musée Alaouï, Suppl. 1*), p. 266.

J. W. Hayes, *Late Roman Pottery*, London, (1972).

V. Hoff et C. Lyon-Caen, 1986.*Catalogue des lampes en terre cuite grecques et chrétiennes*, Musée du Louvre, Paris,

G. Kuzmanov, 1992. *Anticni lampi. Kolekcija na Nacionalnija archeologiceski muzej*, Sofija.

A. Larese & D. Sgreva, 1997. *Le lucerne fittili del Museo Archeologico di Verona*, Roma.

E. Lattanzi, 1972. La nuova basilica paleocristiana di Egnazia, dans Vetera Christianorum, 9.

E. Le Blant, 1875. D'une lampe païenne portant la marque ANNISER, in Revue Archéologique, XXIX,

E. Le Blant, 1886. De quelques sujets représentés sur des lampes en terre cuite de l'époque chrétienne, in Mélanges d'archéologie et d'histoire, Ecole Française de Rome, VI.

C. Leonardi, 1947. *Ampelos, il simbolo della vita nell'arte pagano e paleocristiana*, Rome.

S. Loeschcke, 1919. *Lampen aus Vindonissa*, Zürich.

M. Mackensen, 1980. *Spätantike nordafrikanische Lampen-model und Lampen*, in Bayerische Vorgeschichtsblätter, 45, pp. 205-24.

M. Martin, 1991, *Die beinerne Gürtelschnalle mit Szene aus des Geschichte des Propheten Jonas*, in Archéologie Suisse, 14, pp. 279-288.

E. Marec, 1958. *Monuments chrétiens d'Hippone. Ville épiscopale de Saint Augustin.*

H. Menzel, 1954. *Die antiken Lampen in Römisch-Germanischen Zentral Museum zu Mainz*, Mainz.

A. Merlin, 1912. *Fouilles dans l'îlot de l'Amiral à Carthage*, dans Compte rendu de l'Académie des inscriptions et des belles lettres, Paris.

O. Mitius, 1897. *Jonas auf den Denkmälern des christlichen Alterums.*

A. Mlasowsky, 1993. *Die antiken Tonlampen im Kestner-Museum Hannover*, Hannover.

I. Moderzewska, 1988. *Studi iconologico delle lucerne siro-palestinesi del IV-VIIs. ap. J.-C.*, in Rivista di Archeologia, suppl. 4.

A. Ovadiah, 1974. The relief of the Spies from Carthage, dans *Israël Exploration Journal*, vol. 24, p. 210ss.

M. T. Paleani et Liverani, 1984. *Lucerne Paleocristiane conservate nel museo Oliveriano di Pesaro*, Tomo 1, Roma.

M. T. Paleani, 1993. *Le lucerne paleocristiane* (Monumenti, Musei e Gallerie Pontificie, Antiquarium Romanum), Roma.

J. Palzweig, 1961. *The Athenian Agora: Lamps of the Roman Period.*

L. Pani Ermini-M. Marione, 1981. *Catalogo dei materiali paleocristiani e altomedievali del Museo Archeologico Cagliari*, Roma.

C. Pavolini, 1981. Lucerne, in *Enciclopedia dell'Arte Antica*, suppl., pp. 460-4.

A. M. Ramieri, 1978.*Gruppo di Lucerne tardo antiche da S. Prisca*, in Rivista di archeologia cristiana, 3-4, Roma.

M. Rassart-Debergh, 1978.*"Les trois hébreux dans la fournaise" dans l'art paléochrétien. Iconographie*, dans Byzantion 48.

L. Réau, 1956. Iconographie de l'art chrétien, T, 2,1, Iconographie de la Bible, Ancient Testament.

R. Rosenthal & R. Sivan, 1978. *Ancient Lamps in the Schloessinger collection*, in Quedem 8.

J. W. Salomonson, 1969. *Spatrömische rote Tonware mit Reliefverzierung, aus Nordafrikanischen Werkstätten*, dans Bulletin Antieke Beschaving, 44, Leiden.

S. Schäfer, 1990. *Lampen der Antikensammlung (Frankfrt), Archäologische Reihe, n. 13*, Frankfurt.

A. M. Smith, 1922. *The iconography of the sacrifice of Isaac in the early christian art*, in American Institut of America 26.

I. Speyart Van Woerden, 1961. *The iconography of the sacrifice of Abraham*, in Vigiliae christianae XV.

G. Stuhlfauth, 1898. *Bemerkungen von einer Christlich Archaelogischen Studiereise nach Malta und Nordafrika*, dans Mitteilungen des Kaiserlich Deutschen Archälogishen Institutes, 18, Roma.

P. Testini, 1978. dans Atti del IX Congresso Internazionale d'Archeologia Christiana, Roma 1975, Città del Vaticano, pp. 484-5.

A. Toulotte, 1900. *Le roi Nabuchodonosor sur les monuments africains*, dans Nuovo Bollettino d'Arte, 6, Rome.

G. M. Tourret, 1884.dans Revue Archéologique, 4.

C. Trost et M.-C. Hellmann, 1996. *Lampes antiques, Bibliothèque Nationale Française, III Fonds général lampes chrétiennes*, Paris.

A. Venturi, 1901. *Storia del'arte italiana, t. 1*, Milano.

H. Vincent, 1902. *La grappe d'Echkol*, dans Revue biblique 11, p. 600-1.

A. Zaccaria Ruggi, 1980. *Le lucerne fittili del museo civico di Treviso*, Roma.

Crédits des illustrations:

Les photos des lampes 1, 5, 8, 11, 15 et des réflecteurs 1, 2, 3 sont © Fathi Béjaoui. Les photos des lampes 7, 10, 20 et 21 sont © Musée du Bardo, Tunis. La photo de la lampe 2 est © Musée de Viuz-Favergues. La photo de la lampe 13 est © Musée d'Art et d'Histoire, Genève et A. Gomes. La photo de la lampe 17 est © Musée Historique d'Etat de Moscou. La photo de la lampe 19 est © Museo Archeologico al Teatro romano, Verone et Umberto Tomba. Le dessin de la lampe 3 est tiré de DACL, II, 1910, col. 1802. Le dessin de la lampe 18 est tiré de Garrucci, 1876, pl. 475. Le dessin de la lampe 13 est d'Anna Trifonova (Moscou). Les dessins des lampes 4, 6, 9, 14 et 16 sont de l'auteur.

Fig. 1. Réflecteur 1

Fig. 2. Réflecteur 2

Fig. 3. Réflecteur 2

Fig. 4. Lampe 1

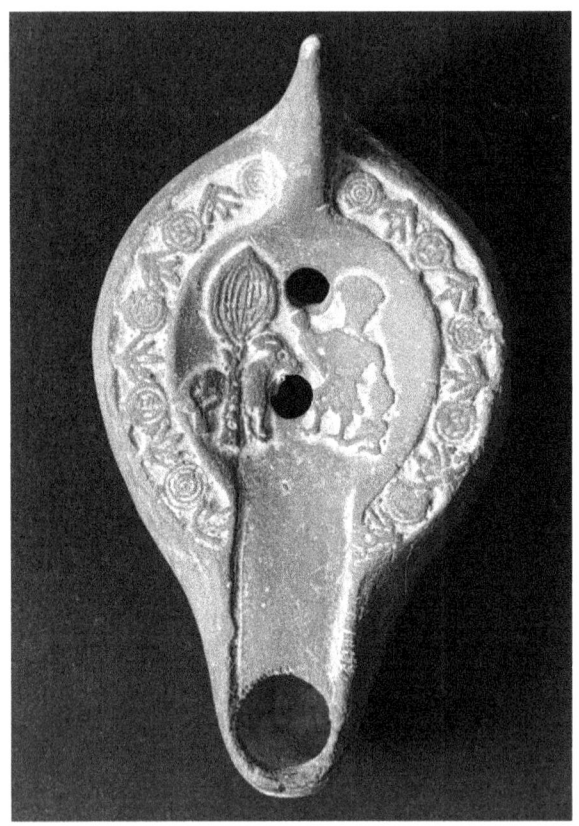

Fig. 5. Lampe 2

Fig. 6. Lampe 3

Fig. 7. Lampe 4

Fig. 8. Lampe 5

Corinne Sandoz : Scènes vetero-testamentaires sur les lampes à huile tardo-antiques

Fig. 9. Lampe 6

Fig. 12. Lampe 9

Fig. 10. Lampe 7

Fig. 11. Lampe 8

Fig. 13. Lampe 10

Fig. 14. Lampe 11

Fig. 15. Lampe 12

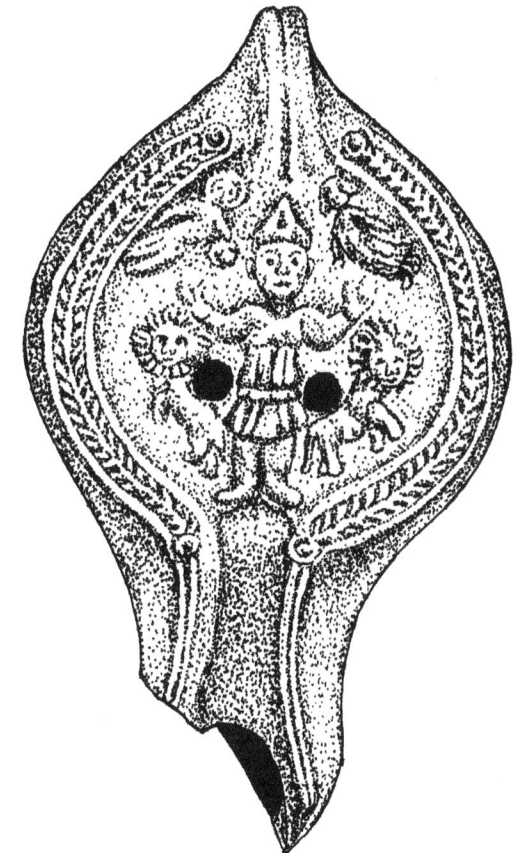

Fig. 16. Lampe 13

Fig. 17. Lampe 14

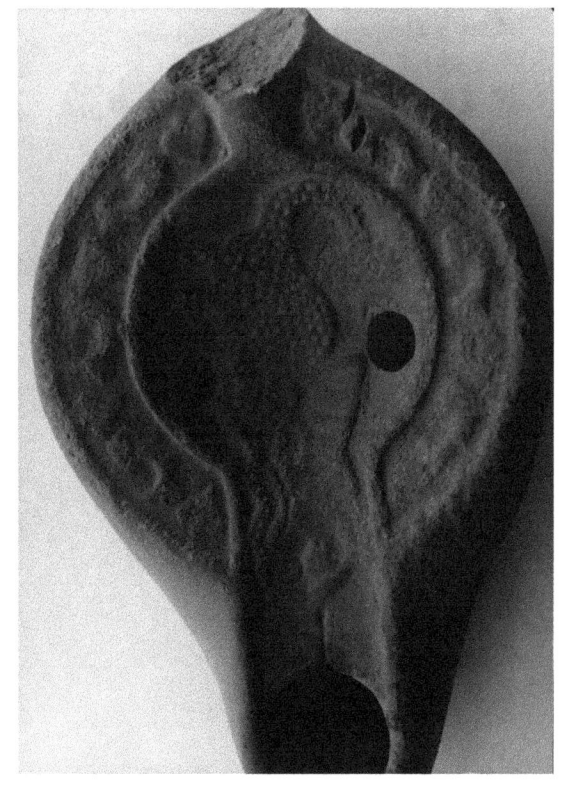

Fig. 18. Lampe 15

Fig. 19. Lampe 16

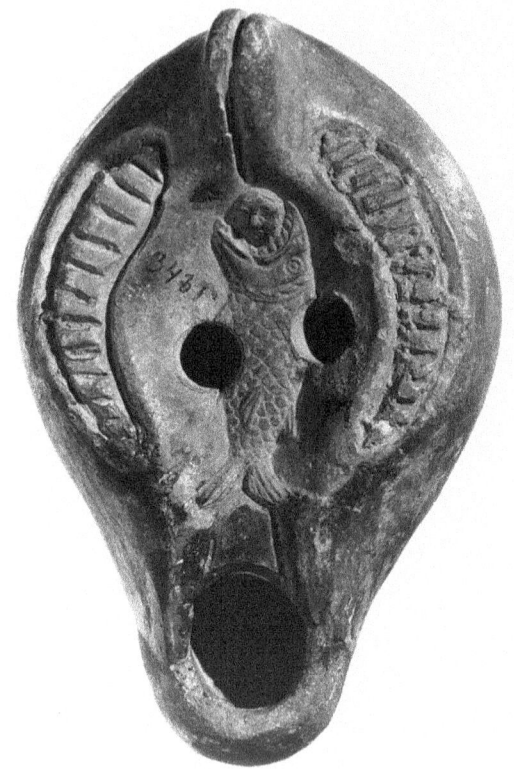

Fig. 20. Lampe 17

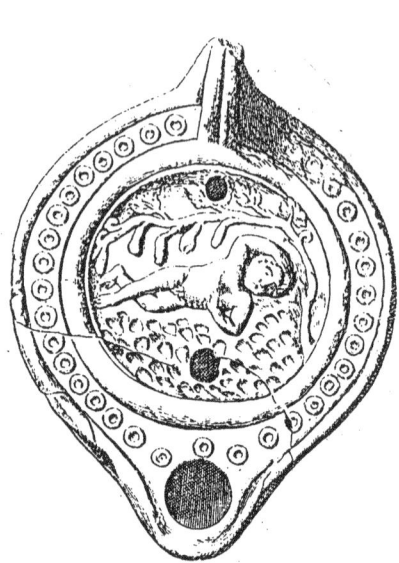

Fig. 21. Lampe 18

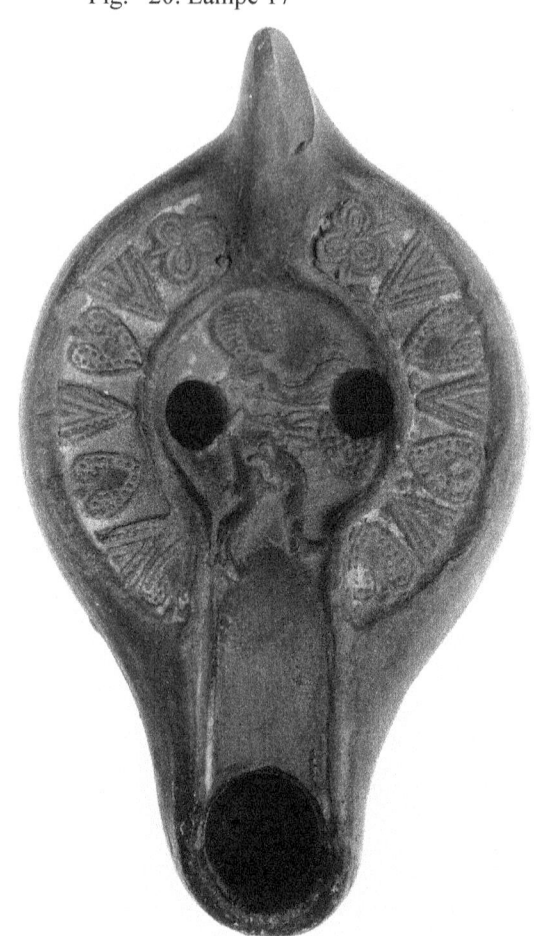

Fig. 22. Lampe 19

Fig. 23. Lampe 20
Fig. 24. Lampe 21

Light for Life and Death in Early Byzantine Empire[1]

Sergey Sorochan
(Kharkov, Ukraine)

What could be more ordinary and habitual for a person of the Greaeco-Roman world than light, dispersing darkness? Ancient people constantly had to use various lighting equipment, to think how to keep this poor light. The centuries were passing by and different changes in this field were taking place. They were summing up bringing a great revolution, sometimes inconspicuously for contemporaries. Is it possible to notice this process now, to understand the causes, the meaning and the gist of the change which occurred when one epoch was replacing the other - this being what is referred to as the Late antiquity and the early medieval period, which is unfairly known as the "dark ages"?

Usually we see this change as a simple scheme: the Byzantine Empire became a successor of the Greek and Roman civilisation and of traditional lighting equipment i.e. clay lamps. Later on lampadas and candles appeared, followed by a silent emptiness of the 7th-9th centuries. After this period problems of lighting seem to dissapear. People solved this problem with the help of different lampadas and torches. That's why historians used to see only the regression here, but not the progression. It is obvious that we have to use a general as well as a detailed view to all the events of this period to try to produce a new opinion, concerning the problem of lighting equipment. Only such a view allows us to notice changes that were mentioned in some short phrases of Byzantine writers and survived in badly preserved physical remains of the Romaine culture.

At the time of the birth of the Eastern Roman Empire a new stage in production of well-known classical lamps of the so-called Roman type began. They were closed oil lamps with an egg-shaped or pear-shaped body and with a little hole for pouring oil into the vessel. In the earlier period, i.e. the 3rd century A.D., the Italian influence to production of clay lamps, usually covered with bad red or brown slip, began to diminish and a lot of new local varieties with some common features appeared.

First of all, the quality of clay, firing and the general proportion of the lamps became cruder. Decorative forms were getting coarser and disproportionality of the whole lamp became the main tendency; in general all the artefacts from this period exhibit a cold stylisation. However, new, easier methods of decoration and new rough elements were born at the same time. Sometimes craftsmen improved unclear details of imprint with the help of retouching, which was made with sharp shaft. A handle was very often made only as a rudimentary, flat (plane) and not perforated projection. All these lamps relied on mass production and consumption by all the population. Some fine objects were also produced at this time, however they do change the general situation and are not considered in this paper. Therefore most of the scholars studying this subject have a common opinion about difficulties in classification of Late Antique lamps, their dating and localisation of workshops (Bernhard 1955:181; Szentleleky 1969; Gualandi Genito 1977:227-228; Chrzanovski & Zhuravlev 1998: 80).

In the 6th century A.D. it is possible to distinguish following centres of Late Byzantine lamp production: Greece (Attic, Corinth), Egypt, Mauritania, Syria, the north and the north-west coasts of Asia Minor and Thrace. The main part of these lamp types existed simultaneously, sometimes during two centuries. According to the numerous finds from Chesonesos-Cherson in Taurica it is possible to note, that by the beginning of the 6th century A.D. the so called "rubchatye" lamps ornamented with sun-rays and produced in workshops of the north Pontic cities, the jug-shaped lamps, that are found with Late Attic, Corinthian, Syrian, Palestinian, Egyptian artefacts and with small crude egg-shaped ones had predominated (Sorochan 1982: 43-45; Kadeev & Sorochan 1985: 96-99, fig.1b, 3-4; Zalesskaja 1988:233-237; Zalesskaja 1987: 308-322; Hayes 1992, Pl. 20, 34-43; Chrzanovski & Zhuravlev 1998, N 59, 63, 67, 68, 70, 75 - 80, 82-84, 89-91; Son & Sorochan 1988: 127-131, fig. 5, 5-6; 6). By the end of the century fine red slip lamps, coming mainly from Alexandria and Carthage, and Coptic lamps with discuses made in a shape of a frog took important place among other imported lamps and they competed well with artefacts from Late Roman workshops of Asia Minor and Attic (Kadeev & Sorochan 1989: 61, 64-65, 69-71, 73-74, fig. 29, 1-2, 5; 30; 32, 1-2; 33, 1, 5; 36). In the 5th – 6th centuries so called Thracian ("Byzantine") lamps with figured handles in the shapes of a human head, a triangle, an oval or a cross, and North African ("Mediterranean") ones, reflecting the obvious influence of Christianity in their motifs, appeared in the North Pontic Area (Sorochan & Schevchenko 1983: 97-100, fig. 5-6; Zalesskaja 1997: 39; Hayes 1992: 86-88, 436, type 11; Chrzanovski & Zhuravlev 1998: 155-174, N 93-105, 108-110).

Clay lamps were used in every house, workshop and shop. They were hanging in front of them, in porticoes, standing in niche inside the walls or on the ground, near entrances; they were put into vaulted mounts (at some cemeteries a third of a quarter of tombs contained them) (Sorochan 1998: 113 -114, 189; Zubar & Sorochan 1984: 149). It is possible to say, that the light of lamps served every living or dead soul. Ammianus Marcelinus wrote that ancient Antioch was lighted during the night not worse than during the day (*Amm. Marc., XIV.I.9*). Byzantine chronicles and other historical works of the 6th-7th centuries A.D. were

---
[1] Translated by Natalia Zhuravleva

still mentioning lamps ("τὸ λαμρόν" or simply "φῶς πῦρ") (Appendix ad Palladii Helenopolitani 1858, col. 181C; Chronicon Paschale... 1832: 725, 17; Leontios Cyprorum ...1864, col. 1709 B) as well as hanging lampadas (kandela) (Ioannis Malalae Chronographia... 1831: 267, 6; 285; 15, p. 468; 546, 17; Beati Ioannis Eucratae... 1976, col. 3056 C; Sophronii Patrarchae Hierosolomitani... 1864, col. 3429 D; Leontios Cyprorum ...1864, col. 1708 D). At that time workshops continued to produce not only clay, but also bronze, sometimes figured lamps, candelabra, lampodoforae, necessary for lighting of large premises, cathedrals, baptisteries, churches, chapels and mausoleums (Bank 1966: 5, Pl. 9; P. 13, Pl. 18-21b, 22, P. 611).

Lamps (λύχνος, λυχνία, λαμπάς, λαμπτήρ) did not disappear from daily life, nor from craft and trade during the next several centuries. For example, they were often mentioned in different variants by Georgiy Monach and by Amartol's Continuer (Georg. Mon. Chron: 279, 292, 353, 614; Istrin 1922: 38, 20). According to Stefan Savvait, it was a burning lamp that monk Sergiy was holding in the cave-church in 796/797 (Stefan Savvait 1907, sec. 44, p. 35, 40). Some clay lamps covered with glaze were found during the excavations of the Large Emperor Palace in the layer of the stage II (Late Isavrian period) that contained coins from Iustinian II (685-695, 705-711) to Leo V (813-820) (Stevenson 1947: 38, pl. 19, 38). They were produced later as well, in the time of Paleolog (Talbot Rice 1958: 120, fig. 29, b). Clay lamps (λυχνα) were mentioned in the letters of Late Byzantian correspondents (Smetanin 1987: 90). Primitive, but glazed open clay lamps with flat handle at the border for wick were found among more numerous clay candlesticks at the excavations of some mediaeval sites of Crimea in the 14th –17th century layers (Aibabina, Bocharov 1998: 195-208). As one of the most necessary things in daily life of ancient people they were never forgotten and remained very important part of the civilisation of Byzantine, the Migration Period and medieval Europe.

However we should note that from the 6th -7th centuries A.D. such archaeological and narrative evidence was becoming rather rare. The most catalogues and publications of lamps end with the ones of this period. The finds of lamps in close contexts of this time, very numerous in previous periods, are becoming also very rare and uninteresting (Romanchuk 1973: 246-250; Romanchuk 1975: 3-14; Golofast 1994 (1995): 217, fig.3, 4). Pear-shaped clay lamps with a broad channel from a discus to a longed nozzle are the last types of lamps and they had finished the evolution of the lighting equipment of this type by the middle of the 7th century.

At the same time the number of glass lamps (λαμπάδες) and "wine-glass vessels", found in excavations, had increased. As the latter ones had little round handles on borders, we might suppose that they were not used only for drinking (Isings 1957: 139). Bronze lustrons (λαμπαδοφορας) of the 5th century with numerous nozzles, ending with horizontal rings were obviously intended for setting of lampadas, but not lamps of Roman type (Lazarev & Bank 1975:15). The earliest chandelier used for holding lampadas and lampadas themselves date to the end of the 4th - the beginning of the 5th century A.D. (Mescheryakov 1978: 132). In the same period clay lamps had finished playing their important role in rituals and had been replaced by another type of lighting equipment. (Zubar & Sorochan 1984: 153). According to Paul Silenciarius (563 A.D.) glass lamps (some of them carved) were among the finest things inside the St. Sofia Cathedral (Schapova 1998: 231). Theofilaktus Simokattus, describing funeral of the Emperor Tiberius II in 582 A.D. in Constantinopolis, remembered singing psalms by burning lampadas during all the night till dawn (Theophylacti Simocattae Historiae... 1887, I,2,4).

From the 4th century A.D. glass beakers with conic or cylindrical bodies, sometimes decorated with drops of dark blue glass, appeared in all the Greek and Roman provinces and were in use the 6th century A.D. (Sorokina 1971: 85 - 101). The finds of such vessels with oil traces on their walls and images of such hanging lampadas at a stone tomb from Rome and on a mosaic in a synagogue from Hammat Tiberias testify to their employment as lighting equipment (Harden 1936: 156). Since the very beginning their popularity was as great as that of oil lamps. People poured water into them, then oil and then put a wick inside. In Chersonesos, the earliest import of glass lamps dates to the second half - the end of the 4th century A.D. when clay lamps were still widely used (Kadeev & Sorochan 1989: 72).

From the 5th to the 8th century a new type of lampadas with hemispherical or cylindrical broad body, convex border and narrow leg which was fixed into a lampadoforus predominated among lighting equipment (Hayes 1992: 400, fig. 150, 37, 38; Foy 1995: 213, fig. 160, 133; Sternini 1995: 260). Remains of such lampadoforus were found in Chersonesos in a context of the third quarter of the 5th century A.D. It had diameter of 24, 5cm and height of 12.5cm. There were 7 holes with diameter of 2.5cm for the placing of lamps and between them in its horizontal border, three oval holes in the equal distances, for hanging (Golofast 1998: 105-106, fig. 8).

L. A. Golofast who was collecting different materials concerning finds of Late Byzantine lamps in Chersonesos distinguishes several types and variants among them with analogies from other regions of Pontic and Mediterranean areas in the 4th-7th centuries. There are lamps with convex spherical base; lamps with convex conical base decorated with drops or buds usually from bright dark blue glass; lamps with three small loop-shaped round or oval handles for hanging on a bracket or a cross (Golofast 1998: 94-106). Such lighting equipment was probably mentioned by the Syrian chronicler Ieshu Stulit who wrote that the new egemon of Edessa, arriving in the town at the turn of 496/497 AD, ordered craftsmen to hang crosses with 5 burning "phanoi" over their shops on the eve of every

Sunday (Joshua the Stylite. 1882, ch. 29).

Since the end of the 4th century people began to use so-called wine-glass vessels (vessels on leg). They were multipurpose vessels, suitable both for drinking in the daily life and for cult purposes in churches. Some articles were obviously used as lamps, as they had small loop-shaped handles for hanging and are often found at the excavations of public buildings, where they could not be used as table ware (Isings 1957: 139-140; Hayes 1975: 86; Foy 1995: 205). In the 6th - beginning of the 7th centuries A.D. these vessels were a dominant type of all the glass vessels in almost all Byzantine cities (Philippe 1970: 72; Golofast 1995: 98; Golofast 1997: 314).

There are some indications allowing us to suppose that from the 9th century A.D. the Church began to persecute the use ritual objects made of glass (Schapova 1998: 53). This must be the reason for the lesser amounts of such vessels, including glass lamps. In spite of this, similar objects continued to be used as lighting equipment as was written by Constantinopolis Patriarch Fotius (858-867, 877-886) mentioning "evening time, ...when lamps were already burning" in one of his letters (Litavrin 1974:12). As it is told in "Miracles of St. Eugenius from Trapezund" "yelions" (as people used to name such lamps) were widely produced in the 9th-10th centuries and imported by workshops of Fasiana in Armenia (Rosenquist 1994: 52-59).

The empire statute book - Basilici and "Book of ceremonies of Byzantian court" mention candelabrae, but we cannot affirm for sure that they were used only for lamps. (Basilicorum libri LX, XV.4.6; XLIV.13.3; 15.19.1; 47, p. 724, 4). Some of bronze hanging candlesticks found in Chersonesos were considered by the excavator Kostiyshko-Valjuzhinich to be holders for lamps with a hole in the centre because candelabrae had sharp pintle (Kostjushko-Valjuzhinich 1905: 80, fig. 37a-b), althougt lamps of such type were produced not later than the very beginning of the Hellenistic period (Cf. Bovon 1966:15-17, N 1; Gualandi Genito 1977: 31-32, N 6-8, 21-22), were not used by Romans and are not obviously found in medieval cities. In this case pintle was necessary for holding thick wax candle.

Another reduction in the volume of lamp production took place after the 9th-10th centuries A.D.; the shapes underwent a radical change, and lamps became rough, simple, and open in form (sometimes mullet-circled (Yakobson 1959: 314-315, fig. 169; Belov 1959: 35, fig. 19; Chrzanovski & Zhuravlev 1998: 177)). The change could be explained by the growing predominance of other types of lighting equipment. If that was not so, we would have to state that from the 7th century Romans used only light of torches and hearths in their houses and churches. Of course torches helped to solve the problem of lighting and there always was a constant demand for them. As it is possible to understand from the story about the Ave Pimene the Great in the 5th century A.D., even monks were making torches for sale and invested this revenue in buying threads and other necessary things in order not to stop their production of this product (Dostopamyatnye predaniya 1821: 318-319). The "Book of Eparchus" - orders for Constantinopolis trade and craft corporations reflecting situation of the 9th century - notes that a part of ergasterion income was intended for acquiring torches (τῶν δαδῶν) (Eparchus, XVIII, 1). Inspite of this there should be something simple and common that could be bought and used by all the population and fill up the emptiness that increased after the disappearence of lamps of Roman type. Besides lampadas whose number also diminished by the 8th century, only candles were able to play such a role and since that time they began constantly to predominate among other lighting equipment.

The Byzantian Empire did not find anything new that concerned lighting. For a long time people were acquainted with candles, which caused a great, but not rapid change From the 4th century A.D. many types of sources contained numerous mentions of candles (cereus, cerula, κηρός, κηρίολος, κήρινος) (S. Athanasius Alexandrinus 1884, col. 229 C; Nili Ancyranae Opera omnia 1864, II, 205, col. 309 A; Socratis Scholastici...1864, col. 689 B; Sozomeni Historia ecclesiastica 1864, col. 1537 A; Ioanni Monachi opuscula 1976, col. 309 A; Ioannis Malalae Chronographia... 1831, p. 467, 16; Chronicon Paschale... 1832: 530, 7; 605, 3; Istrin 1920: 527, 5; 57, sec. 9, p. 62, 9; Eparchus, XI, 4, 6; p. 65, 12; 125, 25) made from wax, which was signified by the same term (Istrin 1920: 329, 18; Eparchus, XI, 3). However, Georgii Amartol used the other, much rarer term ("φάτλιον") (Istrin 1920: 538, 14).

Even in the time of Ioannis Chrisostom, when lamps of Roman type were among the most popular lighting equipment, candles were widely used in daily life; they were used for lighting the houses and for funeral processions (Ioannis Chrysostomi ... 1862, col. 560). We can see candlesticks on frescoes in vaulted burials dating to the 4th century found in the West Pontic Area - Osenovo, Plovdiv, Silistria, Pech (Velkov 1959: 146-147; Dimitrov 1961: 19-21; Milcev & Georgiev 1981: 9-12). The author of the Life of Pahomii remembered that numerous candles were among the most necessary things on archbishop's travels in Phivaida (Troitskiy, 1907: 113-114). According to Socrates Scholastics candles were used during prayer, they were lit on Saturdays and also during religious singing that were held by Christians at night in the streets (Socrates Scholastics, V.22; VI, 8).

The greatest demand for wax candles was in the time of sacral holidays, during festive events, funeral processions and fairs where many people gathered. For example, in 459 when bishop Martirius and stratilatus Ardavurius were preparing the body of Simeon Stilit to be buried, "it was not possible to see a mountain because of the crowd, candles and lampadas...when all the people of the town came to meet the procession with candles and singing" (μεθ κερῶν καὶ υμνων) (Antonin, sec. 23, 28; p.83-85).

Candles were bought for everyday religious services, liturgies, sometimes even by clergymen themselves as it was done by a deacon of the Church of St.Sofia (Diegesis ton thaymaton toy agiou ... Artemiou 1909: 25, mir. 21). These candles were different - rather common cheap ones and more expensive candles with special covering (Diegesis ton thaymaton toy agiou ... Artemiou. 1909: 26-28). This early description can be compared with Late Byzantine evidence about simple candles and candles decorated with Christian symbols and designs, made with "gold" (Codinus Curopalata 1864, col. 64). It also should be noted that candles were sold by their weight which proves the mass character of such goods (Eparchus, XI, 9; Sorochan 1998:109).

As Joann Malala and later Byzantine authors informed us, during the reign of Theodosios, in the forties of the 5th century A.D., Constantinopolis eparchus Kir Sophist (Pholosopher) who "used to take care of everything" "invented" (επενόησε) a new way of workshop lighting which had been unknown to Romans before (Joannis Malalae Chronographia... 1831: 361, 5 - 362, 3; Istrin (1913) 1914, XIV.4.15 - 25, p. 12; 66, t. 1, p. 598, 22). This innovation, for which, along other important inventions he was praised, was compared to the renovation (ἀνανεώσαντα) of all the city, which had been damaged after an earthquake and to the construction of the new city wall. This means, that a "lighting reform" was a really serious innovation and the new lighting equipment replaced former oil lamps. We can suppose that the innovation was either hanging glass lampadas or wax candles that were constantly used from the 4th century A.D.

New processes and changes also took place in Late Roman Chersonesos - early Byzantine Cherson, one of the greatest cities of Taurica. Finds of fragments of lighting equipment are treated by archaeologists as one of the types of lamps. As these finds come from the same contexts as Roman lamps, they are considered as their counterparts and are published usually in the same chapters (Kadeev & Sorochan 1989: 96, fig. 4).

However, some peculiarities of their construction leave no doubt that theese are new types of the earlier clay lamps-candle-holders, being used in Chersonesos-Cherson at the same time as Late Roman traditional clay lamps and that they were produced probably in same workshops (fig. 1, *1-3*). They were wheel-thrown open lamps with the height of 4,5-6cm and the diameter of 9-12cm with a hollow shaft in the centre of the bottom, 6-7cm high and with the diameter of 4,5-5cm. A candle of the same or slightly smaller diameter was put into the centre; wax was accumulated in the bottom. The candle remains were easily extracted by heating the candleholder. As a result of that wax was poured out through the hole made near the end of the tube and then through the channel in the border of a candleholder. Wax, as an important and rather expensive material was obviously reused.

Such candle holders were known in Late Roman Moesia, Capidava and Tomae as well as in early Russian settlements of the $11-13^{th}$ centuries A.D. (Kadeev & Sorochan 1989: 96; Petasuyk 1976: 175-178, fig. 1). K.Kostjushko-Valjuzhinich treated them as "lamps of Byzantine time" (Kostjushko-Valjuzhinich 1898: 6; 1902: 85; 1905: 71; 1906: 43-44; 1907:115). Their finds in a tomb with coins of Bosporan King Sauromates II (Kostjushko-Valjuzhinich 1907: 96, N 1960), in a vaulted mount among Chersonesos coins of 211-217 A.D. and Roman coins of Gorodianus III (238-244) (Kostjushko-Valjuzhinich & Skubetov 1911: 55, N 2286), in a cistern containing 4th-century artefacts (Belov, Strzheletskiy, Yakobson 1953: 184-197, fig. 38d) let us suppose that these candle-holders had existed as a special type of lighting equipment from end of the 3rd century A.D. and continued in the following centuries.

The diminishing of lamp finds in the 6th-7th centuries and degradation of their types can be explained only by the increased use of candles in lighting. Burning lamp as a symbol of a soul and a symbol of light, and to prevent evil, was replaced by a burning candle (Cf. Sebeos 1939: 115, chapter 45; Zubar & Sorochan 1984: 148-154) and even in funeral processions people began to use polycandles. The terms "λαμπάς" used before for clay lamps, seems to have been used for candles as well (Socratis Scholastici ...1864, col. 689 B; p. 225). One of the causes for the increase use of candles was the reduction of oil imports, caused by military events against Islamic expansion (Lopez 1959: 72). Oil has been among goods with which government tried to prevent disturbances, connected with the absence of the other most important goods (Codex Iustinianus 1895, IV.41.1; Sorochan 1995:123-124). Many events of that time - annexation of Egypt by Arabs, evacuation of Romans leaving Alexandria by last boats and the loss of the north African territories that were main exporters of oil, by the end of the 7th century A.D. - became catalysts of the process of curtailment of mass lamp production. For the production of candles oil was also needed, but in much smaller amounts than for lamps and lampadas (30-50 grams for a lamp was was only enough for three or four hours of burning). Embargo on oil imports, which was controlled consecualy by Basileuses, proves that such a situation lasted for several centuries.

Evolution concerning the profession of candle-maker, very rare in the 2nd-3rd centuries, should also be noted. The vast corpus of Latin inscriptions has only one mention of cerearius (CIL, Vol.3, N 2112). Candles could appear among goods sold by a wax seller, who was known in Greek and Roman Egypt as a keromatikos (Fihman 1965:31; Fihman 1976:128). Later kyroularioses as well as kyropoluses had obviously the same function.

According to the amount of mentions in different historical sources, the profession of keromatikos had been the most widely spread in the Late Byzantine period. Letters and Latin papyrii of the 6th-7th centuries speak of cereariuses in cities of Byzantine Italy, in Neapolis and Ravenna (Borodin 1991:115). The Miracles of Artemius, written in the seconds third of the 7th century A.D., contain unique details concerning this craft. The story proves with certainty that kyroularios, "working" in a Constantinopolis' porticus, made and sold candles of different types, quality and price. He also repaired broken candles (but not candle-ends) that were returned to him (Diegesis ton thaymaton toy agiou... Artemiou 1909: 26-28, mir. 21; Cf. Eparchus, XI, 6). When deacon Stephanus, on his way to the St. Artemius church bought very expensive candles in a kyroularius' shop, had slipped and broken the candles, he "returned the broken pieces to the workshop".

A kyroularius might have had a rather good income. In the beginning of the 9th century A.D. it was sometimes possible to meet very rich people, whose wealth aroused envy of even noble Byzantians, among kyroulariuses. The first Empire financier - the chief of the tax department Basileus Nikiphorus I Genik, who had a constant lack of money, finally found a person who could always supply him with it. This person was a kyroularius, having a workshop near an agora of Constantinus, who was able to pay 100 pounds (approximately 32 kg of gold) for the honour to be present at the emperor's dinner. This sum allows us to suppose that such people were wealthy enough as compared with other craftsmen (Theoph. Chron.: 487-488). The same amount of money was gathered as a state tax (κομέρκιον πανηγύριον) at the annual fair in Ephesos (Theoph. Chron.: 469). According to the Byzantine Taktikonae of the 9th century, even the greatest Byzantine military leaders commanding the most important regions of the Empire did not earn such sums (Sorochan 1998: 405-406).

The "Book of Eparchus" mentions imposing fines of 40-50 gr. of gold besides physical punishments and goods confiscation for kyroulariuses as a punishment for violation of work rules (Eparchus, XI, 5, 7; VI, 13; XII, 1,3,5; XIII, 3). Kyroulariuses' wealth is proved also by the fact that there were many householders, leasing premises, among them (Eparhus, XI, 7; p. 121-133).

Although mediaeval west European craftsmen made tallow candles (Registr remesel, 1958: 177-178, kol. LXIV), Byzantine kyroulariuses were only able to sell wax (keron e anergaston e eirgasmenon) and wax candles, buy bee wax and pure oil of necessary amounts for these purposes (Eparchus, XI, 1, 3-5). There is no evidence that they produced special "lighting oil" and sold it, as some historians sometimes suppose (Eparchus, 208). Lamps and lampadas were usually filled with normal oil that was sold by people producing it and by the sellers of groceries (Eparchus, XIII, 1). Such oil did not require any special processing. The Book of Eparhus forbade grocers to sell wax (Vizantiyskaya kniga Eparha 1962, XI, 8), but kyroulariuses (at least Constantinopolis ones) were also not allowed to trade in oil (Eparchus, XI, 2). However, the existence of such a prohibition itself refers to the fact that this difference was not so strict in reality and sellers tried to deal with their goods according to desires of customers.

There is a popular opinion among historians that candles were too expensive for everyday using. This contradicts the wide prevalence of the professions of a maker and a seller of candles and wax (κηροπώλης and κηρουλάριος) in Byzantine cities of the 9th and 10th centuries A.D. (Theoph. Chron. 1883: 487; Istrin 1920: 565, 11; Georg. Cedr., Vol. 2, p. 39), as well as a large amount of their workshops and special quarters of craftsmen (Istrin 1920: 540, 12; Theophanes continuatus: 377.10, 420.15, 437, 715.12, 744.19, 870.21; Sorochan 1998:15-16, 58-60). The amount of candles, produced in workshops situated near the St. Sofia cathedral, was enough to supply not only the main cathedral of the Empire, but also most of the houses of Constantinopolis citizens. And this place was not the only one trading with candles in the city.

Finally bronze hanging candlesticks from Byzantine Cherson, mentioned above, also contradict the fact that candles were used only for burning in front of icons and not for lighting even in churches (Eparchus, 208). There are some finds of candlesticks and of their needles from city estates (Ryzhov 1988: 21-22, fig. 79). In general, trade was highly developed in early Byzantine Cherson and it was well known as a great centre of wax re-export (Romanchuk 1981:322; Sorochan 1995:115-120). Basileus Konstantinus VII noted telling his son Romanus, the future emperor, that the citizens of Cherson were keeping in touch with nomads, who used to come to this city and were exchanging various goods. The main goods citizens of Cherson were offering were clothes, belts, pepper, leather etc (Const. Porph. 6. 2-11). On the other hand nomads brought wax and pelts which was exported to Romania afterwards. According to Basileus's words, the city could not exist without such a trade, for it was the main income for lots of citizens (Const. Porph. 53. 530-532). As the term "τα κήρια" could mean not only wax itself, but also some goods made from it, for example candles, I can presume that at least part of all wax brought to the city was used for processing and that local kyroulariuses sold candles to their neighbours, for it was profitable to sell manufactured rather than raw material. Candles might have been among the most common goods, as salt, agricultural products and other necessary things were, and became one of the main objects of local production very soon.

As a conclusion I should note that by the 7th century candles had replaced Roman lamps in daily life. Glass lampadas were also in use, from earlier times, but they could not compete with wax candles. The candles played important role in trade as well as their specialist sellers, kyroupoloses and kyroularies, did. That does not mean a crisis of this craft but only the beginning of new types of production that was caused mainly by economical and profitable changes. We can name this process as a revolution in lighting equipment production and state that a new page was opened in its development.

Bibliography

Aibabina & Bocharov, 1998. Айбабина Е.А., Бочаров С.Г. Керамические подсвечники и светильники XV-XVIII веков из Каффы: In: *Херсонесский сборник. Вып.9.* Севастополь. 195-208. (in Russian)

Antonin — Антонин. Житие преп. Симеона Столпника 1907. In: *Сборник палестинской и сирийской агиологии.* Санкт Петербург. (in Russian)

Appendix ad Palladii Helenopolitani... 1858. Appendix ad Palladii Helenopolitani episcopi Apophthegmata patrum. In: *PG, Vol.65.*

Bank 1966. Банк А. *Византийское искусство в собраниях Советского Союза.* Москва-Ленинград. (in Russian)

Bank 1966а. Банк А. В. *Византийское искусство в собрании Гос. Эрмитажа.* Ленинград. (in Russian).

Beati Ioannis Eucratae... 1976. Beati Ioannis Eucratae liber qui inscribitur Pratum quod floridaam proferat vitarum narrationem coelestis roseti. In: *PG. T.87.*Turnhout,

Belov 1959. Белов Г.Д. 1959. Отчет о раскопках в Херсонесе в 1955 г. In: *Херсонесский сборник. Вып. 5.* Севастополь. 17-69. (in Russian).

Belov, Strzheletskiy, Yakobson, 1953. Белов Г.Д., Стржелецкий С.Ф., Якобсон А.Л. Квартал XVIII [Херсонеса] (Раскопки 1941, 1947 и 1948 гг.). In: *МИА.* 1953. № 34. Археологические памятники Юго-Западного Крыма. Москва. (in Russian).]

Bernhard M.L. 1955. *Lampki starozytne.* Warszawa.

Basilicorum libri LX / Ed. C.G.E. Heimbach, G.E. Heimbach. Lipsiae, 1833. Vol.1 (Lib. I-XII); 1840. Vol. 2 (Lib. XIII-XXIII); 1843.- Vol..3 (Lib. XXIV-XXXVIII); 1846 Vol.4 (Lib. XXXIX-XLVIII); 1862 . Vol.5 (Lib. XLIX-LX)

Borodin 1991. Бородин О.Р. *Византийская Италия в VI - VIII веках (Равеннский экзархат и Пентаполь).* Барнаул. (in Russian).

Bovon A. 1966. Lampes d'Argos. In: *Etudes peloponnesiennes. 5.* Paris.

Chrzanovski L. & Zhuravlev D. 1998. *Lamps from Chersonesos in the State Historical museum - Moscow.* Studia archeologica, 94. Roma.

Chronicon Paschale... 1832. *Chronicon Paschale ad exemptur vaticanum rec. L. Dindorfius. Bonnae, Vol.1*

Codex Iustinianus. 1895. Corpus juris civilis. Vol.2: Berolini / Rec. P. Krueger.

Codinus Curopalata. 1864 . In: *PG. 157*

Diegesis ton thaymaton toy agiou...Artemiou. 1909. Diegesis ton thaymaton toy agiou...Artemiou. In: *Varia graeca Sacra. Сборник греческих неизданных богословских текстов IV-XV веков. Записки СПб университета. Историко.-филологический факультет.* Часть 95 ((in Russian)

Dimitrov 1961. Димитров Д.П. Стил и дата на стенописите от късноантичната гробница при Силистра. In: *Археология (Sofia). Кн. 1 (in Bulgarian)*

Dostopamyatnye predaniya. 1821. Достопамятные предания о Пимене Великом. In: *Христианское чтение.* Ч. 3. (in Russian).

Eparchus — Византийская книга Эпарха: Вступит. ст., пер., коммент. М.Я. Сюзюмова. Москва. 1962. (in Russian).

Fihman 1965. Фихман И.Ф. *Египет на рубеже двух эпох: Ремесленники и ремесленный труд в IV - середине VII вв.* Москва, 1965. (in Russian).

Fihman, 1976. Фихман И.Ф. 1976. *Оксиринх - город папирусов.* Москва. (in Russian).

Foy D. 1995. Le verre de la fin du IVe au VIIIe siecle en France Mediterranienne (premier essai de typo-chronologie). In: *Le verre de l'antiquite tardive et du haut moyen age.- Val d'Oise,*

Georg. Cedr. — Georgius Cedrenus Ioannis Scylitzae Compendium historiarum / Ope ab I.Bekkero suppletus et emandatus. Bonnae,1838-1839. Vol. I-II.

Georg. Mon. Chron. - Georgii Monachi Chronicon (Rec. C. de Boor) Lipsiae, Vol. I-II. 1904.

Golofast L. 1994. Голофаст Л.А. Комплекс VI в. из северо-восточного района Херсонеса. In: *МАИЭТ. Вып.4.* Симферополь. 215-224. (in Russian).

Golofast 1995. Голофаст Л.А. Комплексы стеклянных изделий конца VI - начала VII в. из Херсонеса. In: *Проблемы археологии древнего и средневекового Крыма.* Симферополь, 1995. (in Russian).

Golofast 1997. Голофаст Л.А. К вопросу о стеклоделии в ранневизантийском Херсонесе. In: *МАИЭТ Вып. 6.* 312-326. (in Russian).

Golofast L. 1998. Голофаст Л.А. Стекло ранневизантийского Херсонеса: Дис....канд. ист. наук (рукопись). Институт археологии РАН. Москва. (in Russian).

Gualandi Genito M. C. G. 1977. *Lucerne fittili delle collezioni del Museo civico archeologico di Bologna.* Bologna

Harden D.B. 1936. Roman Glass from Karanis found by the University Michigan Archaeological Expedition in Egypt, 1924-1929.- Ann Arbor University of Michigan Press,

Hayes J.W. 1975. *Roman and Pre-Roman Glass in the Royal Ontario Museum.* Toronto,

Hayes J.W. 1992. The Pottery. In: *Excavations at Sarachane in Istanbul. Vol.2.* Princeton.

Ioannis Chrysostomi ... 1862. Ioannis Chrysostomi Opera omnia quae extunt...Opera et studio B. De Montfaucon (Accurant et denuo rec. J.-P. Migne). In: *PG. - - T. 48*

Ioannis Malalae Chronographia... 1831. *Ioannis Malalae Chronographia ex rec. L. Dindorfii.* Bonnae.

Istrin 1913 (1914). Истрин В.М. Хроника Иоанна Малалы в славянском переводе. Книга одиннадцатая и четырнадцатая. In: *Сборник Отделения русского языка и словесности имп.*

АН. - СПб., (1913) 1914. - Т.90. №2. (in Russian).

Istrin 1920. Истрин В.М. 1920. Хроника Георгия Амартола в древнем славянорусском переводе. Текст, исследование и словарь. Петроград. Т. 1: Текст. (in Russian).

Istrin 1922. Истрин В.М. Хроника Георгия Амартола в древнем славянорусском переводе. Vol.2: *Продолжение хроники Георгия Амартола по Ватиканскому списку № 153. Исследование.* Петроград. (in Russian).

Ioanni Monachi opuscula. 1976. In: *PG 86 A.*

Isings C. 1957. *Roman Glass from Dated Finds.* Groningen; Djakarta,

Joshua the Stylite. 1882. *The Chronicle Composed in Syria A.D. 507* (Ed. by W. Wright). Cambridge,

Kadeev & Sorochan, 1985. Кадеев В.И., Сорочан С.Б. Египетские и сирийские светильники первых веков н.э. из Херсонеса. In: *Вестник Харьковского университета. № 268.* Харьков. (in Russian).

Kadeev & Sorochan, 1989. Кадеев В.И., Сорочан С.Б. 1989. *Экономические связи античных государств Северного Причерноморья в I в. до н.э. - V в.н.э.* Харьков. (in Russian).

Kadeev & Sorochan, 1989a. Кадєєв В.І., Сорочан С.Б. 1989. Херсонес і Західний Понт: проблема контактів. In: *Археологія (Київ). № 4.* (in Ukrainian)

Kostjushko-Valuzhinich, 1898. Косцюшко-Валюжинич К.К. Отчет о раскопках в Херсонесе за 1896 год. In: *ОАК за 1896 г.* Санкт Петербург. (in Russian).

Kostjushko-Valuzhinich, 1902. Косцюшко-Валюжинич К.К. Отчет о раскопках в Херсонесе в 1901 году. In: *ИАК. Вып.4.* (in Russian).

Kostjshko-Valuzhinich, 1905. Косцюшко-Валюжинич К.К. 1905. Отчет о раскопках в Херсонесе Таврическом в 1903 году. In: *ИАК. Вып. 16.* (in Russian).

Kostjushko-Valuzhinich, 1906. Косцюшко-Валюжинич К.К. Отчет о раскопках в Херсонесе Таврическом в 1904 году. In: *ИАК. Вып.20.* (in Russian).

Kostjushko-Valuzhinich, 1907. Косцюшко-Валюжинич К.К. Отчет о раскопках в Херсонесе Таврическом в 1905 году. In: *ИАК. Вып.25.* (in Russian).

Kostjushko-Valuzhinich & Skubetov, 1911. Косцюшко-Валюжинич К.К., Скубетов М.И. Извлечение из отчета о раскопках в Херсонесе в 1907 году. In: *ИАК. Вып.42.* (in Russian).

Kul'tura Vizantii. 1984. *Культура Византии. IV - первая половина VII в..* Москва. (in Russian).

Lazarev & Bank, 1975. Лазарев В.Н., Банк А.В. *Искусство Византии в собраниях Советского Союза. Краткий путеводитель.* Ленинград, (in Russian).

Leontios Cyprorum …1864. Leontios Cyprorum episcopi Vita Sti Symeoni Sali. In: *PG. T.93.*

Litavrin 1974. Литаврин Г.Г. *Как жили византийцы.* М. (in Russian).

Lopez R.S. 1959. The Role of Trade in the Economic Readjustement of Byzantium in the Seventh Century. In: *DOP N 13.*

Mescheryakov 1978. Мещеряков В.Ф. О времени появления христианства в Херсонесе Таврическом. In: *Ежегодник музея религии и атеизма.* Ленинград. (in Russian).

Milchev, Georgiev, 1981. Милчев А., Георгиев П. Раннохристианска гробница съ стенописи край с. Осеново, Врачанско. In: *Известия на народний музей – Варна. Кн. 17 (32. (in Bulgarian))*

Nili Ancyranae Opera omnia. 1864. In: *PG. 79.*

Petasyk 1976. Петасюк Н.П. Свічники з Софійського собору в Києві. In: *Археологічні дослідження стародавнього Києва.* Київ. (in Ukrainian).

Philippe J. 1970. *Le monde byzantin dans l'histoire de la verriere (V^e - XVe siecle).* Bologna.

Registry remesel 1958. Регистры ремесел и торговли города Парижа. In: *Средние века. Т.11.* Москва. (in Russian).

Romanchuk 1973. Романчук А.И. Комплекс VII в. из портового района Херсонеса. In: *АДСВ. Вып.10.* (in Russian).

Romanchuk 1975. Романчук А.И. Слои VII-VIII вв. в портовом районе Херсонеса. In: *АДСВ. Вып.11.* (in Russian).

Romanchuk 1981. Романчук А.И. Торговля Херсонеса в VII - XII вв. In: *Byzantino-bulgarica. T.7.* Sofia. (in Russian).

Rosenquist J. O. 1994. Lamps for St. Eugenios: A Note on Byzantine Glass. In: *Eranos. T. 92*

Ryzhov 1988. Рыжов С.Г. Отчет о раскопках X "А" квартала в Северном районе Херсонеса в 1988 году. In: *Архив НЗХТ. Д. № 2849/1. 45 л.* (in Russian).

S. Athanasius Alexandrinus. 1884. Vol.1. In: *PG. T. 25*

Schapova 1998. Щапова Ю.Л. *Византийское стекло. Очерки истории.* Москва. (in Russian).

Sebeos, 1939. История епископа Себеоса. Пер. с 4-го испр. арм. изд. Ст. Малхасянц. Ереван. (in Russian)

Smetanin V.A. 1987. Сметанин В.А. *Византийское общество XII-XV веков по данным эпистолографии.* Свердловск. (in Russian).

Sokratos Sholasticus — Сократ Схоластик. *Церковная история: Статья, комментарии. И.В. Кривушина.* Москва, 1996. (in Russian)

Socratis Scholastici …1864. Socratis Scholastici Historia ecclesiastica. In: *PG. T.67*

Son, Sorochan, 1988. Сон Н.А., Сорочан С.Б. Античные светильники из Тиры In: *Античные древности Северного Причерноморья.* К. (in Russian).

Sophronii Patrarchae Hierosolomitani… 1864. Sophronii Patrarchae Hierosolomitani Narratio Miraculorum SS. Cyri et Ioannis. In: *PG. Vol.87*

Sorochan, 1982. Сорочан С.Б. Про так звані рубчасті світильники з Херсонеса In: *Археологія (Київ). № 38.* (In Ukrainian).

Sorochan 1995. Сорочан С.Б. О торгово-экономической политике Византии в Таврике VII - IX вв. In: *Проблемы археологии древнего и средневекового Крыма*. Симферополь, (in Russian).

Sorochan, 1995a. Сорочан С.Б. 1995. Случайность или система? Раннесредневековый византийский "меркантилизм". In: *Древности*. Харьков, (in Russian).

Sorochan 1998. Сорочан С.Б. *Византия IV-IX веков: этюды рынка. Структура механизмов обмена*. Харьков. (in Russian).

Sorochan, Schevchenko, 1983. Сорочан С.Б., Шевченко А.В. Западнопонтийские светильники II-VI вв. из Херсонеса. In: *Вестник Харьковского университета. № 238*. Харьков. (in Russian).

Sorokina 1971. Сорокина Н.П. О стеклянных сосудах с каплями синего стекла из Причерноморья. In: *СА. № 4*. (in Russian).

Sozomeni Historia ecclesiastica. 1864. In: *PG. T.67*

Stefan Savvait. 1907. Стефан Савваит. Сказание о мученичестве св. отцов, избиенных варварами Сарацинами в великой лавре преп. отца нашего Саввы. In: Сборник палестинской и сирийской агиологии. Санкт Петербург. Вып.57. Т.19. (in Russian).

Sternini M. 1995. Il vetro in Italia tra Ve - IXe siecoli. In: *Le verre de l'antiquite tardive et du haut moyen age*. Val d'Oise.

Stevenson R. B. K. 1947. The Pottery, 1936-1937. In: *The Great Palace of the Byzantine Emperors*. London; Oxford,

Szentleleky T. 1969. Ancient Lamps. Budapest,

Talbot Rice D., 1958. The Bzyantine Pottery In: (D. Talbot Rice (ED.)) *The Great Palace of the Bzyantine Emperors. Second Report*. Edinburg.

Theophanis Chronographia. 1883. Theophanis Chronographia / Rec. C. de Boor. Lipsiae,.- Vol.1: Textum graecum continens

Theophanes continuatus // Theophanes continuatus. Ioannes Cameniata. Symeon magister. Georgius monachus / Rec. Im. Bekkerus - Bonnae, 1838

Theophylacti Simocattae Historiae... 1887. *Theophylacti Simocattae Historiae / Ed. C. de Boor*. Lipsiae.

Troitskiy 1907. Троицкий И. *Обозрение источников начальной истории египетского монашества*. Сергиев-Посад. (in Russian).

Velkov 1959. Велков В.И. *Градът в Тракия и Дакия през късната античност (IV - VI вв.). Проучвания и материали*. София. (in Bulgarian)

Vita S. Euthymii / Ed. P. Karlin-Hayter. In: *Byzantion.1955-1957. T. 25-27. Fasc.1*

Yakobson 1959. Якобсон А.Л. *Раннесредневековый Херсонес. МИА № 63*. (in Russian).

Zalesskaja V. 1987. Les lampes paleochretienne en terre cuite de la cote septentrionale de la mer Noire. In: *Archeion Pontou. T.41*. Athenes.

Zalesskaya 1988. Залесская В.Н. Два раннесредневековых глиняных светильника из Северного Причерноморья. In: *СА. № 4*. (in Russian).

Zalesskaya 1997. Залесская В. Импортные глиняные светильники IV-VII вв. в Северном Причерноморье. In: *Международ. конф. "Византия и Крым", Севастополь, 6-11 июня 1997 г. Тезисы докладов*. Симферополь. (in Russian).

Zubar, Sorochan, 1984. Зубарь В.М., Сорочан С.Б. Светильники в погребальном обряде античных городов Северного Причерноморья. In: *Античная культура Северного Причерноморья*. Киев. (in Russian).

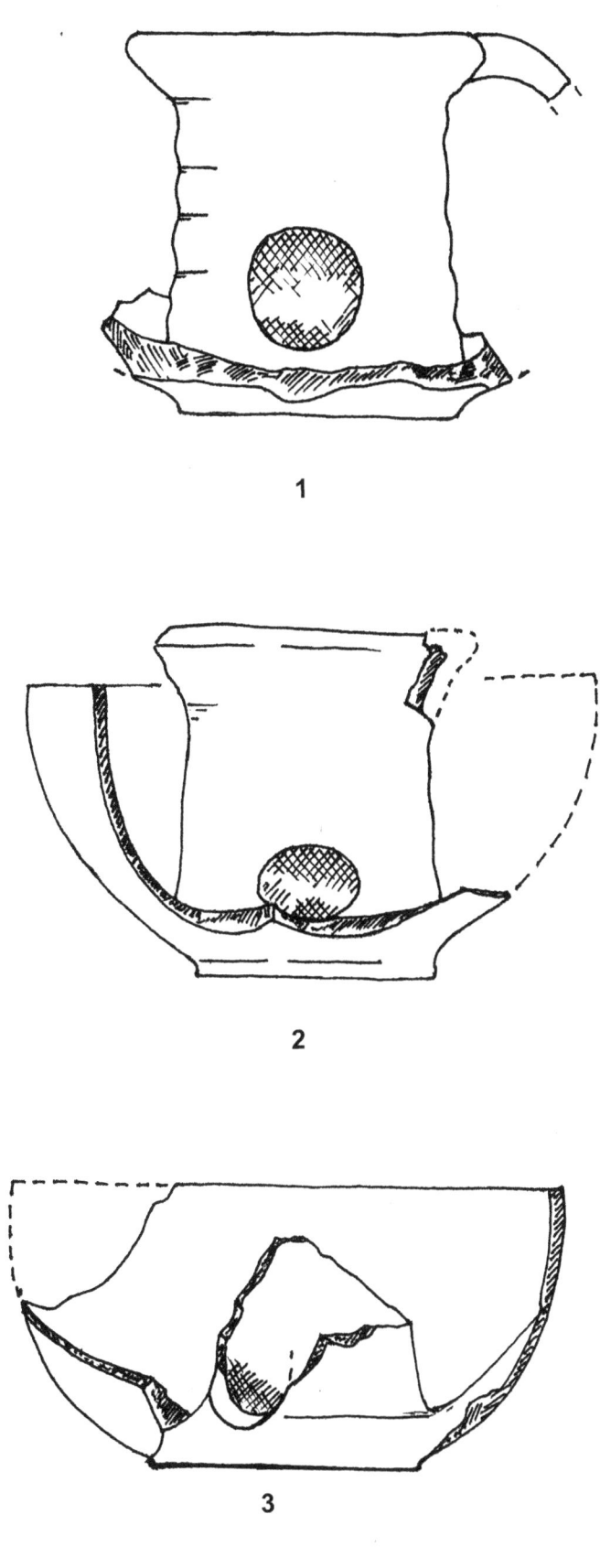

Fig. 1. Early Byzantine lamps. Chersonesos State National Preserve, Ukraine. Inv. N 75/36713, 3/26849, 33/36789.

www.ingramcontent.com/pod-product-compliance
Lightning Source LLC
Chambersburg PA
CBHW041705290426

44108CB00027B/2861